THE SHAPING OF
MODERN IRELAND

THE SHAPING OF
MODERN IRELAND

A Centenary Assessment

EDITED BY

EUGENIO BIAGINI AND
DANIEL MULHALL

IRISH ACADEMIC PRESS

First published in 2016 by
Irish Academic Press
8 Chapel Lane
Sallins
Co. Kildare
Ireland

British Library Cataloguing in Publication Data
An entry can be found on request

978-1-911024-00-2 (Paper)
978-1-911024-01-9 (cloth)
978-1-911024-02-6 (PDF)
978-1-911024-03-3 (Epub)
978-1-911024-04-0 (Kindle)

Library of Congress Cataloging in Publication Data
An entry can be found on request

Contents

List of Contributors

Paul Bew was educated at Cambridge, where he also took his PhD. He has been Professor of Irish Politics at Queen's University Belfast since 2013 – having lectured there from 1991. He is the author of several books on Irish history, including most recently *Ireland: The Politics of Enmity 1789–2006* (2007) and *Enigma: A New Life of Charles Stewart Parnell* (2011). Raised to the peerage in 2007 for his contribution to the Northern Ireland Peace Process, Baron Bew of Donegore (County Antrim) has been an independent cross-bench peer since 2007. From 2013 he has also been Chair of the Committee on Standards in Public Life and, from 2015, Chair of the Speaker's Advisory Committee on the Anniversaries.

Eugenio Biagini was born in Pietrasanta (Tuscany) in 1958, studied at the University of Pisa and the Scuola Normale Superiore di Pisa. He has taught at Newcastle upon Tyne and Princeton, NJ, and is currently Professor of Modern and Contemporary History at the University of Cambridge and a Fellow of Sidney Sussex College. His work has covered Italian, British and Irish history, focusing at first on liberalism and democracy in the nineteenth and twentieth centuries and gradually moving into Irish history since 2007. His main publications include *Liberty, Retrenchment and Reform: popular liberalism in the age of Gladstone 1860–1880* (1992), *Gladstone* (1990), *British Democracy and Irish Nationalism, 1876–1906* (2007) and *Storia dell'Irlanda dal 1845 ad oggi* (2014). With Derek Beales he has published *The Risorgimento and the Unification of Italy* (2002). He is the editor of *Currents of Radicalism* (with A.J. Reid, 1991), *Citizenship and Community* (Cambridge 1996), *Giuseppe Mazzini and the Globalization of Democratic Nationalism 1830–1920* (with C.A. Bayly, 2008) and, with Mary Daly, the *Cambridge Social History of Ireland since 1740* (2016).

Frank Callanan is a Senior Counsel in practice at the Law Library in Dublin and a historian. He edited Edward Byrne: *Parnell, A Memoir*

(1991). He is the author of the *Parnell Split* (1992) and *T.M. Healy* (1996). He has written the entries on Charles Stewart Parnell, John Dillon and T.M. Healy, and more recently, that on Conor Cruise O'Brien, for the *Dictionary of Irish Biography*. His article 'James Joyce and the *United Irishmen*, Paris 1902–3' appeared in the *Dublin James Joyce Journal* 3:2010. He is currently working on a book to be entitled *The Shade of Parnell*, on the course of the Parnell myth, the literary treatment of the myth by Joyce and Yeats, and the formative influence of Parnell and the Parnell split on Joyce's nationalism and on his political relationship with Ireland.

Stephen Collins is the political editor of the *Irish Times*. He has been a political journalist for over twenty-five years and was formerly the political editor of the *Sunday Tribune* and the *Sunday Press*, having started work as a journalist with the Irish Press Group. He has written a number of books on Irish politics, the most recent being *People, Politics and Power: From O'Connell to Ahern* (2007). His other books include, *Breaking the Mould: How the PDs changed Irish Politics* (2005), *The Power Game: Ireland under Fianna Fáil* (2001) and *The Cosgrave Legacy* (1996). He was educated at Oatlands College, Mount Merrion, Co Dublin, and University College Dublin where he graduated with a BA in History and Politics and an MA in Politics.

Richard Vincent Comerford, born at Grangemockler, Co Tipperary in 1945, is a graduate of Maynooth (National University of Ireland) and completed a PhD at Trinity College Dublin under the supervision of T.W. Moody. He was Professor of Modern History and head of department at Maynooth from 1989 to 2010, and oversaw a significant expansion of the department and its programmes. External contributions have included participation in the piloting of the European Credit Transfer System in the early 1990s and membership of the Irish Research Council for the Humanities and Social Sciences. His publications include *The Fenians in Context: Irish Politics and Society, 1848–82* (1985; 2nd ed. 1998) and *Ireland* (2003) in the series *Inventing the Nation* (general editor Keith Robbins). With Christian Noack and Lindsay Janssen he edited and contributed to *Holodomor and Gorta Mór: Histories, Memories and Representations of Famine in Ukraine and Ireland* (2012).

Mary E. Daly is Emerita Professor of Modern History at University College Dublin and President of the Royal Irish Academy; she has written extensively on Irish social, economic and political history. Her many publications include *Dublin, The Deposed Capital: a Social and Economic History, 1860–1914* (1984), *The Slow Failure: Population Decline in Independent Ireland, 1920–1973* (2006) and (as editor with Theo Hoppen), *Gladstone: Ireland and Beyond* (2011). Her latest book, *Sixties Ireland: Reshaping the Economy, State and Society, 1957–1973* (2016), is a major new social, economic and political history of Ireland during the long 1960s which exposes the myths of Ireland's modernisation. With Eugenio Biagini, she is the editor of *The Cambridge Social History of Ireland since 1740* (2016).

Theo Dorgan is a poet and also a novelist, non-fiction prose writer, editor, translator, broadcaster, librettist and documentary scriptwriter. His most recent collection, *Nine Bright Shiners* (2014) won the *Irish Times* Poetry Now Award for the best book of poetry published in 2014. He has edited, among other titles, *Foundation Stone, Notes Towards a Constitution for a 21st Century Republic* (2013), the unique manuscript book *Leabhar Mór na hÉireann/ The Great Book of Ireland* (1991) and, with Máirín Ní Dhonnchadha, *Revising the Rising* (1991). He has been recipient of, among other awards, the O'Shaughnessy Prize for Poetry (USA) 2010 and is a member of Aosdána.

Diarmaid Ferriter is one of Ireland's best-known historians and is Professor of Modern Irish History at University College Dublin. His books include *The Transformation of Ireland 1900–2000* (2004), *Judging Dev: A Reassessment of the life and legacy of Éamon de Valera* (2007), *Occasions of Sin: Sex and Society in Modern Ireland* (2009) and *Ambiguous Republic: Ireland in the 1970s* (2012). His most recent book is *A Nation and not a Rabble: The Irish Revolution 1913–23* (2015). He is a regular broadcaster on television and radio and a weekly columnist with the *Irish Times*. In 2010, he presented a three-part history of twentieth-century Ireland, 'The Limits of Liberty', on RTE television.

Elisabeth Kehoe is a senior research fellow at the School of Advanced Study at the University of London, where she currently lectures. A cultural historian, she specialises in researching British, Irish and American women of the nineteenth and twentieth centuries. She has published two critically acclaimed and commercially successful biographies, *Fortune's Daughters: the Extravagant Lives of the Jerome Sisters, Jennie Churchill,*

Clara Frewen and Leonie Leslie (2005) and *Ireland's Misfortune: The Turbulent Life of Kitty O'Shea* (2008). Dr Kehoe is a frequent broadcaster, presenting popular television programs in Britain and America, for Channel 4, PBS and Smithsonian Films. She was born in Germany and brought up in Europe to third-generation Irish New Yorker parents.

Michael Laffan studied at Gonzaga College, University College Dublin, Trinity Hall Cambridge and the Institute for European History in Mainz. He lectured briefly at the University of East Anglia, Norwich, before taking up what proved to be a long-term post at UCD. He lectured there for over three decades, served in various positions, including that of head of the School of History, and retired in 2010. From 2010–12 he was president of the Irish Historical Society, and he is now an emeritus professor at UCD. He has lectured extensively in Ireland and across the globe and published widely on modern Irish history. His writings include *The Partition of Ireland* (1983), *The Resurrection of Ireland: The Sinn Féin Party, 1916–23* (1999), and *Judging W. T. Cosgrave* (2014), and he has edited *The Burden of German History, 1919–1945* (1988). He hopes to return to his research on Irish political funerals.

John Joseph Lee, born in Tralee, Co Kerry, on 9 July 1942, graduated in 1962 from University College Dublin with first-class honours in History and Economics, and went on to complete his MA on the history of the railways in nineteenth-century Ireland, before taking his PhD at Cambridge. He was Professor of Modern History at University College Cork from 1974 until 2002 and is currently Professor of History and Glucksman Professor for Irish Studies and the Director of Glucksman Ireland House, at New York University. His many publications include *The Modernisation of Irish Society, 1848–1918* (1974) and *Ireland 1912– 1985 – Politics and Society* (1989), one of the most influential books on the subject. He has been a member of the Royal Irish Academy and, in 1993, he was elected to the twentieth Seanad Éireann as an independent member for the National University of Ireland constituency.

Martin Mansergh is vice-chair of the Expert Advisory Group on centenary commemorations. Between 2002 and 2011, he served as a Fianna Fáil senator, a TD and latterly as Minister of State for the Office of Public Works, Finance and the Arts. He served on the British–Irish Parliamentary Body until 2008 and on the Council of State during

President Mary McAleese's second term. A former diplomat, then political advisor to Taoisigh Charles Haughey, Albert Reynolds and Bertie Ahern, he was a back-channel and negotiator during the peace process. A regular book reviewer and columnist, he is author of *The Legacy of History for Making Peace in Ireland* (2003). He is a board member of *History Ireland* and, in 1994, was co-winner of the 1994 Tipperary Peace Prize.

Patrick Maume, born in Cork in 1966, is a senior researcher with the Royal Irish Academy's *Dictionary of Irish Biography*, to which he has contributed 400 entries (including one on Douglas Hyde). He has published extensively on nineteenth and twentieth-century Ireland, with particular reference to print culture and cultural and political nationalism, and is the author of the biographies '*Life that is Exile*': *Daniel Corkery and the search for Irish Ireland* (1993) and *D.P. Moran (Life and Times)* (1995) and of a study of early twentieth-century Irish nationalist political culture, *The Long Gestation: Irish Nationalist Life 1891–1918* (1999). He is a graduate of University College Cork and Queen's University, Belfast, has taught in politics and history departments in University College Dublin and Queen's University Belfast and lived for many years in Northern Ireland. He is now based in Dublin.

Daniel Mulhall was born in Waterford in 1955, and joined Ireland's Department of Foreign Affairs in 1978 after studying history and literature at University College Cork. He has held various positions in Dublin and has had diplomatic postings in New Delhi, Vienna, Brussels, Edinburgh, Kuala Lumpur, Berlin and London, where he has served as Ireland's Ambassador since 2013. Throughout his diplomatic career, he has maintained a strong, personal interest in Irish history and literature and has lectured frequently on these topics during his overseas assignments. He has taught at the University of Limerick and at Murdoch University, Western Australia and is the author of *A New Day Dawning: A Portrait of Ireland in 1900* (1999), along with many other contributions to books, newspapers and journals.

Daithí Ó Corráin is lecturer in Irish history in the School of History and Geography, Dublin City University. He has written on compensation in the aftermath of the 1916 Rising, the Irish Revolution, Irish political violence, twentieth-century ecclesiastical history, ecumenism, church-state relations and the Northern Ireland Troubles. His books include *Rendering to God and Caesar: The Irish Churches and the Two States in Ireland, 1949–73* (2006) and *The Dead of the Irish Revolution, 1916–21* (forthcoming, with Eunan O'Halpin). He is editor of *The Irish Revolution, 1912–23* monograph series of county histories and is currently completing a major monograph, *The Irish Volunteers, 1913–1919 A History*.

Sonja Tiernan is the Peter O'Brien visiting scholar in Canadian Irish Studies at Concordia University (2015–16) and a senior lecturer in Modern History at Liverpool Hope University. She specialises in Irish and British social and political history of the nineteenth and twentieth centuries. Sonja received her PhD from University College Dublin and has held fellowships at the Keough-Naughton Institute for Irish Studies at the University of Notre Dame, at Trinity College Dublin and at the National Library of Ireland where she designed their first research guide for manuscripts relating to women in Irish history. She is a contributor to the *Dictionary of Irish Biography* and has published widely in the area of gender and women's history including most recently *The Political Writings of Eva Gore-Booth* (2015) and the biography *Eva Gore-Booth: an image of such politics* (2012). A co-edited volume, *Sexual Politics in Modern Ireland*, was also published in 2015.

Margaret Ward was the Director of the Women's Resource and Development Agency, a regional organisation for women, based in Belfast, from 2005 until her retirement in 2013. She has worked at Bath Spa University and the University of the West of England and is a former research fellow at the Institute of Irish Studies at Queen's University, Belfast. She is the author of a number of books, including *Unmanageable Revolutionaries: Women and Irish Nationalism* (1983) and biographies of Hanna Sheehy-Skeffington and Maud Gonne. In 2014 she was awarded an Honorary Doctor of Laws by Ulster University, for her contribution to advancing women's equality. Margaret is currently a visiting fellow in the School of History and Anthropology at Queen's University, Belfast.

Preface to
The Shaping of Modern Ireland: A Centenary Assessment

Eugenio Biagini and Daniel Mulhall

1 The Book

The editors of this book met in February 2014 at the Cambridge University Irish History Seminar, as convenor and guest speaker. In conversation at that time, we discovered a shared interest in Irish history, one as a historian and the other as a diplomat with thirty-five years of experience representing Ireland around the world and often drawing on Irish history as an essential resource for understanding and explaining Ireland. Our mutual interests, we discovered, were more specific than this, however. Each of us had a special focus on the thirty years that preceded the attainment of independence in 1922. That shared enthusiasm has led to continued collaboration and to the publication of this collection of essays on prominent figures from the Ireland of a century ago.

Our chance encounter is one aspect of the background to this book. The other pillar on which this volume rests is a book entitled *The Shaping of Modern Ireland*, written more than half a century ago, whose fifteen chapters surveyed the period between 1891 and 1916 through the lives of a set of individuals seen to have helped shape modern Ireland during the years between the death of Charles Stewart Parnell and the Easter Rising. The original chapters were written by leading writers and academics from the Ireland of the 1950s, some of whom would have known the subjects of their essays. The book's editor, Conor Cruise O'Brien, described the collection as 'an interrogation by a cross-section of contemporary Ireland of a significant cross-section of its own past'.

Indeed, all bar two of that book's contributors were significant enough to merit entries of their own in the *Dictionary of Irish Biography* when it appeared in 2009.

The Shaping of Modern Ireland was published in 1960, six years before the fiftieth anniversary of the Easter Rising, and reissued a decade later. As such, it may be seen as an early example of what became an extended reassessment of the causes and consequences of the 'terrible beauty' of 1916. The present volume represents an effort to look afresh at some of the key figures from that formative era in modern Irish history. As editors, we have asked a number of academics and public figures to re-examine the decades leading up to Irish independence through the prism of those figures who featured in *The Shaping of Modern Ireland*.

While, for the most part, adhering to the structure of the 1960 volume, we have made some adjustments and additions to reflect changed perceptions of the period under examination. For example, the original book featured just one woman as a contributor and all of the subjects of the essays were male. Curiously, even Constance Markievicz was not included in the very male bastion of 'shapers' of modern Ireland, despite the significant role she played in the Easter Rising and its aftermath, in particular as the first woman ever to be elected to the Westminster Parliament.

We have sought to redress these inadequacies by increasing the number of chapters and broadening the coverage to include some prominent women from the decades prior to the attainment of Irish independence – Eva Gore-Booth, Constance Markievicz, Hanna Sheehy-Skeffington, Kathleen Lynn and Maud Gonne-MacBride. We have included Dorothy Macardle, the only woman contributor to the 1960 volume, in one of our chapters, reflecting her importance as a historian of this formative era for Ireland. We have also added a chapter on major figures from the world of business, the Jacobs and Guinnesses, the economic influences on the shaping of modern Ireland having been underplayed in the 1960 collection.

The absence of Éamon de Valera and Michael Collins from the earlier analysis of the shaping of modern Ireland seemed to us to leave a gap that needed to be filled. In 1960, de Valera was just one year into his fourteen-year spell as President of Ireland and many of those deeply involved in the acrimonious split over the Anglo-Irish Treaty of 1921 and the bitter Civil War that ensued – a political divide personified by Collins and de Valera – were still active in public life. Now, at a remove of close to a century, it is possible to 'cast a cold eye', or at least a colder one, on the controversies that surrounded the birth of the independent Irish State, though, as Ronan Fanning has recently argued, de Valera remains one of the most divisive figures in the history of modern Ireland.[1] Much the same, indeed, could be said for Collins.[2] Of course, the inclusion of Collins and de Valera involves extending the timeframe of our book to encompass the turbulent years that followed the Easter Rising but, in any case, many of the original contributors dealt with events stretching into the post-independence decades insofar as these related to the lives of the personalities they were assessing.

Some of the individuals included in the earlier collection have been regrouped. The three titans of the Irish Parliamentary Party, John Redmond, John Dillon (who, curiously, was excluded from the 1960 book) and Tim Healy, have been brought into a single chapter in which the Irish Parliamentary Party's partial triumph (in 1914) and dramatic eclipse (in 1918) can be examined. Much scholarly work has been done on these in recent years, not least Dermot Meleady's monumental biography, and the two important monographs by James McConnell and Conor Mulvagh.[3] All of these works show how close to success – a peaceful, but revolutionary success – Redmond and his party were. Meleady goes as far as sketching out the way that an all-Ireland Home Rule might have emerged without violence had England 'kept faith' (as it did, eventually, though by then, in 1920, Home Rule was too little too late). George Russell (Æ), D.P. Moran, two talented editors, and Tom Kettle, a well-known nationalist intellectual who died on the Somme in 1916, have been grouped together for the purposes of comparison. All three were clearly nationalists, but with very different views on their country's future direction.

A striking feature of the 1960 volume is the way in which the various contributors, almost as much as their subjects, seem to come out of a radically different Ireland from the one we know today. The radio programmes on which the original essays were based were broadcast in the mid-1950s, at a time when the performance of the Irish economy was a source of serious disquiet to many contemporaries. This resulted in the publication of *Economic Development*, in 1958, an analysis of independent Ireland's failings that ushered in a fundamental shift in the direction of national policy. Yet, nowhere in those essays is there any meaningful echo of those economic discontents and their putative remedies.

Indeed, Dorothy Macardle's essay on Connolly and Pearse gives the Ireland of the 1950s something akin to a rave review, noting the 'incalculable, almost incredible, difference' compared with what went before. She saw freedom as 'a thing beyond price'. Macardle concluded that 'the Sovereign, Independent Republic of Ireland' was 'a superb reward for all the toil and anxiety and sacrifice, despite its flaws'. These faults could be attributed to the effects of 'long subjection' for which 'political freedom is the cure'.

It is difficult to imagine any commentator today being prepared to offer such a paean of praise to the fruits of political independence.[4] We are now more inclined to weigh up the social and economic balance sheet of the past 100 years of freedom. The mixed bag is probably our preferred metaphor. Looking back on the past half-century, it is hard to ignore the impact of change that has transformed Ireland, its politics, its economy, its culture, its society and its people, but that makes it all the more interesting for us to revisit those formative years prior to the advent of independence.

Is it still possible to view the years between 1891 and 1922 as ones that shaped Ireland? Are there not rival contenders to this title? What about the first decade of independence when the leaders of the Irish Free State created new institutions and consolidated Irish independence in deeply unpromising circumstances? Or the 1930s, when the limitations on Irish independence were gradually removed, a de facto republic created and a policy of wartime neutrality asserted against the odds? Did the decade after 1958 not have a shaping impact on modern Ireland as new policies reoriented the Irish economy and produced an era of relative prosperity?

Membership of the European Union could also be seen as a crucial factor in the making of modern Ireland, and there are those who would see the impact of the Great Recession of 2008 onwards as a game changer for the country, even if it is still far too early for any definitive judgements about our own era.

These rival claimants notwithstanding, it seems to us that there was something special about the three decades after 1891, for the world as a whole and for Ireland. In his introductory essay in *The Shaping of Modern Ireland*, its editor, Conor Cruise O'Brien, described the period as 'a sort of crease in time, a featureless valley between the commanding chain of the Rising and the solitary enigmatic peak of Parnell'. It is no longer possible to see it like that, for the period's hills and hollows are now much more comprehensively explored than they were a half century ago.

This was, after all, an era of considerable ferment characterised by: the founding and impressive development of the Gaelic League; the growth of the Gaelic Athletic Association; the impressive flowering of the Irish literary revival; the passage of a major land act in 1903; the Ulster crisis of 1912–1914; the 1913 Lockout (the most famous Irish labour dispute of the twentieth century); the coming of Home Rule in 1914; and the outbreak of the First World War with its huge implications for Ireland.

It is in the nature of volumes like the present one to be selective in ways which are all too easy to criticise. For example, the North is comparatively neglected, though it is the focus of both the chapter on Carson and – to an extent – of Mary E. Daly's essay on Pirrie and Plunkett. We have not systematically engaged with the structural dimension of change – for example land reform. The neglect of this element in the original *Shaping of Modern Ireland* was, according to Paul Bew, in his essay in this volume, one of that book's main flaws: Conor Cruise O'Brien wrote Irish political history 'without the peasant'. Indeed, the relationship between the land question and nationalism was as important as the relationship between the banking, industrial and business worlds and unionism. While some of our contributors touch on these aspects and their implications, on the whole we have preferred to adhere to the original project's emphasis on key players, using them as the lens through which to view the wider course of Irish history. We can now view these diverse personalities and the influence they brought to bear with different eyes, from the vantage point of our own time and with a century's distance between their world and ours. It is hoped that this collection of biographical essays will contribute to knowledge and awareness of the period in Irish history of which 1916 forms part.

2 The Historical Context

One hundred years ago Europe was in the midst of a devastating war and on the brink of a far-reaching revolutionary crisis comparable to those of 1789–99 and 1848–9. Between the spring of 1916 and the end of 1923 a number of rebellions and revolutions changed the social, constitutional and geo-political layout of much of Europe and the Middle East. The first act of this transformative cycle was played out at Easter 1916, in the westernmost region of Europe, and reached its ideological apex with the 1917 October Revolution, in a very different setting in St Petersburg – Europe's easternmost metropolis.[5]

Although very different in tenor and outcome, both revolutions were inspired by democratic ideas, focusing on popular sovereignty and citizens' equality without distinction of gender. However, while the Bolshevik revolution provoked long-lasting enthusiasm among the masses throughout the world, the Irish revolution – despite favourable echoes in various parts of Europe and North America[6] – seemed to have failed, as the vision of 1916 was lost in the chaos of the Civil War and eventually superseded by the prosaic and conservative realities of the Irish Free State and Northern Ireland. Soon republican intellectuals such as Sean O'Casey and Sean O'Faolain expressed their disappointment and frustration with the new Ireland and surveyed the gap between rhetoric and reality in political and social outcomes. No 'new deal' ensued for the poor and, while many ordinary people were forced to emigrate, those who did not faced endless battles over civil rights, gender roles, health, religion and basic social entitlements. Such problems were compounded by the country's partition – a development which, as the Protestant nationalist Ernest Blythe admitted in 1955, was perpetuated by the aversion that the Irish of the North felt towards the social conservatism and clericalism of the society that had emerged from the Southern revolution.[7]

When the original *Shaping of Modern Ireland* was published in 1960, the IRA Border Campaign (1956–62) seemed to confirm that Ireland would never be able to escape the legacy of revolutionary violence. In this context, Cruise O'Brien perceived the period from 1891 to 1916 'as a lull between storms'.[8] In hindsight, we may take a different view: we must wonder whether it was, instead, the storm between two 'lulls'. For what is striking in the course of modern Irish history is the resilience of parliamentary government in both its pre- and post-1922 varieties, and the extent to which violence was used by rebels and revolutionaries to secure access to the electoral process, rather than to replace it. In terms of this perspective, the key significance of that turbulent period was the assertion of democracy and the principle of popular sovereignty – the establishment of the idea, if we can borrow from the title of a recent major work on the subject, that the Irish were 'a nation and not a rabble'.[9]

If it was largely a *political* revolution, this was not because the *social* revolution 'failed', but because – to an extent – it had been pre-empted by the British state through the Land Acts (1881–1903) and the operation of the Congested Districts Board from 1891. Collectively, these reforms amounted to a great experiment in social and economic engineering that revolutionised Ireland's rural economy and society, though they did so for the benefit of the rural middle classes and largely neglected both the farm labourers and the urban workers.

Was it a 'bourgeois' revolution? This is a loaded notion, similar to the idea of a 'working-class' revolution, in that both are predicated on the naïvely materialistic assumption that, at a given point in time, a whole social 'class' shares in a set of political aspirations, irrespective of regional, religious and cultural differences. In pre-1916 Ireland, land reform had strengthened old aspirations, such as peasant proprietorship, which became central to the Irish collective psyche. In 1960, such values may have looked, if not outworn and archaic, certainly to be associated with the past: 'the future' was the world of technology, free trade, 'economic miracles' and the European Community. Indeed, the political revolution may have delayed economic development through partition and counterproductive policies in the 1930s. While pre-revolutionary Dublin, Cork, Sligo and especially Belfast were major centres of business and industrial activity, each of them suffered severely in the 1920s and 1930s, partly because of strategies adopted by governments which 'dreamed of ... a people who valued material wealth only as a basis for right living ... a land whose countryside would be bright with cosy homesteads, whose fields and villages would be joyous with ... the romping of sturdy children ... and the laughter of happy maidens' – as De Valera famously stated in his 1943 St Patrick's Day radio broadcast.

Yet, the years since 1960 were to show that there was more to Irish peasant culture than the introverted and conservative values of God-fearing patriarchs. There were also key transferable skills – such as self-reliance, managerial talents, and an eye for the market – which, when the opportunity arose, could be deployed in the service of a rapidly modernising society. Thus, as in other parts of Europe, such as Bavaria and Emilia-Romagna, the farmyard became the playground of future generations of businessmen, entrepreneurs and stockbrokers. If, as Tocqueville noted,[10] there is always considerable continuity between the old regime and the revolution, in Ireland's case such continuity took the shape of a culture solidly rooted in the instincts which are central to western modernity.

Ireland's affinity for such instincts – what C.B. Macpherson called 'possessive individualism'[11] – must be borne in mind as we reflect on the reasons why, today, in the age which has seen the triumph of market values and the withering of Marxist experiments, the Republic has become one of the most stable and prosperous democracies in the world, and even Northern Ireland, which was the theatre of a devastating and endless civil conflict for over thirty years, has reached a remarkable degree of stability and economic recovery and is regarded as a model of conflict resolution and peace-making.

This does not mean that, in this book, we present a panglossian assessment of the revolution: on the contrary, several of our contributors hold strong reservations about its dynamics and outcome. Nor indeed does it mean that the contributors necessarily agree with one another or that the editors hold with all the views of their contributors. For this book does not embody a new interpretation or express the views of some new 'school', but instead, it celebrates and affirms interpretative pluralism – though one filtered and disciplined by half-a-century of academic and historical experience. However, it means that, as we examine the men and the women who 'shaped modern Ireland', we are aware that we study, in its light and shadows, what became a major democratic experiment, albeit one consisting of two separate and competing polities, with Belfast and Dublin as their respective capitals.

If asked to name the outstanding Irish figure from the decades following the demise of Parnell, one whose memory remains fresh today, many might choose James Joyce, born in Dublin in 1882. There are good reasons why Joyce was not included in the 1960 volume nor in the present one, even though his work provides a unique window into the Ireland from which he emerged in 1904 at the beginning of an artistic journey that would change the shape of modern literature. Some of the individuals profiled in this book – Michael Cusack, Arthur Griffith, W.B. Yeats, George Russell and Francis Sheehy-Skeffington, Tom Kettle and Tim Healy – make an appearance in Joyce's work or were his direct contemporaries whose lives took different directions. As it happens, 1916, the year of the Easter Rising, also saw the publication of Joyce's *A Portrait of the Artist as a Young Man*, a novel set in late nineteenth- and early twentieth-century Ireland and which covers many of the issues of identity explored in the present collection of essays. James Joyce left Ireland determined to escape the 'nets' of 'nationality, language, religion' that sought to hold him 'back from flight'. The chapters that follow explore those very issues of nationality, language and religion, and provide a variegated portrait of Ireland as an emerging nation. In a memorable passage at the end of his novel, a youthful Joyce looks forward to his new life in continental

Europe 'away from home and friends'. 'Welcome, O life! I go to encounter for the millionth time the reality of experience and to forge in the smithy of my soul the uncreated conscience of my race.'[12] His contemporaries who remained in Ireland were, if less adept with words and images, no less ambitious at the smithy in their efforts to put a better shape on the Ireland in which they lived. Some of their stories are told in the chapters that follow.

Abbreviations used in the footnotes:

SMI   Conor Cruise O'Brien (ed.), *The Shaping of Modern Ireland* (London, 1960).

DIB   James McGuire and James Quinn (eds), *The Dictionary of Irish Biography from the Earliest Times to the Year 2002* (Cambridge, 2009).

Notes

1   R. Fanning, *Éamon De Valera: A Will to Power* (London, 2015).
2   P. Hart, *Mick: The Real Michael Collins* (London, 2007).
3   D. Meleady, *John Redmond: The National Leader* (Dublin, 2014); J. McConnel, *The Irish Parliamentary Party and the Third Home Rule Crisis* (Dublin, 2014); C. Mulvagh, *Sit, Act, and Vote: the Irish Parliamentary Party at Westminster, 1900–1918* (Manchester, 2016).
4   For a recent analysis of Pearse, see J. Augusteijn, *Patrick Pearse: The Making of a Revolutionary* (London, 2010).
5   K. Jeffery, *1916: A Global History* (London, 2015).
6   R. O'Donnell (ed.), *The Impact of the 1916 Rising: Among the Nations* (Dublin, 2008); C. Chini, 'Italy and the "Irish Risorgimento": Italian perspectives on the Irish war of independence', in N. Carter (ed.), *Britain, Ireland and the Italian Risorgimento* (London, 2015), pp.204–25. The global impact of 1916 is the subject of 'The 1916 Easter Rising in a global perspective. The revolution that succeeded?', Churchill College, Cambridge, 3–5 March 2016.
7   E. Blythe, *The Breaking of the Border* (1955).
8   C. Cruise O'Brien, 'Foreword', *SMI*, p.1.
9   D. Ferriter, *A Nation and not a Rabble: The Irish Revolution 1913–1923* (Clays, Suffolk, 2015).
10   A. de Tocqueville, *The Old Regime and the Revolution* (1856, New York, 1955).
11   C.B. Macpherson, *The Political Theory of Possessive Individualism (Hobbes to Locke)* (Oxford, 1965).
12   J. Joyce, *A Portrait of the Artist as a Young Man* (London, 1942 Edition), p. 288.

CHAPTER 1

1891–1916

PAUL BEW

1 Conor Cruise O'Brien at 42

The original edition of *The Shaping of Modern Ireland* was published by Routledge some fifty-five years ago. It had a striking Foreword and survey essay of the period 1891–1916, written by the editor. The essay sought to mark out a new way of looking at modern Irish history. It sought also to insist on the importance of Ireland for the proper study of British history. Written by a successful official in the Department of Foreign Affairs, who had worked on, amongst other things, an anti-partition campaign, it hardly reflected the pieties of the modern Irish state.

It is perhaps worth offering a background note on the life of the author of this essay, Conor Cruise O'Brien (1917–2008). O'Brien's background was hardly typical of the Dublin nationalist intelligentsia. He wrote in 1986: 'I was brought up on the fringes of the Catholic nation, and with ambivalent feeling towards it. My family background was entirely Southern Irish Roman Catholic but my father was what would be called, in the Jewish tradition, as maskil.' He was educated largely outside the traditional spheres of the Catholic Church at Sanford Park School and, in 1936, he entered Trinity College Dublin (TCD) where he had a distinguished academic career. His family's political connections were mostly with the world of parliamentary politics destroyed by the Rising of 1916: his grandfather was David Sheehy, a Parnellite and later anti-Parnellite MP, and his aunt, Mary, was the widow of the Redmondite MP Tom Kettle. Another aunt, Hanna Sheehy-Skeffington was a militant Irish republican who had, nonetheless, sent her son, Owen, along the same educational path as O'Brien.

O'Brien married a fellow TCD student, Christine Foster, in September 1939. She was the daughter of Alec Foster, a liberal Derry Presbyterian and her mother, a Lynd, was a sister of the celebrated essayist, Robert Lynd. O'Brien taught for a couple of months at Belfast Royal Academy in the spring of 1939 where Foster was head teacher. In 1944 he joined the Department of Foreign Affairs and played a key role in Irish support (against the USA line) in the 1950s for the admission of China to the UN.[1] He managed, at the same time, to produce an important book of essays of literary criticism under the pen name of Donat O'Donnell, *Maria Cross: Imaginative Patterns in a Group of Modern Catholic Writers*, and this was published in 1952. In 1957 he published, with Oxford University Press, his brilliant doctoral thesis, *Parnell and his Party*. When he put together *The Shaping of Modern Ireland* for publication in 1959 – the essays were based on Thomas Davis lectures given on Irish radio in 1955–56 – he was on the eve of a dramatic career move. In 1961, the UN Secretary-General, Dag Hammarskjöld, asked the Irish government to release O'Brien to serve as his representative in Elisabethville at the heart of the Congo crisis; an appointment which led to O'Brien's brilliant book *To Katanga and Back* (1962).

2 Against Republican Teleology

The Conor Cruise O'Brien who wrote the essay '1891–1916' for this Routledge collection is, therefore, a most interesting case. While he had worked for the government of the Irish Republic – which had its origins in the 1916 Rising – and authored one of its most spectacular independent acts of foreign policy, he was himself rather more a child of the old Redmondite world. Through marriage – his first marriage began to disintegrate in the mid- to late-1950s – he had, unusually, profound connections with the North and he had even taught for a while in a Belfast school. He belonged, at least partially, to a number of different Irish worlds and his remarkable essay reflects that confluence of experiences.

O'Brien's essay, written in 1959, is a work of considerable intellectual elegance and force, of some classical significance. Its principal device is to attack the idea that those who 'proved to be right' – those who inherited the spoils which flowed from the 1916 Easter Rising in political terms – should be given a privileged place in the account of the history of the era. O'Brien argued that nobody had been 'proved to be right'. The projects of the 1916 revolution had largely failed. Ireland was divided, poor and Anglophone. Northern Ireland here is more absent than present. There is no attempt to reconstruct its political history. Rather it is presented as a symbol of modernity – urban and hard-headed economically – counterpoised against a nationalist Ireland, which is none of those things.

He does say that Unionism also had not been 'proven to be right'. The essay on Sir Edward Carson by R.B. McDowell insists on Carson's sense of defeat at the departure of southern Ireland from the union. But O'Brien was well aware that for his Irish readers, the wrongness of Unionism was a given, and his device is much more subversive of the republican narrative.

This device – or insistence – allows him to break with a teleological vision of history which is obsessed solely with the road to 1916. This is why he insists on the Fairyhouse tradition – by which he means the great affection of the Irish public for horses and sport generally. He argues that sport has, at least, an equal significance in the internal passions of the Irish people. Additionally and more importantly, such a device allows him to open up the way to consideration of constitutionalist as well as revolutionary politicians: so, the 1960 book included discussions of Redmond (by Nicholas Mansergh) and Healy (by O'Brien himself) alongside the revolutionaries – Connolly and Pearse.

O'Brien fully realised that his approach did not impress everyone in Dublin. In a short aside he notes: 'A Dublin publisher refused the collection on the ground that too many of the contributors were from Trinity College.'[2] This sentence perhaps requires comment. At that very moment, Trinity was at the centre of a significant controversy. In 1959–60 there was a proposal to relocate the National Library of Ireland to a site in the grounds of TCD – contiguous to, but independent from, the college library. The proposal had a definite appeal for cash-strapped ministers. Only a small circle of ministers, civil servants and principals from TCD and the National Library participated in the confidential discussions. Then, when agreement to proceed seemed imminent, the proposal was dropped after Seán Lemass, the Prime Minister, talked to the Catholic Archbishop of Dublin.[3] The latter, Dr John Charles McQuaid, was then fundamentally opposed to Catholics attending Trinity – as, of course Cruise O'Brien himself had done many years before. It is clear that McQuaid felt that the placing of Irish cultural treasures on 'Protestant territory' would undermine his ban on Catholics attending Trinity and encourage other Catholics like O'Brien so to do.

O'Brien is well aware that the opening shots against those Catholics who cooperated with Trinity College projects were fired in the 1900s by D.P. Moran, editor of the *Leader*, and the Irish Ireland movement. Dublin's liberal space became constricted. O'Brien wrote: 'For many Irish Irelanders – though not, I like to think for so intelligent a man as Moran himself – Horace Plunkett was a West Briton; Lady Gregory a sourface; Tom Kettle, perhaps a Shoneen.'[4] In fact, though Moran had initially praised Plunkett's book *Ireland in the New Century*, while disagreeing with its criticism of the economic influence of the Catholic Church, to him Plunkett soon became 'Sir Horace Shallow' in the pages of the *Leader*.[5] Moran disliked Yeats even more than he disliked Lady Gregory, but his negativity towards the Abbey project – which Yeats and Gregory championed with a view to renewing Irish drama – increased over time. His relations with Kettle, a professor and Irish Parliamentary Party MP, were strained – Kettle regarded him as a low-grade populist and, at one point, attempted to set up a journal to rival the *Leader*.

O'Brien asked himself what Moran and his friends 'had in mind' when they talked of West Britons? 'I imagine some archetype of a dentist's wife who collected crests, ate kedgeree for breakfast and displayed on her mantelpiece a portrait of the Dear Queen.'[6] This is a nice image, kedgeree being a reheated stodgy meal with imperial (Indian) associations. But, in fact, the category facing Moran's disapproval was much broader. In principle, it would have covered all the products of upper middle-class education at colleges like Belvedere, Castleknock and Clongowes. Moran's real target was a Catholic nationalist politician like Matthew Minch, a director of the *Freeman's Journal* who opposed all schemes for compulsory Irish while sending his sons to Trinity College. O'Brien's nervous reference to the Dublin publisher is a way of conjuring up a world of populist Catholic resentment against elites – including some Catholic elites – not yet extinguished by decades of self-rule.

O'Brien is anxious to insist on the absence of any real sense that Ireland before 1916 felt itself to be living in a pre-revolutionary era. The 'caricatures of Somerville and Ross resemble the brilliant frozen social scenes of *Ulysses* through their intimations of a world both futile and changeless'. On Easter Monday 1916 the focus of middle-class Ireland was not the GPO but Fairyhouse Racecourse. He does acknowledge an 'unusual degree of intensity and self-dedication' – Roy Foster's *Vivid Faces* – but he insisted that it was characteristic of 'quite sizeable groups of people' but 'certainly not the people as a whole'.[7]

O'Brien insists that Ireland 'in the early twentieth century was scarcely oppressed'.[8] This places him firmly alongside John Redmond, who declared in a Wexford speech in October 1914:

People talk of the wrongs done to Ireland by England in the past. God knows standing on this holy spot it is not likely any of us can ever forget, though God grant we may all forgive, the wrongs done to our fathers a hundred or two hundred years ago. *But do let us be a sensible and truthful people.* Do let us remember that we today of our generation are a free people (cheers). We have emancipated the farmer; we housed the agricultural labourer; we have won religious liberty; we have won free education … we have laid broad and deep the foundations of national prosperity and finally we have won an Irish parliament and an executive responsible to it (cheers).[9]

Roy Foster has recently reminded us: 'It is worth remembering that Redmond's claims would have chimed with the opinions of the majority in Ireland in 1915; the radicals were still a minority.'[10] But as Foster admits, many of the attitudes of the 'radicals' were echoed in a 'diluted and contradictory' form in the rhetoric of the constitutionalists. O'Brien's explanation for this is well expressed and central to his analytic framework. 'There is a common basis in all movements of subject peoples: the reaction of the proud and sensitive, not to oppression – Ireland in the early twentieth century was scarcely oppressed – but to contempt and fear, the mutual memory of past oppression.'[11]

Quite brilliantly, he insists on the importance of Irish history for Britain in general. He notes that British historiography was increasingly dominated by issues with an obvious contemporary relevance in the late 1950s – for example the terms of Labour's emergence as a major party of state. But in the actual real history of British politics, Ireland had had a central place between 1880 and 1921. He argues – post-Suez – that a real idea of political understanding had taken place because, for most educated English people, Ireland was now out of sight and out of mind. But the Irish debate had been about the 'Englishman's role in the world' and the emotions aroused were similar to those aroused by the Suez crisis of 1956. He went further: 'Ireland was the first instance in modern times where a nation long subdued won its freedom from a great power which had not been defeated in war.' He believed, entirely correctly, that in the mind of Clement Attlee such a case history was of considerable significance.[12] 'The Irish case was a precedent and it may be supposed that the Labour Government, which after the Second World War conferred independence on India, Pakistan, Burma and Ceylon, had that precedent in mind.' He might also have mentioned the profound impact Ireland had on the ethical language of British politics.[13]

There is at work here a classic revisionist sensibility. That being said, it is worth noting the two key missing elements: the first is any hint of a proper survey of the social foundations of Irish politics. In particular, the connection between life on the land – the occupation of the vast majority of the Irish – and politics. It is telling, perhaps, that the attempted connection is, in fact, an illusion and a rare example of O'Brien himself bowing down before a populist illusion: when he ascribes the 'boycott' as being the key Land League success. In fact, this was an early tactic which could not work in those large parts of the country where farmers were unwilling to be evicted and thus initiated a 'boycott' of anyone who took their land.[14] To overstate the boycott – a weapon of small western farmers – led to a neglect of other more legalistic forms of struggle and, indeed, the role of the rural bourgeoisie during the land war.

The striking weakness in O'Brien's essay and, indeed, the whole book, is the treatment of the relationship between the land and national question. This is the period which saw the United Irish League agitation of 1898–1903 leading to the Wyndham Land Act of 1903 and the ranch war of 1906–10, which led to the Birrell Land Act of 1909. These two acts set the basis for the transfer of ownership of the land of Ireland from one class – the small landlord class – to a mass peasant proprietorship. In the period of the revolution itself from 1916 to 1921, themes of land hunger again re-emerge in a complex way. This weakness in O'Brien's volume remained for some time in the best literature. Nicholas Mansergh's *The Irish Question* (1965) registers that the Wyndham Land Act did not abolish nationalism as British Conservatives had hoped, but says little else. F.S.L. Lyons, in his 1968 extended biography of John Dillon, does not mention the ranch war even though Laurence Ginnel MP, one of Dillon's closest allies, was effectively its leader. This theme – the social base of Irish political life – was to remain neglected until the 1980s.[15] The possibilities of British government devolutionist initiatives - which were received in 1903–04 and in 1907 - were greatly reduced by the unwillingness of a large number of Irish MPs to give up militancy on the land issue. The problem here is that O'Brien's volume in the 1960s is, in essence, Irish politics without the *peasant*: James Connolly and Patrick

Pearse are here, but not the historic personality which determined the early decades of the new state's life. It also helps to explain another obvious 'absence' in his text, the Blueshirt movement of 1933–34 which cannot be analysed without reference to the legacy of rural class tensions.

3 The Black Unknowable North

The other striking weakness here lies in the non-treatment of Ulster Unionism. It is important to note that O'Brien did not see the Northern unionists as simply another part of the Protestant Ascendancy. He notes that nationalists had failed to realise 'that there existed in Ireland another kind of colonist besides the Ascendancy and that these other colonists had built and meant to hold a very non-Ozymandian monument in the shape of Ireland's only modern city'.[16]

While O'Brien makes it clear that the Ulster Unionists are not simply an expression of the 'Ascendancy', he does not really ask what they represented. In 1896 Thomas MacKnight had published his *Ulster As It Is*, the most brilliant Liberal Unionist case ever articulated[17] – political thought delivered in the Irish style of A.M Sullivan's *New Ireland* – potted history, anecdote and an odd mixture of reflection. It is clear that O'Brien had read the Irish nationalist variants, namely the works of William O'Brien, Tim Healy and T.P. O'Connor but not the unionist text which deserves at the very least to be set alongside these.

There is no reference either to W.F. Monypenny's striking volume of 1913, *The Two Irish Nations*. This is perhaps less surprising. I recall as a very young graduate student in 1971 discussing this book's thesis with O'Brien, at a time when he was drafting his *States of Ireland* (1972), a book which was deeply subversive of mainstream nationalist ideology. Even so, he was reluctant to embrace talk of 'two Irish nations', presumably lest it put himself outside the pale of Dublin discourse altogether. In the end, of course, mainstream Dublin discourse now, in effect, concedes the right of self-determination to Ulster Unionists, which was the important implication of the 'two nations' thesis.

There is no attempt, in consequence, to enter the interior world of Ulster Unionism with its economic, religious and political dimensions. R.B. McDowell's fine essay on Carson in this collection continues a useful but broad statement of the entirely forgotten classical unionist case for the Union: 'They believed the Union offered to Irishmen a fuller and richer social life, while it enabled them to make a valuable contribution to the common development of the two islands. If then nationalist opponents accused them of treachery to the national cause, they considered they were fighting for larger loyalties against the offset of a stifling parochialism.'[18] But this general point, while true, hardly deals with the local determinants, which include the sectarianism of the Ulster Unionist case. To be fair, the new scholarly literature on this point really only begins with Peter Gibbons' *The Origin of Ulster Unionism*, published by Manchester University Press in 1975.

The tone of O'Brien's reference to the IRA's doomed 1956 campaign is worthy of note. It is almost as if he welcomes it because it poses questions which should be asked about the IRA; he says, it is both 'absurd' and 'logical'. The shots fired may have awoken a 'number of people from their dogmatic slumber', he declares. In fact, one awakened soul was Éamon de Valera, who stopped talk about British pressure on the unionists and denounced the IRA campaign because it was 'inter Irish' rather than anti British as in 1920–21: 'The solution of the partition question was strictly an Irish problem, one that must be worked out between Irish people north and south. It must be achieved on a satisfactory basis for both sides',[19] de Valera told American journalists in 1957.

Elsewhere in the essay, O'Brien, a fluent Irish speaker with an interest in the classics (he had originally wanted to study Greek at Sanford Park), hails the generosity of the best Irish language supporters who were seeking to create a non-sectarian basis for an Irish nation. But he insists also on the absolute utopianism of such a project. In short, O'Brien's introduction puts everything into play – all the sacred assumptions of Irish history are open to question.

The economic context of this book is worth noting. The Irish economy in the mid-1950s had performed badly. Many blamed Sean McEntee, Fianna Fáil minister for finance from 1951 to 1954,[20] who was to become O'Brien's father-in-law after the collapse of his first marriage. A severe shock had been delivered to mainstream Irish opinion by the preliminary report of the census of 1956. This disclosed that the population, at 2,894,822, was the lowest ever recorded for the state by any census. Although the natural increase between 1951 and 1956 was greater than during any period since 1881, the net emigration was higher at 200,394 (40,000 a year) than at any period since 1881. This caused a population decline of 65,771 compared with the 1951 census.[21] The figures recalled the recommendation of the Commission on Population that to reduce emigration would require large-scale industrial and agricultural expansion. *The Irish Times*, in a leading article, declared: 'If the trend disclosed…continues unchecked, Ireland will die – not in the remote unpredictable future but quite soon.'[22] The only part of Ireland where the population was actually growing was Ireland 'unfree' – the six counties of Northern Ireland, the 'Black North'. The levels of emigration under an independent Irish government were higher than during the later decades of British rule. R.D.C. Black, one of the contributors here, would have been well aware that his head of department in Queen's, Belfast – the liberal unionist Quaker professor, Charles Carter – had been invited to advise the Irish government on ways out of the mess. Professor Carter urged the abandonment of economic nationalism and the introduction of foreign capital. Carter pointed out that the government's target for job creation was wildly unrealistic: 'Now capital of this amount is as far beyond the Irish economy as an ocean-going yacht is beyond the capacity of the Irish family.'[23] From 1957 to 1959, the new Fianna Fáil government directed by Seán Lemass followed suit and repealed the control of manufacturers legislation introduced by the same politician in the early 1930s. In the summer of 1959, Éamon de Valera resigned and Lemass became Taoiseach and the modernisation of Irish society began in earnest. The effects were to be quite dramatic and relatively successful – but this cannot have been apparent to O'Brien as he drafted his essay in late summer 1959. 'Similarly Redmond's failure, though it cannot be seen as anything else but a failure is beginning to be seen as the failure of one attempt to adhere to something which has not yet been attained – a satisfactory adjustment of the political triangle London-Belfast-Dublin.'[24]

This is a remarkable passage. It has to be said that it may be seen as opening up the opportunity for the revaluation of Redmondism, which did not, however, really start to take place until the 1990s. In 1994 the present writer commented:

One final irony. Redmondite home rule was conceived essentially as democratization; a more sensitive, more intimate form of government than Dublin Castle bureaucracy. For Redmond and his colleagues, once this debt owed to history was paid by Westminster then the Irish could for the first time play a full part as equals in wider UK parliamentary and imperial concerns. Ever since Lemass started to unpick the elements of economic nationalism in the 1950s we have been moving back to the world of Redmond. Of course, the intimate Redmondite involvement in Westminster – which would have survived home rule – is impossible to recreate, but a more relaxed, less charged version of Irish political destiny already exists, with Brussels to some degree playing the role Redmond envisaged for London. Redmond would easily recognize a world in which a government in Dublin exists predominantly for political and democratic reasons and in which there is only a low input (save perhaps on the North) from nationalist ideology. Even here the current policy of support for the Anglo-Irish Agreement – direct rule with a green tinge – bears a remarkable resemblance to that pursued by Redmond after 1914.[25]

The point here is that Redmond, having accepted partition in 1914, sought to ensure that a London government – responsible also to nationalist MPs at Westminster – would give fair play to the Catholic minority in the North. The application of violence in 1916 opened up the way to a more separatist settlement in Dublin and a more harsh settlement in Belfast for the minority.

4 Constitutional Contexts

Since these words were written, it is possible to go further. The Belfast Agreement of 1998 substantially remodelled and modernised the Belfast-Dublin-London triangle of relationships. The Agreement created complex new structures on a north/south level and east/west level. In recent years, the Queen's visit to Dublin and the Irish President's visit to London have created a mood of Anglo-Irish harmony which O'Brien could hardly have conceived in 1960. In such a context it is, at least, a matter for serious debate whether Ireland will rejoin the commonwealth. Writing in 1960 he noted that an 'acceptable framework' for north-south relations in Ireland had not been achieved – it had been seriously debated at the Irish Convention of 1918, but without an effective result. It is notable that this acceptable framework for north-south relations was achieved with the 1998 Agreement: despite all gloomy prognostications at the time, the crises of the new settlement were related to other issues, decommissioning, policing and justice and, finally, surprisingly, welfare reform. To employ O'Brien's phrase, is there not now in place a rather Redmonite 'adjustment of the political triangle London-Belfast-Dublin?'[26] Again, though, it is notable how brilliantly and with what precision O'Brien formulated the problems awaiting resolution. It must, however, be noted that he lacked knowledge of the interior life of the North and believed, even to his last days, that Ian Paisley would not countenance power sharing with Sinn Féin.

In his own time Redmond, after all, did 'fail'. In a celebrated sentence, Conor Cruise O'Brien wrote: 'Through the mouths of Carson and Pearse all Ireland heard ancestral voices prophesying war. Different ancestors and a different war.'[27] But it is worth noting – that from 1914 to 1916 Irish people from both traditions supported the same war. By-elections revealed that Redmond faced significant opposition but retained majority support.[28] Even the disaster at Gallipoli, where Irish soldiers were slaughtered in their hundreds before they could even land properly as Father Finn, their chaplain, ran desperately amongst them delivering the last rites before he too was cut down, did not shatter support for Redmond.[29] It took the executions of the 'men of 1916' to do that. As J.L. Hammond wrote:

> Ireland had condemned the rebellion; there was one way of making her forgive it. She has thought it a shameful act; there was one way of making her think it a noble act. The Government took that way. Ministers who had refused to let Redmond bring Ireland into the war a free people, sent her back to the ghosts who had tried to make her a free people. And among the men shot there were rebels of quality, to walk in Elysium with Emmett and Wolfe Tone.[30]

Further Reading:

D.H. Akenson, *Conor: A Biography of Conor Cruise O'Brien* (Montreal and Kingston, 1994)

P. Bew, *Ireland: The Politics of Enmity, 1789–2006* (Oxford, 2009)

F. Callanan, *Tim Healy* (Cork, 1997)

J. Cooney, *John Charles McQuaid: Ruler of Catholic Ireland* (Dublin, 1999)

R. Fanning, *Fatal Path: British Government and Irish Revolution 1910–1922* (London, 2013)

A. Jackson, *Sir Edward Carson* (Dublin, 1993)

D. Meleady, *John Redmond: The National Leader* (Dublin, 2013)

Notes

1   B. Evans and S. Kelly (eds.) *Frank Aiken: Nationalist and Internationalist* (Dublin, 2014), p.221.

2   C. Cruise O'Brien, 'Foreword', *SMI*, p.8.

3   J. Bowman, 'The Wolf in Sheep's Clothing: Richard Hayes's proposal for a new National Library of Ireland, 1959–60', R.J. Hill and M. Marsh (eds) *Modern Irish Democracy* (Dublin, 1993), p.45.

4   See Cruise O'Brien, *SMI*, p.18.

5   P. Maume, *D.P. Moran* (Dublin,1995), p.11.

6   See Cruise O'Brien, *SMI*, p.19.

7   Ibid., p.15.

8   Ibid., p.10.

9   P. Bew, *Ideology and the Irish Question: Ulster Unionism and Irish Nationalism 1912–1916* (Oxford, 1994), pp.123–4. Emphasis in the original.

10   R. Foster, *Vivid Faces: the Revolutionary Generation in Ireland, 1890–1923* (London, 2015), p.2.

11   Ibid., p10.

12   Attlee papers, Bodleian, Clement Attlee to his brother Tom, 3 April 1933, MSS.Eng. 4792.1f.89.

13   E.F. Biagini, *British Democracy and Irish Nationalism* (Cambridge, 2007).

14   P. Bew, *Land and the National Question in Ireland* (Dublin, 1978).

15   P. Bew, *Conflict and Conciliation in Ireland 1890–1910: Parnellite and Radical Agrarians* (Oxford, 1987); F. Campbell, *Land and Revolution: Nationalist Politics in the West of Ireland* (Oxford, 2005); M. Wheatley, *Nationalism and the Irish Party*, 1910–16 (Oxford, 2005).

16   See Cruise O'Brien, *SMI*, p.20.

17   P. Maume, 'Burke in Belfast: Thomas MacKnight, Gladstone and Liberal Unionism' in D.G. Boyce and A. O'Day (eds) *Gladstone and Ireland: Politics, Religion and Nationality in the Victorian Age*, (London 2010), p.181.

18   See Cruise O'Brien, *SMI*, p.83.

19   H. Patterson, *Ireland since 1939: The Persistence of Conflict* (Dublin, 2006), p.154.

20   P. Bew and H. Patterson, *Seán Lemass and the Making of Modern Ireland* (Dublin, 1982), pp.60–78.

21   P. Bew, 'Britain's Modern Irish Question', in *Economy and Society*, vol. 10 1981, pp.481–6.

22   M. McInerney, 'Economic Recovery Plan is Approved', *Irish Times Review and Annual*, 1956, p.52.

23   See Bew and Patterson, *Seán Lemass*, p.122.

24   See Cruise O'Brien, *SMI*, p.8.

25   See Bew, *Ideology and the Irish Question,* p.158.

26   See Cruise O'Brien, *SMI*, p.8.

27   Ibid., p.22.

28   P. Maume, *The Long Gestation: Irish Nationalist Life, 1891–1918* (Dublin, 1999).

29   J.H. Patterson, *With the Zionists in Gallipoli* (London, 1916), pp.87–90.

30   J.L. Hammond, 'A Tragedy of Errors', Reprinted from *The Nation*, 8 Jan 1921, p.14.

CHAPTER 2

Stephens, Devoy and Clarke

R.V. COMERFORD

1 Introduction

In the opening lines of his chapter in *SMI* Desmond Ryan (1893–1964) spells out how James Stephens (1825–1901), John Devoy (1842–1928) and Tom Clarke (1857–1916) are to be considered shapers of modern Ireland by reason of their respective roles in the Fenian movement, a subject on which he did extensive and invaluable pioneering research, editing and writing. In his very first sentence, Ryan conveyed that the Fenian movement, or Fenianism, as he readily named it, had (like many a spiritual essence) gone through three phases, and that the lives of his select trio constituted 'all that need be known of Fenianism'. Some of his readers may have wondered about the place in the scheme of things of Jeremiah O'Donovan Rossa (1831–1915), subject of a famous funeral oration by Desmond Ryan's teacher and mentor, Patrick Pearse (1879–1916). And what about John O'Leary (1830–1907), arbiter of literary taste for advanced nationalists over the decades, and his collaborator Thomas C. Luby (1822–1901)? For men associated with a policy of living by the sword the Fenians had produced an elite of strikingly long-lived greybeards. This longevity of the founding fathers was an element in the mystique of the movement identified by T.W. Moody in the volume of essays he edited to mark the anniversary of the Fenian rising of 1867.[1] Desmond Ryan, in 1959, explains the origins of Fenianism in terms of Famine-era radicalisation, subsequent disillusionment with constitutional politics, republican 'inspiration' from the past and resentment of subordination to Britain. This is fine as far as it goes, but more than half a century later a more structured explanation might be expected.

Since the first quarter of the nineteenth century a politicised Catholic collectivity has been the largest (if not always the most influential) political entity on the island. It achieved remarkable coherence under the leadership of Daniel O'Connell (1775–1847) on the basis of the Catholic parochial structure. By the early 1840s it was functioning as what can be called 'a sub-state nationalism'. O'Connell deployed the rhetoric of intense historical grievance against those he called the English along with a strategy of opportunistic cooperation with respect to the British state. His trademark policy objective was repeal of the Act of Union and restoration of an Irish parliament under the crown. While the interaction between the subordinate nation and the imperial state is a large factor in subsequent political history, it is inseparable from a far more constant, enduring and prolific source of political effervescence, namely the internal contest for leadership of the nation itself.

The endurance of the national collectivity formed in O'Connell's time is not particularly remarkable: most of the European nations and proto-nations that crystallised in the first half of the nineteenth century are still significant polities. What is noteworthy – although not of course exceptional – in the Irish case is the near-continuous hegemony within that national collectivity for a period of nearly two centuries of what may be called constitutional politics. Thus, thanks to an embedded political culture, independent Ireland emerged in 1923 as a parliamentary democracy that proved to have the capacity to weather the after-effects of civil war and several other challenges over subsequent generations. To make the link to the O'Connellite era is not to intimate the working out of a path-determining, unchanging formula. On the contrary, it was only the capacity to incorporate elements eschewed by O'Connell that enabled constitutional politics to prevail in later times.

Along with its strengths O'Connell's formula had several weaknesses. One was that it did not extend to those of the population who were collectively Protestants (using that term to mean members of any of the Reformed churches). From 1842 to 1845 Thomas Davis and others who would be designated as Young Irelanders sought, especially through the pages of the *Nation,* to make a home for all Irish people in the nationalist movement. This was successful only to the extent that many individual

Protestants would subsequently feel free to join the ranks of nationalists, and indeed would be heartily welcome once they made their allegiance clear. As distinct from this nationalising remnant, Protestants generally remained inside their own collectivities, with their own group identities and political dynamics, as in Northern Ireland they largely still do. The entitlement of these Irish people to remain outside the Irish nation was much contested and was not formally conceded by the majority until the ratification by referendum of the Good Friday agreement of 1998.

2 Swords and Clubs

There was principle to O'Connell's policies, but as with all politics his principles are best understood in terms of their function, especially in the never-ending contest for influence within, and leadership of, the collectivity. O'Connell's rejection of armed force as a means to his political ends, by reassuring the government and the Catholic Church, secured him great freedom of movement in his popular mobilisation through the Catholic Association and subsequently the Repeal Association. Utilisation of the parochial structure enabled O'Connell to promulgate his system while at the same time by-passing and discouraging the kind of autonomous popular mobilisation represented in England by Chartism, and in Ireland by the agrarian societies that had flourished for the best part of a century, not to mention the United Irishmen of the 1790s, whose overt revolutionary endeavours had ended only in 1803. O'Connell vehemently opposed combinations and secret societies, but nevertheless he was the unwitting hero of the oath-bound Ribbonmen. Politics would, in the longer term, be unsustainable without such associations. Deploying them was an available tactic in the contest for political influence and leadership. In fact constitutional politics can function in a democratising society only if there are mechanisms that allow ambitious individuals starting from a position of little advantage to make their way through to roles of influence and status in the political system. This requires associational opportunity for those lower down the social system that mimics the functions of elite schools, county clubs, professional bodies, Freemasonry, business associations, golf clubs and other such organisations in the world of the propertied and professional classes. A substantial element of the associational milieu developed by and for the lower middle and working classes in Ireland from O'Connell's time onwards was explicitly nationalist: over generations many would enter on the path of upward mobility through initiation into oath-bound revolutionary nationalist organisations.

The invocation of a policy of taking up arms to secure or defend freedom was a standard leadership tactic in a nineteenth-century nation. O'Connell had forfeited this, to good effect, but in the final years his leadership was challenged by the Young Ireland element in his movement, precisely under this heading. Apart from how convincing or otherwise it might be as practical policy at any given time, the invocation of armed action has the deeper appeal of evoking the spilling of blood for the community that has such an elemental influence over societies of all kinds. Awareness of the rebellion of 1798 and its associated calamities, along with strategic silence on the topic, were fundamental to the O'Connellite mobilisation. This is not to deny that O'Connell made his own use of the imagery of blood. That others could see the potential of open commemoration was demonstrated when the *Nation* in 1843 published a literary ballad, John Kells Ingram's 'The memory of the dead', with the opening line: 'Who fears to speak of '98?'

Already in O'Connell's time, and so even before the Great Famine, the Irish in America were beginning to take a hand in the politics of the homeland. From 1848 onwards there would always be Irish-American cadres whose lives were consumed by Irish politics, living among a large population of fellow-exiles that could be energised betimes to rally and contribute in support of action in Ireland, or the promise thereof. Irish-American attitudes, money and occasionally personnel would be an enduring influence on Irish nationalist politics.

In 1858 James Stephens (a veteran of the attempted rising of ten years earlier and a long-time exile in Paris) launched in Dublin, with the collaboration of like-minded men in New York, a movement that promoted a bundle of the policies and strategies missing from or understated in the then existing politics of nationalist Ireland. At its core was mobilisation for armed insurrection in an organisation subsequently named the Irish Republican Brotherhood (IRB), although from 1863 its members came to be called the Fenians, by reference to its American ally and mentor, the Fenian Brotherhood. In the early 1860s Stephens created a highly impressive movement based on his secret revolutionary society. He was in receipt of moral support from the USA, and also funding, but nothing approaching the sums that had been promised. Stephens absorbed or infiltrated existing organisations and successfully stymied rival attempts at channelling revolutionary nationalist tendencies. He drew in and deployed the support of contemporaries such as Luby, O'Leary, O'Donovan Rossa and Charles J. Kickham (1828–82). They would subsequently deride his bombastic language and dictatorial style. In this denigration they would be joined enthusiastically by the most able lieutenant of the next generation, John Devoy. He had spent a year with the French Foreign Legion, including a stint on colonial service in Algeria, before returning to become an activist with Stephens, who in 1865 appointed him to work at recruiting among Irish soldiers in the British regiments based in Ireland.

Until 1865 the momentum of apparent success secured Stephens from internal criticism, as the American Civil War and its aftermath created a sense of expectancy and tens of thousands of young men in Ireland were available to be called out by Stephens at short notice. However, they were poorly armed and confined to a narrow demographic base. Not only the propertied classes, but almost everyone with a stake in the country, including farmers at every level, feared revolution. In September 1865 and again early in 1866 the government moved to detain the leaders and other identifiable members of the conspiracy. As Desmond Ryan recounts, Devoy subsequently excoriated Stephens for a failure of nerve in refusing to raise the standard of rebellion in February 1866 while the rank-and-file organisation was still relatively intact. Instead Stephens made his way to New York, where he was quickly caught up in the enthusiasm of disbanded Civil War veterans eager to set sail for Ireland and spearhead a revolution. Unable to invoke the language of restraint, Stephens allowed them to convince themselves that he was about to lead a Garibaldi-style descent on Ireland. At an open-air meeting in New York in late October 1866 Stephens indicated that his next public appearance would be in Ireland at the head of a revolutionary army. Dozens, perhaps hundreds, of his listeners sold what they had and equipped themselves for the enterprise. However, while Stephens might be delusional in speech, he was a realist in action. Knowing that the resources were not in place and that the conditions were totally unsuited for an Irish-American invasion of Ireland, Stephens then slipped away for some weeks, to reappear in New York in late December. When he now proposed to his commissioned officers that the invasion be postponed, this generated such outrage and antipathy that it was never forgotten but seldom subsequently mentioned. Indeed, it is passed over by Desmond Ryan in *SMI*. Some of the discommoded would-be invaders made their way not to Ireland (where the ports were being watched closely), but to

England, and participated in the preparations for the ill-fated rising of 1867.

3 Prodigals

Two things happened in 1867 that transformed the place of the Fenians in the wider national collectivity. The first was that the failure of the rising in February and March provided re-assurance that an Irish-American army would not, after all, be coming to restore the Famine emigrants to the land, or otherwise turn the Irish world upside down: indeed that there was no credible prospect of the violent overthrow of British power in Ireland. Secondly, on 23 November three Fenians were hanged at Salford for complicity in the death of a police officer in the course of the rescue of two Fenian prisoners. For Irish nationalists Allen, Larkin and O'Brien became the Manchester Martyrs. By December 1867 churchmen and nationalist politicians, who recently had been excoriating the Fenians, were now honouring them with requiem masses, mock funeral processions and patriotic ballads. There would always be tensions between the interests and strategies represented by Fenian and other versions of national politics, but it had now been established that, however foolhardy their escapades might be, the Fenians were part of the family. Soon they were standing as candidates in parliamentary elections. And when parliamentary nationalism was reorganised by Isaac Butt in the early 1870s, Fenians were involved and Fenian activists were soon proving to be excellent election workers. In 1873 the constitution of the IRB was revised to provide that 'the fit hour of inaugurating a war against England' (for which the organisation would continue to prepare in secret) should be determined in an express decision by 'a majority of the Irish people'.[2] Soon several prominent members of the Supreme Council of the IRB were Home Rule MPs. However, the more common pattern for the generations ahead would be that of individuals rising to prominence as Fenians and using the platform of that prominence to enter the world of politics and leave insurgency behind. A measure of voter indulgence of former rebels is an undeniable feature of Irish parliamentary democracy, and has been in evidence since the Young Ireland rebel of 1848, John Blake Dillon, was elected Liberal MP for Tipperary in 1865. The basis of this favouritism is principally reward for having given up violent ways. Inseparable from this, however, is the instinctive feeling – found in all nations – for the champion who, albeit unauthorised, has borne aloft the sword on behalf of the imagined community. In the 1970s Conor Cruise O'Brien would identify the ambivalence in the *sotto voce* sentiments of Fianna Fáil and Fine Gael supporters admitting to a 'sneakin regard' for the 'boys' of the Provisional IRA.

Fenian leaders jailed in 1865 and 1866 (including O'Leary, O'Donovan Rossa, Luby and Devoy) were precluded from an easy transition to constitutional politics because on release (in 1871) they were excluded from the country for many years. Stephens had never been sentenced, but his notoriety and record – including a Dublin prison escape in November 1865 organised by a subsequently scornful Devoy – meant that he did not feel safe about settling in Ireland until 1891, after which he was encouraged, not least by his friends, to live quietly. So, while the typical Fenian of the 1870s, 1880s and beyond was up for transactional politics, the founding fathers grew in stature as symbols of imprisonment, exile and intransigence.

John Devoy was never content with a merely symbolic role. Following his arrival in New York in 1871 his ability and determination made him a leader in Irish American affairs and from that base he endeavoured ceaselessly, for a period of more than half a century, to influence developments in Ireland. Allied with Michael Davitt he entered, in 1878, into an alliance with the emerging parliamentary leader, Charles Stewart Parnell, to mobilise the country on the basis of exploiting the widespread agrarian distress of the period. A large number of Fenians throughout Ireland, to the disapproval of Kickham and O'Leary, followed Devoy's lead. However, his hope that the outcome would be an armed insurgency under Fenian control was to be disappointed, as Parnell successfully redirected the newly released energy into his own political movement. Nonetheless, the Land War of 1879–82 was to be the occasion of the single most decisive revolution effected with Fenian involvement. This was the socio-economic transformation which saw the balance of power and status in provincial Ireland, countryside and town, tilt against the claims and pretensions of the old landed class and the elites associated with it, to the material advantage of farmers, shopkeepers and publicans, and the psychic advantage of clerks, carmen, labourers and all the others in country and town who identified with the nationalism of Parnell.

In the 1870s O'Donovan Rossa, exiled in New York and desperate to retain relevance and compete with Devoy, grasped the potential of the tactic of terror by explosive for Irish revolutionaries which dawned on the world in the years following the invention of dynamite in 1867.

He was the main inspiration, and indeed the public face, of successive bombing campaigns in Britain between 1881 and 1887 that were directed from the USA. Other Fenian patriarchs denounced the campaign, expressing moral revulsion against a form of warfare that threatened civilians. But the dynamite policy attracted the sympathy and money of a sufficient number of Irish-Americans to make it profitable. Devoy's lack of enthusiasm for the campaign was a factor in his loss of control of the leading Irish republican society in the USA, Clan na Gael, in the early 1880s. The die-hards who not only supported the campaign but offered their services included a fairly recent arrival from Dungannon, Tom Clarke. Arrested in London in the course of his mission, Clarke was convicted of treason-felony and, in June 1883, sentenced to penal servitude for life. He was released on licence in 1898, spent a few restless years in Ireland, and then moved to New York. Here he formed a close and enduring bond with Devoy, now restored to the leadership of Clan na Gael. Clarke returned to Ireland in 1907 and set up in Dublin city as a tobacconist and newsagent, ideal cover for a revolutionary conspirator with the resources of the Clan to call upon. It was Clarke's single-minded response to unfolding events that, more than anything else, brought about an armed rising in Dublin on Easter Monday 1916.

4 Rising

One of the instruments used by Clarke was the IRB. For decades before 1907 the IRB had been the totem of a largely amorphous, if still significant, sub-culture. Joining ('taking the Fenian oath') was a rite of passage for unknown numbers of young men with a modicum of independence finding their feet in the world, such as Tom Clarke himself was when he joined in 1878. But, as Clarke discovered to his disappointment, he had not thus become a cog in some great nation-wide machine. The taut and relatively cohesive paramilitary body controlled by Stephens for a few years down to 1865 was a thing of the past. Locally or at county level the brotherhood might, for a time, have an effective militant arm or a cohesive clique of conspirators ready to infiltrate the management of other organisations to which they, in any case, tended to belong, such as debating societies, sporting organisations or social clubs. From time to time brothers might be moved to help one another find work or give preferential trade to a friendly businessman. Nationality in its rituals and other semiotic mechanisms mattered among them, as it mattered also to others who had not taken the oath. And of those who had taken the oath, dedication to any republican ideal, or to any life-orienting ethos, was but a minority option. There was seldom any one driving force and there was nobody in overall control, as distinct from holding nominal authority. The IRB had a countrywide organisational template, but most of the time much of the network was down.

Clarke did not attempt a general revivification of the IRB. He promoted revitalisation of certain elements, especially the supreme council. These he used for his own purposes, eventually side-lining even the supreme council. Through the IRB he recruited a small number of key individuals for what was his project. Clarke could not have engineered the circumstances that resulted in the formation of two large armed volunteer forces in Ireland in 1913, but he had the resources in tactics and personnel that enabled him to become master of the Irish Volunteers, which even when reduced in 1914 following the outbreak of the Great War, exceeded in every respect any force he could have conjured up out of the IRB.

Launching his movement in 1858 Stephens had endeavoured to create a sense of urgency by highlighting the temporarily very credible case for the imminence of Anglo-French conflict. Through the years of his high success until 1865 the prospect that a victorious Union side in the American Civil War would engage in, or at least countenance, war with Britain was a major factor in Fenian morale. Devoy had devoted restless energy over subsequent decades to finding a chink in Britain's international relationships, at various times unsuccessfully approaching French, Spanish, Russian and American governments with suggestions for Irish involvement in joint score-settling with the British. When Clarke and a small number of associates resolved, in November 1914, that they would stage a rebellion in Ireland before the war's end, they were conscious of how rare were the possible opportunities for successful involvement of a foreign power in the affairs of Ireland. Devoy was already engaging with German agents and interests in the USA. In the end the foreign aid once again failed and, despite Clarke's resort to tactics of ruthless deception in order to keep his plans on course, the proportion of the potential revolutionary body actually available on the day was small. The determination of the socialist James Connolly to launch a rebellion with his Irish Citizen Army had forced Clarke's hand, while also adding just over two hundred participants, men and women.

In addition to the originally unintended blood sacrifice, the enduring emotional impact of the Easter Rising owes much to the impressively conceived and poetically worded proclamation of the Irish Republic with which it was launched. The received wisdom is that Patrick Pearse read the proclamation outside the General Post Office (GPO) on Easter Monday. Writing in 1949, Desmond Ryan says as much, but the authority he cites is at second or third hand.[3] The failure to bear personal testimony to such an iconic moment is surprising, given that Ryan was Pearse's secretary and himself a member of the GPO garrison. Some pieces of evidence have recently come to light that must raise further doubt. In particular, there is the direct evidence of an anonymous journalist published within three weeks of the event, but little noticed since, stating that the proclamation was read by 'a small man in plain clothes' who came from the GPO and stood at Nelson's Pillar. This could not have been Pearse or Connolly, both of whom were in military uniform. On this evidence the reader of the proclamation is more likely to have been Tom Clarke, whose name was first and set apart on the printed list of seven signatories to the document by unanimous insistence of his fellows. Before presenting the proclamation the reader harangued the small crowd of chance onlookers about 'Ireland's wrongs and England's oppression'.[4] That could have been O'Connell addressing a monster meeting in the 1840s. Like Repeal in 1843, and Home Rule in 1886, the Republic proclaimed in 1916 was an authentic reflection of its *Zeitgeist*. In 1886 autonomy within a multi-state polity, as represented by Home Rule, constituted a very acceptable status for the self-esteem of a small European nation. By 1912 that acceptability was still there, but was wearing very thin. Even before war began in 1914 there were those who could see that only self-determination could meet the demands of popular democracy in the small states of Europe, an assessment soon reinforced by the shaming of the empires on the battlefields.

But for one or two chance events the *Aud* – a German ship transporting weapons for the revolutionaries – might have landed its cargo in Kerry in April 1916, thus enabling a more general rising on Easter Sunday. The dynamics of such a rebellion, especially if it lasted long enough to unsettle Irishmen in the British army, might have led the Irish nationalist collectivity to abandon the habits of a century and accept armed revolutionary leadership. This was the kind of rebellion that Tom Clarke had in mind. The rebellion that actually occurred from 24 to 29 April 1916 attracted scarcely any active support and was widely condemned by nationalists, albeit sometimes more in sorrow than in anger. What followed was a re-run of the paradigm of late 1867. Once it was clear that the country had escaped armed revolution and the inevitable miseries to follow, and martyrs from the failed effort became available for commemoration, the defeated warriors became objects of irresistible sympathy within the nationalist family, and a new cult was engendered among Irish nationalists. This cult transformed the survivors of the Rising, together with their associates, into a cadre inspired with a sense of entitlement to rule that was given political form in the new Sinn Féin party of 1917. However, there is no reason to believe that without Easter Week, other events, violent or otherwise, would not have produced other cadres (or perhaps more or less the same cadres) to lead the nation into the brave new world of President Wilson's Fourteen Points in which the Home Rule formula was hopelessly out of date.

In the event, the mobilisation that set up Sinn Féin for victory in the December 1918 general election was provoked by the proposed extension of military conscription to Ireland earlier in the year. This government initiative owed nothing to the Easter Rising, and would, of itself, have impacted disastrously on the hold of the Irish Parliamentary Party on nationalist opinion. (The departure of sons and scarce labour for military service would have played havoc with the war-time prosperity of small and middling farmers.) The mobilisation against conscription was promoted by bishops and priests and was based, once again, on the Catholic parish. It enhanced the credibility of Sinn Féin enormously. The majority of Irish nationalists voted in December 1918 not for any revolutionary programme but (as so often before and after) for the party that seemed best equipped to look after their interests, including their country's place in the world. The fact that the Sinn Féin leadership identified with the rebels of Easter Week is no evidence that Sinn Féin voters in general (or even Sinn Féin leaders in general) were eager for any kind of reprise.

5 Returning to Earth

Michael Collins (1890–1922) was president of the supreme council of the IRB in the closing years of his life. Speaking in September 1917 at the funeral of a predecessor in the role, Thomas Ashe, Collins referred laconically to the deceased as 'a dead Fenian'. But already the term Fenian was being replaced in common parlance by Republican, which had a long usage ahead. However, when Collins himself met his death in August 1922, he would be hailed neither as a Fenian nor as a republican, but as a statesman. He was the recently discovered – and unlikely – hero of a nationalist majority weary of upheaval and violence they had never bargained for, and who yearned for peaceful democratic government. Collins was perhaps the most startling case of the transformation of insurgent into pillar of the constitutional establishment, but the pattern was deeply engrained. The overwhelming public opinion of independent Ireland over the following generations would display its commitment to constitutional government. This was able to function successfully because of the operation of mechanisms for the integration of newcomers to the system, including many who entered by the route of militant nationalist association generally denominated as republicanism, and fuelled by irredentism with respect to Northern Ireland. There scarcely has been, between 1872 and 1918 a Westminster parliament, or since then a Dáil Éireann, that did not include members who, at some stage, had dabbled in Irish rebellion.

Whether in or out of the Dáil Irish nationalists from 1918 onwards lived with a dominant political ideology. It supported the cult of the 1916 Rising as the apogee of national being, in due course extending the style of 'War of Independence' to the national/republican side in the conflict with crown forces in the period 1919–21. Freedom fighters, their associates and others sufficiently adroit to climb on board, constituted the newly entitled political elite. State commemoration as perfected by de Valera in the mid-1930s put the capstone on the cult. Like all such cults it involved much distortion of the historical record. A prime casualty was the memory of Tom Clarke. From de Valera's perspective Patrick Pearse was a more presentable icon. He had left a legacy of quotable poetry and rhetorical prose, and he was an Irish speaker. Very importantly, unlike the infidel Clarke, he had received the sacraments of the Catholic Church before facing the firing squad: the new Irish elite needed a political ideology that would not challenge an older and even more fundamental loyalty.

Of Desmond Ryan's Fenian trio only Devoy lived to see the reality of independence in the form of a twenty-six county Irish Free State. Driven by a visceral detestation of de Valera, he supported the Treaty and the new Dublin regime. When Devoy came to visit in 1924 (for the first time since 1879) Cosgrave designated him a guest of the state and he was welcomed with honour by local authorities on a tour of the country.

But there was an undeniable awkwardness about the business. Devoy affirmed his support for the regime, but his presence was a reminder to both his hosts and himself of the clash between generations of imagining and dreary reality. The mask slipped for a minute at an official reception to mark Devoy's eighty-second birthday. He had just been presented with a silver cigar case on behalf of a grateful nation when he declared that 'he had often wished that he had succeeded in coming over [in 1916] and getting shot with Tom Clarke and Sean McDermott'.[5] Coming from the most practical and unromantic of men this retrospective yearning for a place in a *Götterdämmerung* that neither Stephens, Clarke nor himself would ever have envisaged as their goal, illustrates strikingly the function of the Easter Rising myth in enabling Cosgrave and, in due course, de Valera to get on with day-to-day politics by casting the world of 'bold Fenian men' in a different order of reality.

Further Reading:

R.V. Comerford, *The Fenians in Context: Irish Politics and Society, 1848–82* (Dublin, 1985)

T. Dooley, *The Greatest of the Fenians: John Devoy and Ireland* (Dublin, 2003)

M.T. Foy, *Tom Clarke: The True Leader of the Easter Rising* (Dublin, 2015)

J. Horne and E. Madigan (eds), *Towards Commemoration: Ireland in War and Revolution, 1912–23* (Dublin, 2013)

M.J. Kelly, *The Fenian Ideal and Irish Nationalism, 1882–1916* (Woodbridge, Suffolk, 2006)

O. McGee, *The IRB: The Irish Republican Brotherhood from the Land League to Sinn Féin* (Dublin, 2005)

M. Ramón, *A Provisional Dictator: James Stephens and the Fenian Movement* (Dublin, 2007)

C. Townshend, *Easter 1916: The Irish Rebellion* (London, 2005)

N. Whelehan, *The Dynamiters: Irish Nationalists and Political Violence in the Wider World, 1867–1900* (Cambridge, 2015)

Notes

1   T.W. Moody (ed.), *The Fenian Movement* (Cork, 1968).

2   T.W. Moody and Leon Ó Broin (eds), 'The I.R.B. supreme council, 1868–78' in *Irish Historical Studies*, no. 75 (Mar. 1975), pp.286–332 (ref. pp.313–17).

3   Desmond Ryan, *The Rising: The Complete Story of Easter Week* (Dublin, 1949), p.127.

4   *Dublin Saturday Post* cited in Ann Matthews, *The Irish Citizen Army* (Cork, 2014), p.85.

5   *Freeman's Journal*, 4 September 1924, p.5.

CHAPTER 3

Redmond, Dillon and Healy

Frank Callanan

1 Introduction

Each of the three figures who are the subject of this chapter was defined, and inter-defined, by their position in relation to Parnell. All three were close in age. The oldest was John Dillon, born in 1851 who, as the son of John Blake Dillon, had the most exalted nationalist pedigree. He had joined Isaac Butt's Home Rule League and had become heavily engaged in the land struggle before his election for Tipperary at the 1880 general election. Timothy Michael Healy was born in Bantry in 1854. While not without political connections he still had to make his own way, working as a clerk in Newcastle-on-Tyne while contributing a parliamentary letter to the *Nation*. John Edward Redmond was born in 1856, the son of William Archer Redmond, who sat for the borough of Wexford from 1872–80. He met Parnell at the turbulent meeting at Enniscorthy during the 1880 election. Redmond was knocked down and his face cut. Smiling, Parnell said: 'Well, you have shed your blood for me at all events.'[1] When Redmond's father died in November, Parnell preferred Healy over Redmond, but Redmond was returned for New Ross in February 1881.

Of the three, it was Dillon who was pre-eminent through the 1880s. While emphatically not a socialist (as was Michael Davitt), he stood to the left of Parnell. From 1886 he and William O'Brien were the principal instigators of the Plan of Campaign, a scheme for the withholding of rents on individual estates which was intended to revive the agrarian struggle.

Healy proved a parliamentary master of the land question and, with O'Brien, co-edited the innovative and highly influential Parnellite weekly, *United Ireland*. Healy's deteriorating relationship with Parnell became a source of growing anxiety within the Irish Parliamentary Party. Parnell never admitted Healy into his confidence: what is now known of Healy's dealings with Joseph Chamberlain while Parnell was in Kilmainham Jail, and with Henry Labouchere in the prelude to the 1885 general election,[2] tend to bear out Parnell's extraordinary intuitiveness where Healy was concerned. In both instances Healy had ludicrously underestimated Parnell, misconstruing his holding back as an avoidance of incurring responsibilities which might jeopardise his standing in Ireland.

Healy's suspicions of Parnell's disinterestednesss were accentuated by Parnell's relationship with Katharine O'Shea. This led to the so-called 'Galway mutiny' of February 1886 in which Healy and Joseph Biggar journeyed to Galway to oppose Parnell's imposition of Captain W.H. O'Shea as the nationalist member, only relenting when Parnell himself descended on the scene. The consummation of the Healy–Parnell rift was Parnell's withdrawal in October 1888 of Healy's brief to appear for the Irish members before the Special Commission, established in response to Richard Pigott's forgeries of Parnell's signature on correspondence which appeared to show that Parnell had prior knowledge of the 1882 Phoenix Park murders. This was a deeply humiliating affront to Healy as the pre-eminent jurist of the party.

2 The Split

On 17 November 1890 Captain O'Shea, who had been central to the rift in Galway, obtained a divorce decree *nisi* from his wife on a petition in which Parnell was named as co-respondent. The immediate response was a closing of the nationalist ranks around Parnell. Healy endorsed Parnell in a speech at the Leinster Hall in Dublin on 20 November that he was never permitted to forget. In Britain the 'Nonconformist Conscience' was aroused, and opinion in the Liberal Party moved ineluctably against Parnell. Gladstone temporised (as did the Irish hierarchy), in the hope that Parnell would resign or that the Irish Parliamentary Party would take the initiative in compelling his withdrawal. Forced to act, Gladstone wrote a letter to John Morley on 25 November in which he asserted that Parnell's retention of the Irish leadership would render his own leadership of the Liberal Party 'almost a nullity'. Morley failed to find Parnell or Justin McCarthy to show them the letter, before the Irish Parliamentary Party met later that day and re-elected Parnell as its sessional chairman. Gladstone responded by releasing his letter to the *Pall Mall Gazette*. Events on the nationalist side were now thrown unedifyingly into reverse. Parnell's leadership was now under threat. A reconvened meeting of the party the next day was adjourned to 1 December. Parnell retaliated with his inflammatory 'Manifesto to the Irish People', published on 29 November.

John Dillon was in the United States. He and William O'Brien had broken bail two months previously and made their way from France to America. He had, prior to the Gladstone letter, recognised the implications of the Nonconformist opposition to Parnell. Committed to the instrumentality of the Liberal–Nationalist alliance, Dillon had leaned strongly against Parnell from the outset of the divorce crisis, without seeming fully to grasp the magnitude of what was at stake. The manifesto affirmed his opposition to Parnell. The cable of the Irish delegates in the United States, with the exception of the staunch T.C. Harrington, sent on 30 November condemning Parnell's 'rash and fatal path' was published on the morning the Irish Parliamentary Party met, and dealt a severe blow to Parnell's rapidly diminishing prospects of retaining his leadership. Healy, who had been ill in Dublin, reached London on 27 November.

The debate on Parnell's leadership took place in Committee Room 15 of the Houses of Parliament over the week 1–6 December 1890. Parnell, composed but vehement and unyielding as it became apparent that he was in the minority, was the central figure. Healy marshalled the opposition. The debates were prolonged by the stratagem, set in train by the Parnellites, of seeking assurances from the Liberals on the disputed issues of the manifesto, on which Gladstone would not be drawn. In the strange way in which political careers are forged, Redmond, as a result of his measured defence of his leader, moved from the top of the second to the first tier of parliamentary leadership. In the committee room John Redmond 'like Parnell himself put the Parnellite case upon a basis of cold reason'.[3] A grim tension prevailed on the last day that the unbroken Irish Parliamentary Party met. The occasion was dramatised by a heckle and counter-heckle. In a speech by an anti-Parnellite, Redmond interjected that Gladstone was 'the master of the party'. Healy rose to enquire: 'Who is to be the mistress of the party?' In the scene that ensued Parnell seemed about to strike Healy, 'that cowardly little scoundrel there who dares in an assembly of Irishmen to insult a woman'. Soon afterwards the schism was consummated. Justin McCarthy led a majority of the Irish members out of the committee room.

In Ireland the split ran its unremitting course. Michael Davitt, whose advocacy of a radical Liberal–nationalist alliance was touched with a certain puritanical sanctimony, was credited with Parnell's first defeat, in North Kilkenny. There ensued negotiations in Boulogne in which Parnell strove to exploit the residual susceptibilities of William O'Brien, and warred with Dillon who arrived from the United States a little later. Healy, the ascendant anti-Parnellite leader after Kilkenny, bitterly resented the negotiations, declaring a little later that 'Mr. Parnell was hanged in Kilkenny, but was cut down again in Boulogne.' Healy came to blame Dillon rather than O'Brien for what had transpired at Boulogne. He saw Dillon's actions as owing much to his objection to Healy moving to the fore in the split, temporarily disarranging their pre-split ranking. It was in the Boulogne negotiations, under the shadow of Parnell, that Dillon and Healy's mutual antagonism crystallised.

After Boulogne, Dillon and O'Brien surrendered to the authorities and were incarcerated while the split raged in Ireland. The launch of the anti-Parnellite *National Press* in March 1891 was a serious threat to the Parnellite *Freeman's Journal*. Through the paper and his platform speeches, Healy coined and circulated the ferocious anti-Parnellite idiom of the split. He relentlessly assailed Parnell's relations with Katharine O'Shea, and accused him of forsaking the principles of constitutional action. Parnell went down to defeat in North Sligo and Carlow.

In Galway jail, Dillon's resolve prevailed over O'Brien's misgivings, and when they were released on 30 July they pronounced unequivocally against Parnell. Dillon thereby put himself in a position to challenge Healy's hegemony, but at the price of forbearing to condemn Healy's excesses. The spiralling lunacy of O'Brien's later political course has its origins in his remorseful agonising over what had transpired in Boulogne and after he left Galway jail. On the death of their leader, many Parnellites were as unforgiving of Dillon and O'Brien as they were of Healy.

John Redmond remained steadfast, as did his brother and fellow MP William H. K. ('Willie') Redmond. Though Parnell frequently gave the impression of a man perfectly prepared to fight on alone, Redmond's support continued to have an especial importance for the perceived viability of Parnell's campaign to reconstitute his leadership. He had been at Boulogne, dismayed at Parnell's intransigence as well as that of the Liberal leadership. He was later accused of waning in his allegiance to Parnell, and his enemies made much of his absence from Parnell's last meeting at Creggs. Redmond had held back in the hope that some compromise might be brokered with Dillon and O'Brien on their release. He returned to the fray in a speech the *National Press* characterised as 'the shriek of a lost soul', and spoke on a platform with Parnell for what was to be the last time on 20 September at Cabinteely.[4]

3 After Parnell's Death

On 6 October 1891 Parnell died at Brighton, in the home he shared with Katharine, whom he had married four months previously. Redmond was elected leader of the Parnellites amid the chaos and recriminations that ensued. He resigned his North Wexford seat to contest Cork city, the seat that Parnell's death had left vacant. It was a ferocious contest which Redmond lost. A vacancy arose shortly afterwards in the city of Waterford which Redmond won against Michael Davitt on 23 December. This was the seat Redmond held for the rest of his life, and the Redmondism of Ballybricken, Co Waterford, endured long after his death.

The general elections of 1892, when the Parnellites won nine (against seventy-two anti-Parnellite) seats, and 1895, when they won twelve, affirmed the ascendancy of the anti-Parnellites. The ostensible triumph of the anti-Parnellites was almost negated by the fact that they were themselves utterly riven between partisans of John Dillon and Tim Healy. Formally the parliamentary nationalist ranks were split between Parnellites led by John Redmond and anti-Parnellites led by Justin McCarthy. In reality the division was tripartite. The first theatre of combat in the anti-Parnellite party was for the control of the *Freeman's Journal* which had been amalgamated with Healy's *National Press* in March 1892. The temper of the conflict within anti-Parnellism is conveyed in a letter Healy wrote to his brother and fellow parliamentarian, Maurice, two months later after a shareholders' meeting. 'You will see we finished our bastard Room Fifteen today. Dillon's cold egotism surpasses belief, and he did and said meaner things, without Parnell's justification, than Parnell himself in Room Fifteen. I will never have the smallest regard for his character again, and I believe he is a thorough tyrant at heart.'[5]

The antagonism between Healy and Dillon is politically and psychologically compelling. Healy had always more or less realised he would not be able to maintain the hegemony he had attained at the height of the contest with Parnell. This was not merely because the ferocity of his assaults on Parnell effectively disqualified him from the leadership of the anti-Parnellites. It seems evident that he realised that he lacked the temperament and the skills to lead. His growing intimation that he was not *capax imperii* derived from his long tutelage to Parnell. The most obvious reflection of this fatalistic realisation was in his pursuit of his professional career as a barrister. Called to the bar in 1884, he had, almost from the outset, a markedly successful practice which was adversely affecting his parliamentary attendance as early as the late 1880s. (Redmond, by contrast, who was called to the bar in 1887 and had all the aptitudes for professional success, never allowed his legal practice to circumscribe his political role.) The assessment of the impact of his legal career could be carried a stage further: that his conception of politics mirrored, in its championship of sectional interests, the relationship of a lawyer to his clients. He remained, nevertheless, existentially a politician in a way that his later confederate William O'Brien did not.[6]

No politician is to be expected to accept with equanimity the idea that he was disqualified from leadership. In Healy's case the psychological resolution took the form of an unswerving determination to ensure that John Dillon did not prevail, to deny him the fruits, as Healy saw it, of his own facing down of Parnell. This was a psycho-political strategy of displacement which Healy pursued with almost manic remorselessness. He was emboldened by the knowledge that Dillon was encumbered by an austere sense of political vocation, and incapable of responding humorously. (Francis Cruise O'Brien numbered him among Anatole France's 'hommes qui n'ont jamais ri'.) He knew he could provoke Dillon and his confederates, and then protest at the heavy-handedness of their response. He set out to personalise the contest with Dillon, achieving a large measure of success. This found its clearest expression in his sustained polemic against Dillon, *Why Ireland is not Free*, published in 1898 after anonymous serialisation in the *Irish Catholic*. He perpetuated the refrain 'John wants the chair' as the chief explanation of what had transpired in Irish politics since Parnell's death, and exulted in Thomas Sexton's characterisation of Dillon as 'the melancholy humbug'. It was a bizarre *reprise* of the Parnell split directed against Dillon. The subjective impact on its target was greater than on the lucidly impassive Parnell, exacerbating Dillon's temperamental pessimism and provoking near-apoplexy among his allies.

By the mid-decade, Healy was ceasing to be a serious contender for the leadership of, or for a hegemonic role within, parliamentary nationalism. The 1895 election saw the defeat of a number of his allies and shifted the balance of power within the anti-Parnellite party. His support of William Martin Murphy's dissentient candidacy in Kerry South led to his expulsion from the National Federation, which he had been instrumental in establishing, and from the committee of the anti-Parnellite party. Through the 'People's Rights Fund' and latterly the People's Rights Association which drew on the support of the disaffected Irish clergy and others, Healy championed constituency rights against the supposedly tyrannical anti-Parnellite machine. The ultra-Liberal individuals of the split of 1890–91 came increasingly to champion collaboration with the Conservative government. Healy retained considerable influence, if of a negative kind.

John Dillon toiled on, still a grimly commanding figure, not so much loyal to the Liberals as opposed to the Conservatives, and antagonistic to the manifestations of 'constructive unionism' in Ireland. In January 1898 he attended, with misgivings, the launch in Westport of William O'Brien's neo-agrarian United Irish League which, in the prevailing stasis within nationalism, rapidly acquired momentum. In a gesture intended to facilitate the reunion of the Irish Parliamentary Party Dillon formally resigned the chairmanship of the anti-Parnellite party in February 1898.

4 Reunion and After

The ferocious schism within the anti-Parnellite ranks, which bore out Parnell's prophesies, which had seemed, at the time, exorbitant, that his adversaries would, in turn, fall out among themselves, favoured Redmond. Redmond fared better than Dillon or Healy in the 'long split' of 1890–1900, demonstrating an imaginative resourcefulness as the leader of an embattled minority that he foreswore in his later more settled and inhibiting role as leader of the reunited party. He displayed considerable skill in the debates on Gladstone's Third Home Rule Bill of 1893, carried in the House of Commons before going down to inevitable defeat in the Lords. He held together the disparate Parnellite factions. There was a certain dissonance between his accommodation of the opportunistically volatile Fenian wing of Parnellism and his own belief in the British empire which found expression in a speech to the Cambridge Union in February 1895 in which he declared that Home Rule was not a demand for separation, but 'a demand for a Federal Union, one of the essential constituents of which was the preservation of the unity and integrity of the Empire'.[7] In Arthur Griffith's copious archive of newspaper cuttings the Cambridge speech was a particular favourite of his, and he put it to good use.

The vicious quarrel among the anti-Parnellites probably did greater injury to the repute of constitutional nationalism than the original Parnell split. Yet it did not create the immediate disillusionment which might have been expected, and is conventionally ascribed to it. The dilemma of the nationalist polity ran deeper than the mutual antagonisms of its political leaders, though it is hard to separate from them.

The re-unification of the party on 30 January 1900 after a decade of recrimination was both a fraught and a subdued event. Redmond, supported by Healy but not by Dillon, was elected its chairman on 6 February 1900. The United Irish League became the national organisation of the Irish Parliamentary Party at a party convention in June from which Healy stood aloof. From inauspicious beginnings an enduring relationship developed between Redmond and Dillon. Dillon was more viscerally nationalist than Redmond, and was suspicious of southern landlords and of the pursuit of conciliation, which Redmond was not. Redmond was forced to defer to Dillon's views. While their collaboration provided the central axis of the re-united party, their relations remained strangely distant. On land purchase, in particular, Dillon continued to enunciate his own position, as if oblivious to Redmond's. The leadership of the Irish Parliamentary Party might be crudely characterised as a diarchy in which Redmond directed strategy at Westminster while Dillon toured the platforms in Ireland and directed the United Irish League machine.

At the general election in October 1900 the Healyites stood as independent nationalists. Though Healy held his own seat in North Louth the result marked the end of Healyism as a discrete political force. At a convention in Dublin in December William O'Brien, who had compared Healy's continued presence to 'a poisoned bullet in the body of a man', carried Healy's expulsion from the Irish Parliamentary Party.

Dillon expressed his implacable opposition to the Wyndham Land Act in what became known as 'the Swinford Revolt' in August 1903. As a fervent apostle of 'conciliation', O'Brien broke with Dillon and Redmond. The way was thereby opened for the phased reconciliation of Healy and O'Brien, throwing into reverse a notorious public antagonism that had come into being on Parnell's death.

The general election of January 1906 resulted in a Liberal landslide. Healy opposed the new goverment's ill-fated sop to the Irish Parliamentary Party – the Irish Council Bill of 1907. Following tortuous negotiations the party was briefly re-re-united with the admission of O'Brien and Healy in January 1908, but in the wake of the 'Baton Convention' of the United Irish League in February 1909 an infuriated O'Brien resigned his parliamentary seat, which was filled by Healy's brother, Maurice, out of parliament since 1900.

The general election of January 1910 left Redmond's Irish Parliamentary Party with the balance of power. The domestic British constitutional crisis engendered by Lloyd George's 'People's Budget' came suddenly to encompass Irish Home Rule. Seven O'Brienites had been returned, and Healy scraped back in North Louth. O'Brien established his All-for-Ireland-League in March 1910. The relatively strong showing of the O'Brienites was attributable, in part, to Irish opposition, fanned by O'Brien and Healy, to Lloyd George's budget which included taxation measures opposed by the Irish publicans and distillery interests. The Liberal imperialists in the cabinet were aghast at the prospect of depending on Irish votes. Redmond held fiercely to the 'no veto, no budget' tenet, and was demonised in the British press. The British parties failed to achieve a compromise, and the general election of December 1910 left the Irish Parliamentary Party still holding the balance of power. The Parliament Act of 1911 replaced the veto of the House of Lords with a suspensive power under a procedure of forbidding complexity.

O'Brien, abetted by Healy – who mostly sought to exercise a restraining influence on O'Brien – pursued an irresponsible and opportunistic course, continuing to attack Lloyd George's budgetary provisions (O'Brien condemned 'this Radical–Socialist government') and unsuccessfully attempted to undermine Redmond's leverage at Westminster. The O'Brienites sustained a major reversal in the December 1910 election, and Healy's alliance with O'Brien cost him the clerical support he needed to hold North Louth. He was out of parliament until March 1911, when he was returned for the O'Brienite fief of Cork North-East.

5 Home Rule Crisis

On 11 April 1912, a quarter century after the defeat of Gladstone's First Home Rule Bill, the government introduced its Government of Ireland Bill. This is not the place to rehearse the familiar sequence of events that followed: the burgeoning resistance in Ulster, abetted by the Tories; Redmond's resistance to a partitionist 'mutilation' of Ireland; and his coerced agreement to the opting out of individual Ulster counties for six years. By late July 1914 the issue had effectively come down to how many of the Ulster counties were to be excluded. The dilemma of Redmond and Dillon was clear. They held a winning hand on Home Rule for Ireland outside the north-east. On the inclusion of most of the Ulster counties, they had a weak hand. Public opinion in Ireland, long nurtured on a rhetoric in which Home Rule might be deferred in time but not territorially circumscribed, was unprepared for the exclusion of the north-east. The danger was that partition, and the experience of Ulster resistance, would affirm the idea, previously held only by a small minority in nationalist Ireland, that the paradigm of Home Rule had become, in the long interval from Parnell's death, historically superseded and conceptually inadequate. Without the war, Redmond and Dillon could probably have pulled it off, reconciling a nationalist majority to partition as part of a Home Rule settlement. Conversely the Easter Rising can be viewed as a last chance bid by the insurgents to thwart nationalist inclinations to be satisfied with a Home Rule Ireland. The dualism of the rising was obscured in the *éclat* of martyrdom: if it was a ritualistic confrontation of British power, it was equally the symbolic initiation of a proxy civil war directed against Redmond and the Irish Parliamentary Party.

Neither the Great War nor the rising alone sealed the fate of the Irish Parliamentary Party. The party continued to win the seats it was expected to win in the artificially prolonged war parliament up to the Cork West by-election of November 1916. On 3 August 1914 Redmond rose in the House of Commons to advocate the withdrawal of British troops from Ireland: the nationalist and loyalist volunteer forces would defend the island. The Government of Ireland Bill was enacted on 18 September, but suspended for the duration of the war and subject to amending provision for Ulster. On 20 September Redmond set off from Dublin for Aughavanagh, Parnell's old hunting lodge in Wicklow, which was his Irish residence. Nearing home he stopped off to address

Irish Volunteers drilling at Woodenbridge. He urged them 'to account yourselves as men, not only in Ireland itself, but wherever the firing line extends, in defence of right, of freedom, and of religion in this war'. Redmond's unstinted support of the allied war effort was, in its time, less controversial than might be thought. In the split in the Irish volunteers that ensued the overwhelming majority supported Redmond. Dillon did not dissent, while he did not share Redmond's ardour and held aloof from recruitment. Healy and William O'Brien both advocated enlistment, though Healy could not suppress the temptation to refer – if only privately – to the Redmondites as 'the Bridgeguards'.[8]

No one had reckoned on the bloody protractedness of the war. Redmond was ill-paid for his magnanimity, and was denied an Irish division by the War Office suspicious of the National Volunteers. Redmond refused cabinet office when the coalition government was formed in May 1915, while Carson entered the cabinet as Attorney General. He did secure the exemption of Ireland from conscription, imposed in Britain in January 1916.

6 The Rising and After

Redmond badly underestimated the resolve of the insurgents of Easter 1916. Dillon, who lived in North Great George's Street, was in Dublin throughout the Rising. In the Commons on 11 May he re-found the voice of his agrarian youth. Defending the courage of the rebels, he condemned the Dublin executions which were still in progress, and protested: 'you are washing out our whole life work in a sea of blood'.

The immediate political sequel to the Rising involved negotiations conducted by Lloyd George with unionists and nationalists to give effect to Home Rule. These eventuated in an agreement to exclude six counties, which included Tyrone and Fermanagh. This, Lloyd George represented to Redmond, would be on a temporary basis. Later accusations of perfidiousness against Lloyd George were both well-founded and beside the point – it was never going to be possible to dis-assemble separate arrangements made for the excluded Ulster counties. The assent of the northern nationalists to what transpired to be an abortive accord was secured at a meeting in Belfast in June only by the suasions of the northern nationalist leader, Joseph Devlin, and Redmond's threat to resign.

It all turned to dust. The government resolved on permanent exclusion: as Stephen Gwynn put it, 'we were thrown over'. With the death of his brother Willie, who had heroically enlisted at the age of fifty-four, on the front in Belgium in June 1917 personal tragedy was added to unremitting political adversity. Dillon despaired of Westminster politics without abandoning parliamentarism. He held aloof from the Irish Convention of 1917, Redmond's last gambit. He participated in the broad nationalist resistance to the threat of conscription, encountering, presumably for the first time, his adversaries Éamon de Valera and Arthur Griffith at the Mansion House Conference of April 1918.

William O'Brien's standing was destroyed by the rising and he renounced standing at the general election; Healy hoped to hold on. He believed no less strongly than Dillon that Sinn Féin's policy of abstention was utterly misconceived, but was less intolerant of Sinn Féin than his brother Maurice whom he tried to bring round. Outmanoeuvred by Sinn Féin, Healy was forced to make good on an offer to resign in October 1918. On a Sunday in November he had a visit at his home in Glenaulin in Chapelizod from two Sinn Féiners, whom he realised were Michael Collins and Harry Boland, who were curious to see how far he could be drawn.

John Redmond died on 6 March 1918. Dillon delivered the funeral oration at his grave in Waterford, and assumed the leadership of the Irish Parliamentary Party. The general election of December 1918 marked the triumph of Sinn Féin, even if its sweep of the parliamentary seats under the straight vote belied the still very substantial vote for the Irish Parliamentary Party. Dillon lost the East Mayo seat he had held since 1885 to Éamon de Valera by a margin of two to one. Irish politics was truly a cruel game. He cleaved obstinately to the conviction that Lloyd George had deliberately sought to bring about the defeat of the Irish Parliamentary Party. He died on 4 August 1927.

Redmond, Dillon and Healy were creatures of the great Irish Parliamentary Party of Parnell. What united them might seem to render the divisions between them across the course of their political careers petty, but they were not. Each of them responded in divergent ways to the common *problematique* of parliamentary nationalism after Parnell. That was not merely the loss of a commanding leader, but the transformation of Irish and British politics which had begun to take effect in his lifetime. These issues might be summarised as the satiation of Irish agrarian grievances, and the creation of a class of peasant proprietors; the post-split ascendancy of the Catholic Church in Ireland; the duration of conservative government until 1906, and the uninhibited radicalisation of conservative resistance to Home Rule in opposition thereafter; as well as the sharply diminishing Liberal commitment to home rule after Gladstone. Ulster unionist resistance to Home Rule was always there, anticipated by Parnell, but not mobilised in 1886 or 1893.

The massive electoral ascendancy of the Irish Parliamentary Party gave a somewhat misleading impression of its actual political strength. Francis Cruise O'Brien, in 1908, shrewdly assessed the party's dilemma: 'The Irish Party... has concealed the fact that the Irish people, what with their land question settled, and their little local grievances to be ventilated, take no practical or living interest in Home Rule, and it has concealed it by lashing and whipping the Irish people into an appearance of interest, or rather, of adhesion to the demand.'[9]

Ireland had also changed culturally, or more accurately was undergoing a process of cultural change. Warre B. Wells, the author of the first, impressively objective, full biography of Redmond wrote that 'while intellectually the Home Rule policy was to a large extent sterile, intellectually *Sinn Féin* was fertile'. Redmond, like others, had failed to realise that 'the machine had broken down'. The Irish Parliamentary Party had been conceived as a transitional entity. Parnell had repeatedly asserted that he did not believe in the permanence of an Irish Parliamentary Party at Westminster. The relationship of the Irish Parliamentary Party to 'Ireland' – meaning both the prospective Irish state, and the actual people of Ireland – was as central to the self-definition of parliamentary nationalism as the pursuit of Home Rule itself. The reunited Irish Parliamentary Party needed, from 1900, to enter into a more fluid, less seemingly imperious relationship to contemporary Ireland. Weighed down with a crushing burden of expectation, and engaged in what they believed to be the final push for Home Rule, the reconceptualisation of the party's role was the last thing on Redmond and Dillon's mind. Healy openly questioned the role of the party, but his cheerfully cynical critique came close to espousing the abandonment of any serious pretensions to the exercise of political authority through parliamentary nationalism.

7 Conclusion

In the original *Shaping of Modern Ireland* John Dillon did not feature as a subject. The amends made in this volume are fully merited. He was, in his time, a dominant personality in Irish politics, more present on the Irish terrain than John Redmond: Francis Cruise O'Brien wrote 'Ireland has *felt* Mr. Dillon. The wave of his enthusiasm has crossed it in fire.' Dillon had come to political maturity in the agrarian struggle and in the early Parnell era, and he never deviated from that ardent trajectory. Cruise O'Brien wrote that there was about him nothing of the contemporary: 'He does not strike one as a present-day European statesman, nor as a professional politician, as one understands the term in our modern system. He does strike one as an antique Roman.'[10] Dillon was not altogether unconscious of change, but little disposed and ill-equipped to adapt to it. In a rare moment of semi-introspection he wrote to his friend and collaborator, T.P. O'Connor, after the election of January 1910: 'The truth is that Irish politics is and has been for a considerable time a much more complex problem than it used to be.'[11] Of all the figures in the Irish Parliamentary Party, his career has the longest historical reach, connecting Young Ireland (through his father) with the Ireland of Sinn Féin. D.P. Moran characterised him as 'a political fossil' – if he was it was of the most remarkable kind.

The coda belongs to Healy, who alone survived to play a role in the politics of the independent Irish state. He intervened on the periphery of the treaty negotiations in London. After the death of Arthur Griffith, who could never forgive his role in bringing down Parnell, Healy was sworn in as the Governor General of the Irish Free State on 6 December 1922, and held that office until 1928. It is ironic that Healy should alone have been the survivor of the *ancien regime* of the Irish Parliamentary Party to hold high office in the new state. His appointment, which required British assent, and was vaguely intended to reassure southern Irish unionist opinion, was made politically possible by his record of conspicuous dissentience from the leadership of the Irish Parliamentary Party across the preceding two decades. Tim Healy died on 26 March 1931.

The contest between Sinn Féin and the Irish Parliamentary Party endures in Irish political memory. It commands continuing attention among historians, who struggle to transcend the schism precipitated by the Rising.[12] The honourable failure of the Irish Parliamentary Party is as significant for the democratic legitimacy of Sinn Féin and of the independent Irish state as the outcome of the 1918 election. The graceless disparagement of the role of the Irish Parliamentary Party of Redmond and Dillon (and of Healy) on one side of Irish nationalist politics, and the diffidence in acknowledging it on the other, is yielding slowly to a consciousness of the continuities of Irish politics through successive ascendancies. This enhanced sense of the cyclical was prefigured by James Joyce, who on the first page of *Finnegans Wake* evoked Parnell's displacement of his predecessor Isaac Butt: 'a kidscad buttended a bland old isaac'.

Further Reading:

F. Callanan, *The Parnell Split* (Cork, 1992)
C. Cruise O'Brien, *Parnell and his Party 1880–90* (Oxford, 1957)
S. Gwynn, *John Redmond's Last Years* (London, 1919)
D. Gwynn, *The Life of John Redmond* (London, 1932)
P. Maume, *The Long Gestation: Irish Nationalist Life 1891–1918* (Dublin, 1999)
D. Meleady, *Redmond: The Parnellite* (Cork, 2007)
M. O'Callaghan, *British High Politics and a Nationalist Ireland* (Cork, 1994)
W. B. Wells, *John Redmond: A Biography* (London, 1919)

Notes

1   R. Barry O'Brien, *The Life of Charles Stewart Parnell 1846–1891* (New York, 1898), pp.i, 213.
2   F. Callanan, *Tim Healy*, pp. 66-72, 114–50.
3   W.B. Wells, *The Life of John Redmond* (London, 1919), p.75.
4   D. Meleady, *Redmond: The Parnellite* (Cork, 2007), pp.182–9.
5   See Callanan, *T. M. Healy*, p.412.
6   The late Michael O'Leary, former Tánaiste and leader of the Labour Party, told me that a lady in Cork who had read my biography of Healy commented that I had got Healy all wrong, treating him as a villain whereas he was a rogue.
7   *Irish Daily Independent*, 27 February 1895.
8   See Callanan, *Tim Healy*, p.511.
9   *Leader*, 6 June 1908.
10   *Leader*, 12 March 1910.
11   F.S.L. Lyons, *John Dillon: A Biography* (London, 1968), p.313.
12   Studies devoted to Redmond and the later Irish Parliamentary Party are almost inescapably prone to counterfactual drift. James McConnel's *The Irish Parliamentary Party and the Third Home Rule Crisis* (Dublin, 2013) is alert against the stereotyping of the Irish Parliamentary Party but does not substantially reframe the narrative; Ronan Fanning's critique of the Irish Parliamentary Party in *Fatal Path: British Government and Irish Revolution 1910–22* (London, 2014) by contrast is informed by a somewhat exorbitant Sinn Féin – Irish Free State legitimism. A point that tends to be lost in the preoccupation with 1916 is that there was more to Sinn Féin than its embrace of the Rising, even if the Sinn Féin victory in the 1918 general election is scarcely conceivable without it.

CHAPTER 4

Douglas Hyde

PATRICK MAUME

1 Introduction

At the 1938 inauguration of Douglas Hyde as first President of Ireland, which took place in St Patrick's Hall of Dublin Castle, Éamon de Valera declared: 'In you we greet the successor of our rightful princes, and in your accession to office we hail the closing of the breach that has existed since the undoing of our nation at Kinsale.'[1] As always with de Valera's statements, this contains layers of meaning which are not apparent at first glance. One is site-specific; the ceiling of St Patrick's Hall is decorated with a painting of Irish kings paying homage to Henry II, executed in the late eighteenth century to affirm the unbreakability of the connection between Britain and Ireland whose evanescence was signalled by the inauguration of an elected Irish head of state. The second was more straightforward. In proclaiming Hyde, a Protestant and descendant of colonists, to be an embodiment of a resurgent Ireland founded on the Gaelic tradition in whose revival Hyde had played a central role, de Valera was affirming that this Irish nationalism encompassed and included the Protestant minority north and south. (This message was sadly lost on the parish priest of St Paul's, Arran Quay – the Catholic parish in which Áras an Uachtaráin is located – who wrote to the government demanding that Hyde should pay his parish dues on the grounds that whatever his private convictions, he was president of a Catholic nation.)

Myles Dillon's essay on Hyde in *The Making of Modern Ireland* is shaped by Dillon's own consciousness of what Ireland – and he himself, as a Celtic scholar – owed to Hyde in the revival of popular awareness of the Gaelic tradition and the creation of an infrastructure to sustain and revive the language. At the same time,we must bear in mind that Dillon's candidacy to succeed Hyde as Professor of Irish in 1932 was turned down partly because of his outspoken opposition to the regulations which made Irish compulsory both for matriculation in the National University of Ireland (NUI) and for a variety of professional and governmental employments. This suggests that Hyde and the Gaelic League were partly responsible for the triumph of a narrow version of national identity which had supplanted a broader nationalist vision supposedly represented by the parliamentary nationalism incarnated by Dillon's father, John; he had outspokenly opposed the compulsory Irish requirement for the NUI at its inauguration. In discussing the extent to which Hyde himself was a product of the colonial tradition, Dillon implies that Hyde's own limitations helped to create the oversimplification which, in Dillon's view, marred the implementation of the Gaelic Revival.

Zealous Irish-Ireland admirers of Hyde, such as Daniel Corkery, who recalled the 1903 experience of watching Hyde perform in one of his own Irish-language plays both as 'my first glimpse of the Gaeltacht'[2] and the first time he laid eyes on a living writer and possible role-model for his own literary aspirations, saw in Hyde the exemplary Anglo-Irishman who cast off the derivative and exploitative culture of the Ascendancy to identify with the richness of Irish folk culture and to explore and express the lives of the people. Dillon's personal acquaintance with Hyde at University College Dublin – which he draws on in a series of fascinating vignettes – made him aware of the extent to which Hyde retained many of the tastes and habits of the small gentry among whom he grew up, including a certain easygoing amateurism disconcerting to Dillon's rigorous scholarly training and middle-class work ethic.

2 Family Background

Hyde was conscious of his descent from a junior branch of the Hydes of Castlehyde in Co Cork; he was related to the Lords De Freyne, whose estate (where the young Hyde regularly went shooting with his father and brothers) was the scene of periodic and bitterly-fought land agitation between the early 1880s and the sale of the estate under the 1903 Wyndham Land Act (when Hyde's summer residence, Ratra House, was bought and presented to him by the Gaelic League). His brother, John Oldfield Hyde – to whom Hyde was not particularly close – served as an officer in the Royal Irish Constabulary during the Land War and applied unsuccessfully to become a Resident Magistrate before his death in 1896. Some aspects of this background were used against Hyde in periodic whispering campaigns throughout his career, with some republican critics of his presidency claiming that, rather than the first president of a sovereign Ireland, he was simply the latest Governor-General.

As son of the Rector of Tibohine (Frenchpark, Co Roscommon) who had encouraged his youngest son's interest in the Irish language in the hope that it might assist Douglas in following his father into the Church of Ireland ministry and securing a living in the West of Ireland, Hyde exemplifies Vivian Mercier's point that many of the leading figures of the Irish Revival were children or grandchildren (Yeats, Synge) of Church of Ireland clerical families, and that their cultural pursuits can be seen as a secularised mutation of ancestral religiosity, though Rev Arthur Hyde, unlike the Synges and the father of Standish James O'Grady, was not particularly evangelical. Hyde never formally abandoned Anglicanism, though he was determinedly heterodox and anti-dogmatic, feeling that organised religious bodies too often functioned as a disguised form of political rivalry and regretting that evangelical attempts to use Irish as an instrument of proselytism had actively harmed the language; he was vaguely anti-materialistic, noted in his diary that the survival of Scots Gaelic in the Highlands was assisted by its connections with democratically-organised Presbyterian religiosity, and combined diplomatic relations with the Irish Catholic clergy and genuine friendship with some priests such as Eugene O'Growney, with privately-expressed exasperation at the hostility of many West of Ireland clergy to the language and the belief that Irish priests would maintain excessive intellectual restrictions over their followers for decades to come. (As Gaelic League president, Hyde periodically expressed private apprehensions that clericalists such as the lexicographer Fr Patrick Dineen and the polemical editor D.P. Moran were systematically plotting to take over the organisation; these fears were probably exaggerated but contained some substance.)

Later scholarship, notably Dominic Daly's extracts with commentary from Hyde's diaries[3] and the standard biography by Janet and Gareth Dunleavy has underlined the importance of Hyde's family and social background and the extent of his participation in the 1880s political and intellectual debates in student circles around Trinity.[4] His association with the Contemporary Club and the *Dublin University Review* – dominated by Protestant intellectuals such as C.H. Oldham who supported Irish nationalism in principle while avoiding submission to the populist simplifications, rigid discipline and priestly influence of Parnell's party and other nationalist political movements – might be seen as supporting Dillon's assumption that Hyde's political position was always a lukewarm nationalism so far to the right of the Parliamentary Party as to be almost indistinguishable from unionism. Dillon himself regards late-Victorian Irish unionism as simply socially and intellectually barren; he remarks that the Gaelic League 'gave to the Protestants the opportunity for which they must often have longed in vain, to be able to identify themselves with a great national interest other than Big Business and the activities of the Turf Club'.[5] This view assumes that Hyde's achievement was simply to emancipate himself from this background and that his limitations stemmed from failure to complete the process. Hyde himself, as we shall see, shared much of this contempt for late-Victorian would-be cosmopolitan unionism; but while this contempt reflected the real social and political blindnesses of that world, it was not altogether justified. Hyde's annoyance at the declaration of the Trinity don George Francis Fitzgerald that he would do all he could to discourage the use of Irish because he believed its survival was harmful to the country was justified. What it tells us about Hyde's low regard for science was almost tragic, in that he made no allowance for Fitzgerald being a great Irish physicist whose discoveries in due course were to contribute to Einstein's achievement.

Dillon's view, however, overlooks the ways in which the young Hyde was a radical by the standards of his background. The fact that he was educated at home rather than at a boarding-school meant that he was less insulated from the people around him than many of his contemporaries – though such elite participation in popular culture might have been more common a generation or two previously than by Hyde's day. Many provincial gentry and Protestant clergy were ambivalent about the cosmopolitan Dublin metropolitan culture centred on late-Victorian Trinity, seeing it as dangerously infected by the religious scepticism represented by such figures as W.E.H. Lecky, whose election as Trinity MP was met by a revolt of backwoods graduates. (Douglas himself recorded his father's complaint that Trinity had turned Douglas's two elder brothers into an agnostic and a good-for-nothing.)

The Dunleavys suggest that Hyde's youthful fascination with the Irish language and folk-stories of local people around Frenchpark, and his apparent view of the local storyteller and old Fenian, Seamus Hart, as a father-substitute reflected a desire to create an alternative persona to shield himself from the intermittent verbal and physical abuse of his father; they argue that his youthful writings in English reflect a different persona as Anglo-Irish squireen, and that occasional jottings in French suggest a third, more hedonistic persona.[6] (Perhaps Dillon's own background should have made him more sensitive to such cultural osmosis influencing elite children; the Dillons were brought up by a nurse after their mother's death in 1906, and Maurice Manning, biographer of Dillon's younger brother James, has suggested that James was permanently influenced by the fervent devotional Catholicism of this substitute mother-figure.)

3 Nationalism and the Language Question

The early Irish-language publications of Hyde's late teens and early twenties, which appeared in nationalist journals under his pen-name An Craoibhín Aoibhinn (the Pleasant Little Branch), reinvent his background as that of a native-speaking peasant whose (fictitious) grandfather fought on the rebel side in 1798. In the early Gaelic League days, separatists were sufficiently aware of Hyde's literary celebrations of rebellion to see him as one of them. Arthur Griffith's satire on the enemies of the Gaelic League, 'The Thirteenth Lock', featured a scene in which 'D.P. Hooligan' (Moran) lies in wait by the roadside to knife Hyde as part of a clerical takeover of the League; the unsuspecting Hyde's patriotic credentials are emphasised as he sings his own 'Lament for the Croppy'. Even these youthful celebrations of rebellion, however, show a certain suspicion of the ability of physical force to achieve concrete results; 'O'Mahony's Lament', spoken in the persona of the exiled Fenian leader, John O'Mahony, whom Hyde admired as a Gaelic scholar, is an expression of despair as well as an assertion of personal honour. Equally, while Hyde respected O'Donovan Rossa as a person and as a language enthusiast (as a native speaker and famine survivor Rossa embodied the cultural traumas which Hyde's Gaelic revivalism sought to address), Hyde's verse 'eulogy' for Rossa covertly criticises him for inciting the people to a rebellion for which they are wholly unprepared.

As a Trinity student Hyde drew attention by his outspoken advocacy of nationalism and expression of sympathy for Home Rule and land agitation at a time when the dominant forces within Trinity saw themselves as faced with a civil war in which obscurantist mob violence threatened their classicist humanist civilisation. Hyde later believed that

Trinity dons such as Provost George Salmon had covertly sabotaged his academic career because of his political views, and his later clashes with Trinity dons (including his successful resistance to the attempts of Mahaffy and Atkinson in 1899 to abolish Irish as an intermediate examination subject, and his 1903 satirical play *The Bursting of the Bubble* in which Mahaffy and his colleagues are forced by magic to speak only Irish during a viceregal visit to the college) were given added sharpness by resentment. The older Hyde may have felt a certain satisfaction when, in 1931, accepting election as president of Trinity's Historical Society, he remarked 'I will be a very poor successor of statesmen and men of affairs like Ashbourne, Ross and Glenavy' – the latter were unionist lawyer-politicians who had been criticised for using the college as a stepping-stone to judicial advancement.[7]

Hyde's collections of folklore and folk-poetry, with his limpid translations (some of the 'original' lyrics, such as the famous verse 'Mise Raifteri an File', Hyde is suspected of having written himself as exercises in covert self-expression) and his revivalist journalism paved the way for his advocacy of the language as the key to Irish identity in his famous October 1892 lecture 'The Necessity for De-Anglicising Ireland', which led to the creation of the Gaelic League. Although Hyde was only one of several individuals involved in organising the League – and admirers of Eoin MacNeill later complained that the role of Hyde had overshadowed MacNeill's centrality to the hard work of organisation – and although there had been previous advocates of language revival (notably Thomas Davis) and a thin trickle of Irish-language journalism in nationalist newspapers, Hyde played a decisive role in making the language a popular cause. He proved an indispensable leader to the League because of his combination of literary, social and academic credentials and his skill as an inspirational speaker and diplomat. All of these attributes were on display in the way in which he mustered testimonials from continental scholars to the literary value of spoken Irish to rebut Mahaffy and Atkinson's attempts to deploy their own academic authority in support of the proposition that the language lacked academic value because it lacked standardisation and that much of the ancient literature was silly or obscene.

Without Hyde's skill in raising funds for the League in America and holding together its disparate factions, it is unlikely that it would have achieved as much as it did in rousing enthusiasm for the language and bringing about its belated development as a medium of print culture. Publicly professed – often genuinely felt – admiration for Hyde helped to hold together the League despite divisions over such issues as the rival merits of Munster and Connacht Irish, folkloric or literary genres for future Irish-language literature, reliance on vernacular Irish or the creation of an artificial literary standard modelled on early modern literature ('the native speaker is the worst enemy the language possesses and it must be saved from him before he destroys it completely' declared Fr John O'Reilly in advocating a return to the language of Geoffrey Keating). Likewise, it contributed to contain attempts of rival political groupings to infiltrate the League, control it and subordinate it to their own political projects. Whatever Hyde's private denunciations of the Munster-oriented and generally dissident Keating Branch as 'footpads' and the suggestions by some of those brought into close contact with him that Hyde's geniality masked a more complex and somewhat unknowable personality facetiously compared to Jekyll and Hyde, he nonetheless held it together. The fact that the League managed to remain independent for so long is itself a reflection of the breakdown of the hegemony over the nationalist public sphere which the Irish Parliamentary Party had exercised in its Parnellian heyday. Despite Dillon's view of the Irish Parliamentary Party as representing a broader nationalism, it is unlikely that a Gaelic League subordinated to and 'vampirised' by the Party (with Hyde elevated and marginalised to a seat at Westminster, which he was actually offered at one point) would have been more broadminded than the Gaelic League as adjunct to the separatist movement which emerged after Hyde's defeat by the Irish Republican Brotherhood and its allies over its explicit commitment to nationalism led to his resignation as League president in 1915. (The Irish Parliamentary Party contained its share of enlightened statesmen, but it was also a populist movement with its own intolerances; in suggesting that his father was correct in opposing the imposition of compulsory Irish for National University of Ireland matriculation, Dillon occludes the fact that the decisive showdown at which his father was defeated took place not within the Gaelic League, but at a national convention of the Party's support organisation, the United Irish League.)

4 Unwanted Legacies?

There were, of course, limitations to Hyde's achievement. As Roy Foster has argued, the cultural revival, of which the Gaelic League was part, was seen, in retrospect, as turning away from a parliamentary nationalism discredited by the Parnell Split and preparing the way for a renewed physical-force separatism (this view was not confined to those who thought it a good thing; it is implicit in Dillon's ambivalent assessment of Hyde's legacy), but at the time it was presented as trying to create a common ground where not only the nationalist divisions of the 1890s but the bitter unionist/nationalist divisions of the 1880s could be reconciled in a broader vision of Irishness. Hyde's appeal to Irish – something in the background of which most were only vaguely aware – as transcending the divisions of contemporary Ireland came as a revelation to many, but the revelation was filtered through the pre-existing attitudes of those who received it. D.P. Moran stated: 'once Ireland had home power, she could laugh at those who would deny her home rule' and his view of cultural self-confidence as key to social and economic revival were legitimate extrapolations from Hyde's vision; but as the example of Moran shows, Hyde's vision was all too easily reinvented in terms of the nativist chauvinism already visible in nationalist popular politics in the 1880s.

Hyde's biting analysis of the cultural impact of language change in terms of shame and cultural trauma coexists with what can be termed facile antimodernism; it is noteworthy that some of the forces he criticises for undermining the language – the dissemination throughout the country of a popular newspaper press, the development of mass political agitation – were also major forces for social and economic modernisation. J.J. Lee notes that many features of Irish life whose displacement by recent British fashions Hyde deplored – such as the wearing of kneebreeches – were themselves imported from Britain at an earlier date, and facetiously suggests that Hyde's sartorial lamentations might have been summed up in the slogan 'down with trousers'.[8]

Again, the romanticisation and exaltation of the peasant associated with the Gaelic Revival needs to be seen in its contemporary context – a society in which a large majority of the population either worked the land or were closely descended from those who had done so, and with a sense that significant portions of the elites were in denial about the dependence of their prosperous bourgeois lives on the grimier realities which their social proprieties were designed to shut out; hence, the League's appeal to discontented young bohemians such as those described in Roy Foster's *Vivid Faces*. In its heyday the Gaelic League was celebrated as a great democratic educational movement, with commentators pointing out, for example, that student numbers at the League's summer college in Ballingeary in West Cork far exceeded those at the moribund Edwardian Queen's College Cork, and compulsory Irish for NUI matriculation was being advocated on the grounds that the plebeian nature of the Irish-language movement meant that compulsion would assist poorer students to offset the advantages of their more fortunate competitors. This could easily develop into fantasy and anti-intellectualism, as with the tendency for Irish-language writing to be treated as a record of the spoken tongue ('Tá Gaeilge maith san leabhar seo') instead of a literary artefact. Dillon's description of Hyde as an academic, turning his lectures into easygoing conversation classes, is not only the attitude of a trained scholar of Old Irish towards a folklorist and vernacular conversationalist, it also reflects the fact that academics of Dillon's generation were accustomed to keeping a greater distance between themselves and their undergraduates than was the case in later decades, and Hyde's accessibility was relatively unusual. Indeed, some of the older Roscommon people, interviewed by the Dunleavys, who recalled Hyde at Ratra, remarked that one facet of his approachability was precisely that he was at ease with himself and did not pretend not to be a squireen (in contrast to some other patrician Leaguers who reinvented themselves as bekilted synthetic Gaels).

While Dillon is correct in noting Hyde's participation in League campaigns encouraged a mentality of censoriousness, compulsion and division between true Gaels and West Britons, he judges exclusively by the public record and so misses the complexities of Hyde's role. Like other patrician leaders of Irish popular movements, he combined the channelling of popular resentment with elite diplomacy at the opportune moment, was less involved in initiating the protest than his critics supposed and, in private, was more flexible than his public rhetoric would suggest. The Dunleavys note, for example, that Hyde was initially reluctant to support the campaign to force the post office to accept letters and parcels delivered in Irish (which Dillon vividly describes) but they also emphasise the scale of the victory achieved – to a significant extent through Hyde's diplomacy – over the principle of the post-office as an imperial service conducted through English. Similarly, they note that Hyde paid little attention to grammar in dealing with learners, believing that it was better to encourage the wavering than to draw hard and fast lines which would simply provoke opposition.[9] The most conspicuous example of Hyde's ambivalence towards the 'ban' mentality came when he was removed from his position as patron of the GAA because, in his official capacity as president, he attended an international soccer match and thus transgressed the GAA ban on foreign games – an episode whose impact and ramifications are explored by Cormac Moore.

4 Conclusion

Dillon's criticisms of Hyde, then, are probably too harsh and reflect the limited understanding of the Anglo-Irish milieu by Dillon's own social formation – a Catholic-nationalist middle class which equated itself and its own nation-forming projects with the Irish people as a whole. He wrote when Hyde was only a decade dead and when the conflicts of the 1912–23 era, and even the Land War, were still living memories. How does Hyde's legacy seem today, fifty years after Dillon, when the cultural protectionism Dillon reproved and Hyde, however inadvertently, helped to create, has largely been supplanted by globalisation? It is marked both by success and failure; an Irish-language subculture has survived and modernised, but the abandonment of the project of mass Gaelicisation through compulsion has meant that it remains a subculture, insulated from large sections of the population by the very success with which Irish has been developed as a modern medium. Only a writer fluent in Irish can deliver a comprehensive verdict; but perhaps it may be suggested that Douglas Hyde deserves commemoration not as the discoverer of a single authentic Irish identity, but for having expanded the repertoire of resources through which an identity could be developed and reinvented. Dillon's final verdict, that Hyde's great achievement brought him personal integration and contentment, remains valid.

Further Reading:

R. Dudley Edwards, *Patrick Pearse: The Triumph of Failure* (London, 1977)

G. Dunleavy and J. Dunleavy (eds), *Selected Plays of Douglas Hyde* (Washington, DC, 1991)

D. Hyde, *The Love Songs of Connacht* (Dublin, 1904)

D. Hyde, *A Literary History of Ireland* (Dublin, 1899)

C. Moore *The GAA versus Douglas Hyde* (Dublin, 2012)

B.P. Murphy, *Patrick Pearse and the Lost Republican Ideal* (Dublin, 1991)

B. Ó Conaire (ed.) *Douglas Hyde: Language, Lore and Lyrics – Essays and Lectures* (Dublin, 1986)

B. Ó Conaire (ed.), *Douglas Hyde: The Songs of Connacht*, Nos. 1–3 (Dublin, 1985)

P. O'Leary *The Prose literature of the Gaelic Revival, 1881–1921: Ideology and Innovation* (University Park, PE, 1994)

B. Stewart 'On the Necessity of De-Hydifying Irish Cultural Criticism', *New Hibernia Review*, Vol.4 No 1 (Spring 2000)

Notes

1   C. Moore *The GAA v. Douglas Hyde: The Removal of Ireland's First President as GAA Patron* (Cork, 2012), p.64.

2   P. Maume, *Life that is Exile: Daniel Corkery and the Search for Irish Ireland* (Belfast, 1993), p.13. The original reference is Daniel Corkery 'My First Glimpse of the Gaeltacht', *An Gaedheal*, December 1937, pp.6–7.

3   D. Daly, *The Young Douglas Hyde* (Shannon, 1974).

4   G. Dunleavy and J. Dunleavy, *Douglas Hyde: A Maker of Modern Ireland* (Berkeley and Los Angeles, 1991).

5   Dillon, 'Hyde' in *SMI*, p.55

6   See Dunleavy and Dunleavy *Douglas Hyde*, pp.26–41, 48–58.

7   See Dunleavy and Dunleavy, *Douglas Hyde*, p.359.

8   J.J. Lee, *Modernisation of Irish Society 1848–1918* (Dublin, 1973), pp.137–41.

9   See Dunleavy and Dunleavy, *Douglas Hyde*, pp. 228–243, 357–9.

CHAPTER 5

Arthur Griffith

MICHAEL LAFFAN

1 Introduction

Terence de Vere White began his contribution to *The Shaping of Modern Ireland* with a vivid allegory. He identified Arthur Griffith as a playwright who worked for ten years writing a drama that no one would put on. Eventually it became a popular success, but in a form that bore little resemblance to the work he had composed. De Vere White went on to describe him as a leading actor in this distorted version of his own play, and some people saw this role as the great achievement of his life. Others viewed it as an anti-climax. De Vere White's chapter ended as it had begun, with more than a hint at the drama of Griffith's varied life: 'The theatre had gone up in flames and was blazing round him when he died.'

De Vere White provided a balanced account of Griffith's character and achievements. He wrote elegantly, painting a vivid picture for us of one of the great characters in the shaping of modern Ireland: 'he sat down, without fortune, friends, influence or any form of higher education, to work out a political philosophy for his country'. In general his assessment has worn well. Apart from Pakenham's *Peace by Ordeal* and a scholarly biography – written in Irish and, therefore, not widely accessible – little of value had been published until he gave his Thomas Davis lecture in 1956. But in the decades since then, many new manuscript collections, government records and other sources have become available to scholars. Our understanding of the events of 1921 has been enriched by the publication of the private Dáil debates on the Anglo-Irish Treaty and of Thomas Jones's *Whitehall Diary*. (According to one reviewer, thanks to these diaries 'Lloyd George's Irish policy can be followed in more detail than any other episode in British history.'[1])

As a consequence, de Vere White's contribution has been overwhelmed by the volume and quality of later writings. In the past sixty years Griffith has been the subject of a short but valuable booklet, a brief life and three full biographies. Historians have scrutinised his role as editor, journalist and architect of political programmes and historical parallels. The successive Sinn Féin parties and the Dáil governments of 1919–21 have been examined in detail. Much attention has been devoted to the treaty negotiations and the divisions that followed. The Civil War, which had long been neglected by historians, has, belatedly, attracted research.

2 Journalist and Politician

In countless articles, monographs and general surveys a broadly consistent picture of Griffith has emerged. Above all, he was paradoxical. He was modest and unworldly, yet self-confident, pugnacious and even arrogant. According to one authority he was 'prejudiced, puritanical and extremely partisan, but also determined, courageous and unselfish'. Some years after writing his chapter for *The Shaping of Modern Ireland* de Vere White portrayed him as 'a brave, faithful, dedicated, studious, cantankerous, selfless, narrow man'.[2]

Although a devoted Parnellite, Griffith rejected two basic aspects of Parnellism: the cult of the leader and the commitment to parliamentary methods.[3] He excluded the use of force to achieve independence but he was personally aggressive – physically, as well as on paper. He has been described as a vicious and unscrupulous polemicist, and he submitted those who refused total allegiance to his definition of Ireland to unlimited abuse and slander.[4] Yet he devoted much of his life to constructing a model that he hoped would reconcile different Irish political traditions. His newspaper articles were written 'in a uniquely strident, scornful tone that conferred great authority; though in person he was more self-effacing'.[5] He was one of the most narrowly nationalist of Irish political thinkers, and also one of the most European in outlook.[6] The fact that he had (briefly) been an emigrant did not prevent him from attacking emigration. He was a busy, energetic man who enjoyed the absence of pressure while he was in jail. He was apolitical, unambitious, quarrelsome and a poor judge of people, but he nonetheless became leader of a political party and later an acting head of government.

He denigrated home rulers, republicans and many others, and he had a particular loathing of 'Englishmen' such as James Larkin and Erskine Childers. He was sociable despite his shyness; he had a devoted circle of friends with whom he drank pints in the Bailey public house; he composed and sang ballads; and he won the respect of many critics and opponents – ranging from Childers and Patrick Pearse to Augustine Birrell and Lloyd George.

He rejoiced in the independence of other small European countries such as Norway and Montenegro. He also shared a casual racism that was common at the time. He supported the Boers against Britain, but not indigenous Africans against the Boers. He disliked Jewish cosmopolitanism and associated Jews with usury, yet he sympathised with Zionism and had Jewish friends (including his own solicitor). Zionists offered the attraction of wanting to build a nation-state. He was both a man of broad literary tastes and a puritan who denounced Synge's *Playboy of the Western World*.

Critics have treated him harshly in these and in other areas where he displayed intolerance or bigotry, while often glossing over the comparable or greater prejudices displayed by many of his contemporaries.

Some of his writings have been described as containing 'dangerously anti-democratic elements'; in particular, he believed that the nation existed independently of the people who composed it and that they had no right to take certain actions.[7] Like many others – including his opponents and some of his allies in 1922 – he had little respect for majority opinion when he disagreed with it, and he viewed with 'a lofty and boundless contempt' the necessary compromises of John Redmond's Home Rule Party.[8] But he always tried to win over his opponents and – again like his allies and enemies in 1922 – 'he proved quite flexible when given mass support and the prospect of political achievement'.[9] He ended his life as a champion of majority rule.

Griffith came from a poor background and lived in poverty for most of his life. He sympathised with the suffering of the Dublin working class, but he insisted that Irish trade unionists should spurn assistance from – or even cooperation with – their British counterparts. He rejected class conflict, looking instead to the state to ensure that capital did not oppress labour and that both groups would serve the whole community. Disputes should be resolved by enforced arbitration. In some respects his ideas anticipated the corporatism that characterised the 1930s.

Until 1916 he argued that rebellion against Britain would be futile; he believed that he had learned the lesson of the Boer War, and that independence could be achieved by peaceful means. Yet, without the Easter Rising – which he had tried to prevent, by distributing Eoin MacNeill's countermanding order – it is improbable that he or his ideas would have had much influence in later years.

Like de Vere White, later historians have seen Griffith as an unenthusiastic and unsuccessful party leader; at heart he remained an editor and writer. He was a man with a mission, not a politician.[10] Even when he was acting president of the Dáil and of the underground Irish government he devoted much of his time to propaganda. There is universal agreement on his brilliance as a journalist, and although he indulged in muckraking he developed an ideology of Irish nationalism that inspired the revolutionary generation. Many of his converts would subsequently condemn him for what they saw as his unacceptable moderation.

Griffith's political philosophy was grounded on an interpretation of the Irish past, and his historically-based arguments were 'firmly held, strongly felt, and widely influential'.[11] His approach was that of a propagandist rather than a scholar; he was frequently wrong or even dishonest in his writings and he ignored inconvenient evidence. For example, he revered both Henry Grattan and John Mitchel while playing down the incompatibility between their aims and methods. He distorted the two models he offered to the Irish people, Grattan's Parliament and the Austro-Hungarian dual monarchy, choosing and rejecting whatever suited his purpose.

In defining Irish nationality he had no time for sentimentality, he paid no attention to race or religion and, in particular, he refused to identify Irishness with Catholicism. He took a utilitarian and functional rather than a mystical view of what constituted the nation.[12] But along with the great majority of nationalists he was a geographical determinist who believed that all inhabitants of the island should be citizens of an Irish state, whatever their wishes might be.

He rejected the idea that Ulster was more advanced than the rest of the island, and – like most of his contemporaries – he dismissed as bluff the unionists' threats of rebellion before the First World War. Yet, even though he continued to view their objections in economic rather than in cultural, religious or historical terms, he was exceptional in making compromise proposals designed to lessen their objections to Home Rule.

He proposed that parliamentary sittings should rotate between Dublin and Belfast (which was then the largest city on the island), that Ulster should be over-represented in the new Irish parliament, and that its MPs should be given a near-veto on economic and industrial questions. Later, in 1920, he opposed the Dáil's Belfast Boycott because it implicitly recognised partition.

While he believed that nothing should deflect attention from the achievement of national independence, he supported women's involvement in Irish public life. They were eligible for membership of his party and he upheld their right to vote. He also believed in proportional representation, even when it was used against Sinn Féin in 1920–21.

Griffith was obsessively anti-British and he tended to support any individual or any cause, however obnoxious, if it might damage Britain's interests. Yet unlike numerous other Irish nationalists he did not react against 'modernity'. On the contrary, he wanted Ireland to catch up with richer countries, he wished to emulate the achievements of British and other advanced societies, and he was criticised for trying to turn his country into an Irish Manchester. He was preoccupied with bread-and-butter questions; his concerns included efficiency, over-taxation, exports, afforestation and the exploitation of marine resources. But his vision of Ireland's economic prospects was absurdly optimistic; he claimed that it possessed vast mineral resources and that it could support a population of twenty million.

Prominent among his objectives was reform of the educational system, particularly at university level – and, characteristically, he emphasised not merely Irish studies but also economics, commerce and agriculture.

Despite his dogmatism he could be pragmatic, and he modified his views according to changes in his own and his country's circumstances. He was prepared to accept subsidies for his papers from the Irish Republican Brotherhood (IRB) while continuing to reject its methods. In 1910 he antagonised many of his allies by his readiness to contemplate an opportunistic electoral agreement with William O'Brien's All-for-Ireland League. Despite his relative lack of commitment to the Irish language, in the early years of the twentieth century he adapted his paper to placate or attract the powerful Irish-Ireland lobby.[13]

It has even been claimed that Griffith, the founder of Sinn Féin, was no Sinn Féiner: 'he had little Irish and was sceptical about much of the general ideological package concocted by the Gaelic League and the clerics.[14]

3 After the Rising

In *The Shaping of Modern Ireland* de Vere White suggested that Griffith's work was effectively done when he completed *The Resurrection of Hungary* in 1904. Yet he chose to ignore the volume's 1916 cut-off date and he went on to discuss – if in a somewhat desultory manner – Griffith's 'second career' after the Easter Rising.

In 1917–18 many former rebels decided to postpone their plans for another rebellion and to engage in political activity – of the sort that they had hitherto despised. They took over the Sinn Féin party and adopted much of its programme. In the words of one historian, 'the creation of an open organization not committed to violence, representing a broad coalition of nationalist factions, was an astonishing sequel to a violent and conspiratorial insurrection.'[15] Griffith was a central figure in bringing about a synthesis between the political and military wings of radical Irish nationalism. His plan for a dual monarchy was abandoned (just in time; its Austro-Hungarian model collapsed a year later) and he stood down as president of the party in favour of de Valera, but he remained prominent in Sinn Féin's struggle with the home rulers. Its electoral landslide in December 1918 and the creation of the Dáil in January 1919 represented the triumph of his beliefs and the implementation of his policies.

Subsequently, for a period of nearly eighteen months, he became acting president of the underground Irish government. Despite his long-term reservations about the use of force, by 1920 it was obvious to everyone that violence had achieved results; his office of acting president offered sufficient proof that bloodshed had provoked substantial change. In his post during this period, he was able to ensure that democratically-elected civilians exercised at least a theoretical control over the army, and he overcame or concealed whatever distaste he felt at some actions of IRA units and Collins's 'squad'.

Griffith was an inefficient administrator and he was not successful as acting head of a revolutionary executive. He was not identified with any single scheme that it initiated, yet everything that it did formed part of the programme that he had outlined many years earlier.[16] In these years Irish rebels did not merely take arms against British rule, they also achieved a degree of success in creating the counter-state that he had advocated. When the British commander, General Macready, examined captured correspondence laying down the Dáil government's policy he noted that 'it is almost word for word what Arthur Griffith foreshadows in that book of his "The Resurrection of Hungary"'. But after his arrest in November 1920 and de Valera's return to Ireland a month later the Dáil cabinet was led with greater firmness and authority.

Historians have appraised Griffith's roles as leader of the Irish delegation that negotiated the Anglo-Irish Treaty and as one of the principal pro-treaty leaders from January–August 1922.

De Valera has been widely blamed for not leading the delegation to London, for appointing a divided team, for his tardiness in providing it with an 'Ulster' policy', and for being elusive when the negotiations neared their climax. As chairman of the delegation Griffith was faced with an exceptional range of problems. Nonetheless he fought loyally for de Valera's policy of external association, an objective that (rightly) he saw as being unfeasible. He was consistent with his earlier beliefs in not being prepared to 'break' on the question of the crown; even more than de Valera, he was not a doctrinaire republican.

As a negotiator he could be imperturbable, and Thomas Jones recorded him as showing no alarm when threatened with chaos, crown colony government and civil war: 'he keeps himself well in hand'. But he agreed not to create difficulties for Lloyd George if the prime minister proposed a boundary commission; he acquiesced when the original suggestion was widened to envisage transfers of territory in *both* directions; and he did not pass on word of these developments to other members of the delegation or to those members of the cabinet who remained in Dublin. He imagined that in essentials a boundary commission was the same as a plebiscite and he fell for Jones's argument that 'if Sinn Fein cooperated with the P.M. we might have Ulster in before many months had passed'.[17]

Griffith shared the widespread nationalist delusion that Lloyd George could deliver some sort of Irish unity, and he failed to appreciate – or even to concern himself with – the realities of power in Britain. The prime minister had limited freedom of manoeuvre and a faction in the Conservative Party, which formed the dominant force in the government, was committed to defending the interests of Ulster unionists. It may be the case that James Craig called Lloyd George's bluff and Griffith did not but, with partition already in place and with powerful allies in London, Craig's position was considerably stronger.

At the beginning of December 1921, when Griffith returned to Dublin from London with a draft treaty proposed by the British, he was warned that its boundary commission clause was too vague and that it left too much power to the commission. Local plebiscites should be held. He saw the point of this argument but – possibly wrongly – he thought that it was, by then, too late to change the text. The question seems not to have been discussed at a deeply divisive meeting of the Irish cabinet, and Griffith may have been the only member who was concerned about the matter. On that occasion he declared himself prepared to sign the draft treaty – although soon afterwards better terms were obtained in the final round of negotiations, partly thanks to his efforts.

His readiness to sign a revised version of the treaty, even if none of the other delegates did so, has been denounced as vain and naïve; in effect he sided with Lloyd George.[18] It was undoubtedly a blunder. But he believed that the settlement was a good one and that no better terms were available.

Unlike Collins, he gave whole-hearted support to the treaty. It conceded most of what he had sought for twenty years – apart from the exclusion of Northern Ireland, the reasons for which he had come to appreciate and the extent (and duration) of which he hoped to mitigate. It was, therefore, ironic that the establishment of an independent Irish administration in January 1922, with a dual monarchy of the kind he had advocated for so long, should have been accompanied by grief and disillusionment.

Griffith fought robustly for the treaty, defending the delegates' right to sign it and stressing the impossibility of securing a republic. After the Dáil had voted narrowly in its favour he was elected president in place of de Valera, although power gravitated towards Collins's provisional government. He did not belong to this body, but he attended many of its meetings. He was characteristically determined and courageous in ignoring threats to his safety as he continued to justify the settlement with vigour (and sometimes also with venom).

Griffith was impatient to exploit the powers granted by the treaty. He was frustrated by what he saw as Collins's procrastination and his reluctance to take action against rebellious former comrades; the government should assume its responsibilities. He refused to negotiate with the dissidents. He was dismayed by Collins's electoral pact with de Valera (which ultimately benefited the pro-treaty side), yet with characteristic loyalty he went to London to defend it against an onslaught by the British government. Widespread civil war broke out soon after pro-treaty candidates won a massive majority in the general election of June 1922. Griffith was driven to despair. Although his health had been a matter of concern for some time his sudden death in August, probably of a heart attack, was unexpected.

4 Legacy

Griffith's legacy was mixed. His commitment to the principle of majority rule was vindicated, but at a heavy cost. The dual monarchy established by the treaty was retained, at least in theory, for almost thirty years – even if it became increasingly threadbare after Cumann na nGaedheal lost office in 1932. His pro-treaty colleagues discarded his economic views, although, ironically, his policy of protecting Irish industries was partially implemented by his opponents in Fianna Fáil. The Free State government treated his memory with little respect.

Griffith has attracted much criticism. His combination of political moderation with an almost obsessive nationalism ensured that he would be distrusted by two very different groups of people. A man who castigated Synge, Larkin and de Valera was bound to make enemies, both in his lifetime and posthumously. He has been the victim of sustained abuse and casual disparagement; notoriously, a Fianna Fáil Taoiseach dismissed him as 'a civil war figure'.[19]

Yet Griffith deserved his inclusion in *The Shaping of Modern Ireland*. He was one of the most original nationalist writers of his time, and he influenced a generation of revolutionaries, many of whose opinions were more radical than his own. He was a writer with imaginative ideas whose impractical schemes, nonetheless, ultimately provided a framework for a revolutionary government.

In many respects he was modern and progressive, he looked to the outside world, and he was concerned not merely with the achievement of independence but also with its use – with the construction of a prosperous Irish state. He founded a party that, in circumstances he did not envisage, became the principal voice of Irish nationalism. Its successors have dominated the political history of independent Ireland. In 1919–20 he presided over the implementation of many ideas he had advocated years earlier. He had a mixed record as principal Irish negotiator of the treaty; he made mistakes, but they probably did little serious damage, and in other respects he made the best of a bad situation. In the circumstances of 1921 the British were unlikely to make significant further concessions. And, in the final months of his life, he was a determined, even impassioned defender of the Irish people's right to decide their own destiny.

One study of him, sometimes deeply critical, concluded: 'the fact that Ireland, unlike many subsequent revolutionary regimes, established a viable democracy is largely due to Griffith ... [he was] the greatest architect of modern Ireland'.[20] Not everyone would endorse this verdict, but sixty years after de Vere White's chapter was written almost all would agree that Griffith was among the principal shapers of the Irish revolution and the independent Irish state.

Further Reading:

T. K. Daniel, 'Griffith on his Noble Head: the Determinants of Cumann na nGaedheal Economic Policy, 1922–32', *Irish Economic and Social History*, 3 (1976)

R. Davis, *Arthur Griffith and Non-Violent Sinn Féin* (Tralee, 1974)

A. Dolan, *Commemorating the Irish Civil War: History and Memory, 1923–2000* (Cambridge, 2003)

V.E. Glandon, *Arthur Griffith and the Advanced-Nationalist Press, Ireland, 1900–1922* (New York, 1985)

M. Laffan, *The Resurrection of Ireland: The Sinn Féin Party, 1916–1923* (Cambridge, 1999)

B. Maye, *Arthur Griffith* (Dublin, 1997)

O. McGee, *Arthur Griffith: A Biography* (Dublin, 2015)

S. Ó Lúing, *Art Ó Gríofa* (Dublin, 1953)

F. Pakenham, *Peace by Ordeal: An Account, from First-hand Sources, of the Negotiation and Signature of the Anglo-Irish Treaty, 1921* (London, 1935)

S. Pašeta, *Before the Revolution: Nationalism, Social Change and Ireland's Catholic Elite, 1879–1922* (Cork, 1999)

W.I. Thompson, *The Imagination of an Insurrection: Dublin, Easter 1916* (New York, 1967)

C. Younger, *Arthur Griffith* (Dublin, 1981)

Notes

1   A.J.P. Taylor, *The Observer*, 17 October 1971.

2   A. Mitchell, *Revolutionary Government in Ireland. Dáil Éireann 1919–22* (Dublin, 1995), p.50; *The Irish Times*, 14 December 1959.

3   O. MacDonagh, *States of Mind: A Study of Anglo-Irish Conflict 1780–1980* (London, 1983), p.61.

4   R. Davis, *Arthur Griffith* (Dundalk, 1976), p.3; P. Maume, *The Long Gestation: Irish Nationalist Life 1891–1918* (Dublin, 1999), p.50.

5   R.F. Foster, *Vivid Faces: The Revolutionary Generation in Ireland 1890–1923* (London, 2014), p.155.

6   D. McCartney, 'The Political Use of History in the Work of Arthur Griffith', *Journal of Contemporary History*, 8, 1 (January 1973), p.14.

7   P. Maume, 'The Ancient Constitution: Arthur Griffith and his Intellectual Legacy to Sinn Féin', *Irish Political Studies*, 10 (1995), pp.123, 128, 133.

8   See Foster, *Vivid Faces*, p.156.

9   See Maume, 'Ancient Constitution', p.134.

10 J.J. Horgan, cited in P. Colum, *Ourselves Alone! The Story of Arthur Griffith and the Origin of the Irish Free State* (New York, 1959), p.61.

11 See McCartney, 'Political Use', p.4.

12 C. Townshend, *Easter 1916: The Irish Rebellion* (London, 2005), p.12.

13 O. McGee, *The IRB: The Irish Republican Brotherhood from the Land War to Sinn Féin* (Dublin, 2005), pp.300, 305–6, 347.

14 T. Garvin, *Nationalist Revolutionaries in Ireland, 1858–1928* (Oxford, 1998), pp.154 and 94–5.

15 D. Fitzpatrick, *The Two Irelands 1912–1939* (Oxford, 1998), p.66.

16 See Mitchell, *Revolutionary Government*, p.52.

17 T. Jones, *Whitehall Diary Volume III. Ireland 1918–1925* (Oxford, 1971), pp.156–7, 163.

18 R. Fanning, *Fatal Path: British Government and Irish Revolution 1910–1922* (London, 2013), p.309.

19 J. Lynch, *Dáil Debates*, vol. 253, col. 3 (20 April 1971).

20 See Davis, *Griffith*, pp.43–4.

CHAPTER 6

Michael Cusack and the Rise of the GAA

Stephen Collins

1 Introduction

When the Queen of England was welcomed to Croke Park on a beautiful day in May, 2011, it was hard to avoid wondering what Michael Cusack, the founding father of the Gaelic Athletic Association (GAA), would have made of it all.

Queen Elizabeth's visit to the stadium and the warm welcome she received from the leaders of the organisation under the Cusack Stand reflected the central role the GAA plays in twenty-first century Ireland and the openness of spirit that generally characterises it.

In fact, the GAA is one of the few national institutions in independent Ireland whose reputation has survived intact in recent decades. Half a century ago the three great national institutions, which helped to shape modern Ireland, the Catholic Church, Fianna Fáil and the GAA were still powers in the land. Today two of them are badly damaged but the GAA's reputation has not only survived, it has been enhanced.

In his introduction to the first edition of this book in 1960 the editor Conor Cruise O'Brien wrote:

> More than the Gaelic League, more than Arthur Griffith's Sinn Féin, more even than the Transport and General Workers' Union, and of course far more than the movement which created the Abbey Theatre: more than any of these the Gaelic Athletic

movement aroused the interest of large numbers of ordinary people throughout Ireland. One of the most successful and original mass movements of its day, its importance has not perhaps even yet been fully recognised.[1]

Since O'Brien wrote that passage more than half a century ago the influence and reach of the GAA has expanded even further. It has moved from being a predominantly rural organisation to one with a significant presence in the major urban centres including Dublin.

The annual hurling and football championships are among the sporting highlights of the year, attracting enormous crowds to key matches but the roots of the organisation go much deeper than the summer crowds in Croke Park or Semple Stadium in Thurles. The GAA is embedded in almost every community and is probably the best run sporting organisation in the country.

In 2013 it had around 2,300 clubs in Ireland with more than 400 scattered all around the world not only in the traditional destinations for Irish emigrants like the United States, Britain and Australia but in continental Europe and Asia.

The adult membership of the GAA is estimated at around 300,000 which makes it far bigger than any other sporting body in Ireland. Its spread of members across age groups, social classes, regions and gender is wider than any other sports organisation.

Although it is an amateur sport the GAA has a more impressive network of stadiums and club facilities than its professional rivals, soccer and rugby. Its headquarters, Croke Park in Dublin, was redeveloped between 1992 and 2005 into one of the finest stadiums anywhere in the world at a cost of €260 million, even if a significant portion of that came from the national exchequer.

It has been estimated that over 60 per cent of total attendances at sporting fixtures in Ireland are accounted for by hurling and Gaelic football. In 2013 the total attendances at the annual championship matches was 1.5 million.

2 Cusack's Role in Founding the GAA

Michael Cusack's role in the founding of such a durable and powerful institution was crucial. Yet the man, as portrayed by James Joyce in the shape of the Citizen in *Ulysses*, was a bigoted, aggressive nationalist who fulminated against foreigners, with particular emphasis on the British. It is hard to imagine him welcoming any member of the House of Windsor to Ireland, never mind the headquarters of the GAA. It is easier to envisage Cusack consorting with the handful of loutish demonstrators who took to the Dublin streets to object to the visit.

While it is probably true to say that the GAA would never have got off the ground without Cusack's combination of organisational skill and fanaticism, the enduring strength of the organisation has been based on its ability to outgrow its founder's limitations and adapt to the changes in Irish society.

Yet the historians and writers who have chronicled the history of the GAA have little doubt that Cusack was the driving force in the founding of the organisation in Thurles on 1 November 1884.

A native Irish speaker from Clare, he qualified as a teacher and taught at some of the elite Catholic schools in the country like Blackrock College and Clongowes College before setting up his own academy in Dublin to prepare students for civil service examinations. He had been a successful athlete and played rugby and cricket in the 1870s, but became more disillusioned with the way sport was run in Ireland and particularly its domination by what he saw as elite, British values. He claimed that sports in Ireland were organised by people 'hostile to the dearest aspirations of the Irish people'.

His sporting journey began with an attempt to revive hurling which, by the 1880s, was on the point of extinction. After a couple of false starts he founded the Dublin Metropolitan hurling club and, on Easter Monday 13 April 1884, he arranged a match against a team from Killimor in east Galway which was played in Ballinasloe. Each team had twenty-two players and after a lot of confused play the Galway men scored a goal. Cusack then took his team off the pitch claiming that Killimor were engaged in dangerous play. Nonetheless, modern hurling was born on the field in Ballinasloe.

3 Hurling and the Story of Ireland

It is worth taking a moment to look back at the history and development of hurling and Gaelic football before the GAA. A considerable amount of research has been undertaken into the history of the games in pre-modern times, but the vast majority of football and hurling fans have little idea of how the games evolved.

When it comes to hurling all of the authorities cite 'Sceal na hIomana' by Liam Ó Caithnia as the definitive work on the development of the game. The book, published in 1980, was written in Irish which has limited its accessibility but a number of historians and writers have mined it for information about the history of hurling.

The game has an important role in the Irish nationalist myth and is often traced back to the mythical hero Cú Chulainn who supposedly lived around the first century AD and who, as a young boy, famously drove his hurling ball down the throat of the savage hound who was about to tear him limb from limb.

There is an even older story of a hurling match that preceded the Battle of Moytura between the mythical Fir Bolg and the Tuatha De Dannan in 1272 BC. It is recorded in the Book of Leinster compiled in the 1150s AD, more than 2,000 years after the events it describes.

Whether hurling in these ancient times was anything like the game in the sense that we now know it is a moot point but the Cú Chulainn story has given hurling a special status as a game that has been played in Ireland since prehistoric times.

There is more concrete evidence that hurling was a popular game in Ireland in the seventeenth and eighteenth centuries. At that stage two forms of hurling were played across the island. One version, now extinct, was played with a narrow crooked stick and, like modern field hockey or the Scottish game of shinty, did not allow handling of the ball. A hard wooden ball was used and the game was played mainly in winter. This game, called camán (anglicised to 'commons'), was confined to the northern half of the country.

The second version of the game, played in south Leinster and Munster, was called iomán or báire. In this version the ball could be handled or carried on the hurley which had a round flattened head. The ball was soft and made of animal hair; the game was played in summer.

Records from the eighteenth century show this form of hurling was patronised by the gentry, as a spectator and gambling sport, associated with fairs and other public gatherings, and involved a much greater degree of organisation.

The great sports writer Con Houlihan used to argue that this form of hurling, which became the standard version following the establishment of the GAA, had evolved in the rich pasture lands of the south where farmer's sons had the leisure time to practice its intricate skills. By contrasts 'commons' and football did not require the same level of practice and skill and so were played by poorer people living on poorer land.

When newspapers began to expand their range in the eighteenth century many reported on big hurling matches which were attended by leading members of the gentry and at which big wagers were a common feature. The Dublin correspondent of the *Corke Journal* reported that, on 22 September 1755, there was a great match of hurling played between the gentlemen of Dublin and Kildare, which was attended by the Lord Lieutenant the Marquis of Huntington and 'a most brilliant appearance of nobility and gentry were present'.

The *Hibernian Journal* in 1792 reported that a hurling match in the Phoenix Park was 'honoured with the presence of Her Excellency the Countess of Westmoreland, and several of the nobility and gentry, besides a vast concourse of spectators'.

During the nineteenth century, however, hurling went into decline. After the Act of Union it lost the patronage of the gentry and after the Famine it ceased to be played over most of the country. If Cusack had not taken it by the scruff of the neck first by getting the game played and then by establishing the GAA it could well have disappeared.

4 Popularity of Football

Gaelic football does not have the historic resonance or the sheer beauty of hurling when played but football has long been the more popular game with a much greater reach into all parts of the country. It was probably introduced into the country by the Old English settlers and there is a legal reference to a football match in Newcastle, Co Dublin as early as 1308. A statute of Galway from 1527 makes reference to hurling, football and handball, the three major GAA sports. The statute recorded in Liber states: 'at no tyme the use ne ocupye the horlinge of the litill balle with hockie stickes or staves, nor use no hande ball to playe without the walles, but onely the great foote balle, on payn of the paynis above lymittid', (at no time the use nor occupy the hurling of the little ball with hockey sticks or staves, nor use a handball to play outside the walls, but only the great football on pain of the pains above limited).[2]

The banning of hurling (and handball) and the preference expressed for football would indicate which game was played by the Old English. By the seventeenth century football, like hurling, was patronised by the gentry and large wagers were made on the outcome of matches.

The earliest record of a recognised precursor to the modern game dates from a match in Co Meath in 1670, in which catching and kicking the ball was permitted. The match is described in a poem entitled Iomainn Na Boinne which was written by Séamus Dall MacCuarta. The match involved two teams of twelve players and appears to have been a relatively civilised affair with a set of rules.

A similar game called caid was common in Kerry in the early nineteenth century. The object was to put the ball through goals formed from the boughs of two trees. The ball was usually made using a pig's bladder which gave it buoyancy.

The more common form of football played in the seventeenth and eighteenth centuries, usually between parishes, was a much rougher affair. It involved most of the adult males of the parish and the object was to carry or kick the ball across the parish boundary of the opposing team. It was a free for all involving wrestling, tripping and punching. This game could easily have evolved into rugby, but with the formation of the GAA and the codification of a common set of rules the various forms of football played in rural Ireland were transformed into Gaelic football.

My maternal grandfather, William Farrell, from Ardagh in Co Longford, who was born in 1882, was a fine footballer and played for his county. He showed me how a football was made in his youth by twisting a hay rope tightly into a round shape and then sewing it into an old piece of sacking. This ball didn't bounce so the game was inevitably one of catch and kick quite similar to Australian Rules. When he saw Australian Rules played on the television in the 1960s he recognised it as being closer to the game he played in his youth in the 1890s than modern Gaelic football. He recalled that it was normal to use four goalposts as in Australian Rules rather than the one set of goalposts with a crossbar which became standard as the GAA developed.

While football was and remains a more popular game played in all of the counties in Ireland, it was hurling that prompted Cusack to get involved with Maurice Davin in founding the GAA in Hayes Hotel, Thurles, in November 1884, under the patronage of Archbishop Croke of Cashel. The trials and tribulations of Cusack over the following few years and his feud with Croke have been well documented.

One of the leading historians of the GAA, Paul Rouse, sums him up: 'Michael Cusack's unique personality was both his making and his undoing. At his best he was extraordinary and brilliant, capable of great warmth, humour and generosity. His life's work is clearly that of a man of considerable vision. But Cusack's flaws were as outlandish as his talents. He was impetuous on a cartoonish scale. He also thrived on confrontation and managed to find it in most quarters.'[3] Cusack's personality was such that he was dismissed from the organisation he founded in the summer of 1886.

Rouse convincingly argues that, in creating the GAA, Cusack turned Irish sport on its head. He also says that Joyce's portrait of the Citizen was unfair to Cusack but the man that emerges from Rouse's own description bears a striking resemblance to the Citizen.

The GAA was not founded in a vacuum in 1884, but as part of a movement across the western world to codify and organise sport. It was part of the process of modernisation that saw rapid urbanisation and the emergence of the mass market and the mass media. Soccer, rugby, American football, Australian Rules, cricket and baseball all emerged in the 1860s and 1870s. An array of new organisations was established to codify and record sports as different as tennis, rowing, hockey and swimming. Britain's role as the greatest world power in the second half of the nineteenth century saw its sporting organisations dominate the globe far beyond its own borders. Only the United States proved an exception.

Had it not been for Cusack, it is almost inevitable that the traditional Irish games would have disappeared and been swallowed up in the international trend. For instance, research has shown that in the mid-nineteenth century cricket was the dominant game in Co Kilkenny, which was transformed into the greatest hurling power in the land after the birth of the GAA.

The streak of fanaticism that drove Cusack played a significant part in creating the sense of solidarity with the GAA. The identification of Gaelic sports with the national movement was a key element of its success but it also limited its appeal. For a start it excluded the bulk of the Protestant population who regarded themselves as British and remained deeply attached to the union and the crown. That fissure in Irish life meant that the GAA was regarded with great suspicion by the unionist population of the island.

It was not only unionists who were excluded from the organisation. A significant segment of the Catholic/nationalist population was also deliberately excluded. For a start members of the Royal Irish Constabulary or British army were banned from playing the games. While that became irrelevant in the South after independence, it remained an enduring sore in Northern Ireland.

More important than the ban on those who worked for the British state was the exclusion under Rule 27 of the significant section of the population who played games like rugby, soccer and hockey. The segregation of sport was divisive and those who played the so-called 'garrison games' were deemed to be inferior nationalists. This involved the exclusion of the mainly upper middle-class people who played rugby and the urban working class who generally played soccer. The ban on members of the GAA from playing 'foreign games' enshrined this sense of national exclusiveness which gave the organisation its sense of identity, but to those excluded from its ranks it conveyed a bigotry that limited its appeal.

The ban led to some absurd developments. Éamon de Valera, whose nationalist credentials could hardly be impugned, was a rugby supporter who was on record as saying that rugby was the sport best fitted to express the Irish character. He dutifully turned up for major GAA events, but it was no secret that he got more enjoyment out of attending rugby internationals in Lansdowne Road – not surprising for a former Blackrock College boy and teacher. Other prominent Fianna Fáil figures like Todd Andrews and Brian Lenihan preferred soccer and made no secret of it during the ban years.

More significantly, the ban reinforced a fault line in Irish life between a narrow definition of national identity and a more cosmopolitan outlook. It reinforced the tendency in the decades following independence for the country to turn its back on the world and retreat into a closed conception of what it meant to be Irish.

Mind you the ban on foreign games, like the ban on mainly foreign books which lasted until the mid-1960s, was widely ignored and a blind eye often turned to open breaches. When the Kerry player Mick O'Connell, one of the greatest footballers of all time, was photographed at a soccer match in the 1960s, at the height of his fame, the Kerry county board looked the other way and wisely pretended that they had no definitive evidence that it was him.

Eventually the absurdity of the ban was confronted, mainly due to the courage of Tom Woulfe who died in 2015 shortly before his one hundredth birthday. Woulfe, a Kerryman and a public servant first put forward the idea of dropping the infamous Rule 27 in 1959 but it took a long and bitter campaign at the GAA congresses of 1962, 1965 and 1968 before it was eventually abolished in 1971 following a plebiscite of all club members throughout the country.

The ending of the ban paved the way for the GAA to become a more inclusive organisation, although it took some time for the generations of suspicion to ease. The ban created a bigoted image of the GAA which it has still not fully lived down. However, the mutual suspicion between supporters of Gaelic games and other codes has now largely disappeared. It is not unusual to see fans at Leinster rugby matches in the RDS wearing blue Dublin jerseys or Dublin supporters at Croke Park sporting Leinster jerseys. The jerseys of English premiership teams, particularly Manchester United, are worn by GAA fans from different counties on days when the colours match.

The decision of the GAA to allow international rugby and soccer matches to be played in Croke Park during the redevelopment of Lansdowne Road was a huge step on the road to mutual tolerance. At the first rugby international between Ireland and England at the stadium the playing of 'God Save the Queen' was treated with due respect. As the Union Jack flew over Croke Park alongside the tricolour, the anthem was sung lustily by the English supporters (and even some of the Irish ones).

Before the match the English team was briefed on the special place of Croke Park in Irish nationalist mythology, particularly in the light of the Bloody Sunday massacre of 1920. Ironically, some of the English players attributed their defeat on that occasion to their desire to be too respectful to their hosts.

5 The Credit of the Little Village

The ending of the ban nudged the GAA into being a more tolerant organisation and also helped to widen its appeal. It evolved from being a mainly rural organisation which was strongest in the farming community to one that was able to expand its appeal in a society that was undergoing rapid urbanisation from the 1960s onwards. Its real achievement was to adapt its model based on the rural parish club into an urban setting.

By the end of the nineteenth century the GAA had taken root across most of rural Ireland. It is arguable that the key to its success from the beginning was not so much its nationalist appeal but its ability to become the expression of local loyalties. Such loyalties had been a feature of Irish rural life going back centuries. The faction fights of Munster in the early nineteenth century were a violent expression of such feelings but they were also found in organised and unorganised sporting events up and down the country.

The hugely influential sportswriter Con Houlihan was fond of quoting a passage from 'Knocknagow' or 'The Homes of Tipperary', by Charles J. Kickham, published in 1879 and one of the most popular novels ever published in Ireland. In the book's climax, the village hero, Matt Donovan, who was known as Matt the Thrasher, is competing against an outsider, Captain French, in a hammer throwing contest. As he wound himself up for his throw Matt gazed at the mud walls and thatched roofs of the cottages that constituted his native place and uttered the phrase: 'For the credit of the little village'. He then threw the hammer farther than anyone had ever managed before.

The GAA managed to harness that deep and sentimental loyalty to native place and give it direction and meaning. It established a club structure based on the parish which fed into a county structure based on the thirty-two counties of Ireland. Winning a county championship became the ambition of every club team and winning a provincial or even All Ireland title is the holy grail for every county.

The rhythm of the annual inter county GAA season is captured beautifully by sports writer Tom Humphreys in his book 'Green Fields'. The sense of anticipation as the championship begins in May with the drama steadily building as teams move towards the provincial finals or through the new innovation of the qualifiers.

It builds towards the first and third Sundays in September for the football and hurling All Ireland finals which represent the great sporting events of the year for GAA fans and inevitably impinge on the national consciousness.

The beauty of the championship is that it involves more than the die hard football and hurling fans. If a county, particularly a weaker one not used to winning, gets a good run in the championship it generates an air of excitement that gets virtually the whole population of the county behind the team. This element of community involvement is a critical part of the GAA's appeal.

One of the most remarkable developments of recent decades is the way the organisation has expanded its reach in Dublin as the capital itself expanded in all directions. Vibrant GAA clubs are now a feature of Dublin life in a way that was definitely not the case half a century ago.

Growing up in south County Dublin in the late 1950s and early 1960s there was little evidence of the GAA in the community. Soccer was the game on the streets and rugby the game of the better-off kids who attended private schools. The Christian Brothers kept the GAA flag flying in their schools but many pupils resented having to play the game and couldn't wait to play soccer outside school.

My Limerick-born father regularly took me to big hurling and football matches in Croke Park. In the 1960s and 1970s you could pay in at the turnstile for all matches except the All Ireland finals and even for those you could still pay in to stand on the terraces.

Our favourite seats were in the upper deck of the old Cusack Stand near the centre of the pitch and there was little difficulty getting them on most days, even when Dublin was playing. Tickets were only required on All Ireland final day and, even up to the 1990s, it was still possible to pay in on the day to the terraces.

The expansion of the GAA in Dublin began in the 1960s with the founding of clubs like Kilmacud Crokes. They were started by country people who had come to live in the capital but in the decades since then they have become embedded in the local communities. Many players on the current Dublin hurling team, the most successful for more than half a century, come from Southside clubs as do members of the county football team. This contrasts with previous generations of Dublin teams made up of a majority of players from a few Northside clubs.

The GAA has moved with the times in other ways. One of the big developments over the past forty years has been the involvement of women. Hurling for women, known as camogie, began as long ago as 1904 and the first All Ireland championship was played in 1932. It was the founding of the Ladies Football Association in 1974 that widened the appeal of the sport for women and there are now thriving competitions in both sports.

The GAA has always had an appeal for Irish emigrants and helped them hold on to their Irish identity. At times of significant emigration teams from New York and London were capable of troubling some of the weaker Irish counties in the championship. New York even won the National League on three occasions, the last in 1967, having received a bye into the final.

In more recent decades the GAA has adapted to the modern Irish diaspora which includes many young people who do not regard themselves as permanent emigrants.

There are now GAA clubs not only in the traditional destinations for Irish people in the big US and British cities but across Europe and Asia as well.

One of the attractions of the GAA for so many people is that, despite the hype around big championship matches, it caters for the average player and not just elite sports people. The club structure is a vital element of this appeal and one of the big developments in recent decades has been the emergence of the annual All Ireland club championship involving the football and hurling champions from every county.

6 Conclusion

To survive as a sporting organisation that captures the imagination of so many people in one small country has been a remarkable feat. To thrive and expand in the face of the competition from international sports like soccer and rugby has been remarkable, given the enormous resources that have poured into such sports. Television revenues have transformed professional sport and extended its reach into every corner of the globe.

Over the past few decades people have regularly questioned the ability of the GAA to survive in the globalised world. When the Irish soccer team began a successful run under Jack Charlton in 1988 it was widely predicted that the popularity of Gaelic games would soon wane. It didn't happen.

More recently the success of the Irish provincial rugby teams and a good run by the international team has prompted another set of predictions about the decline of the GAA. That hasn't happened either, but it doesn't mean that there are not grounds for worry. Soccer has always been a professional game that proved an attractive career for some of the best athletes in the country. However, the number who could make it in the English leagues has always been limited and is becoming even more so in the Premiership era. The league of Ireland has never managed to challenge the GAA's grip on local loyalty and attendances at its matches are far inferior.

In the past two decades rugby has emerged as a potentially more serious threat. The success of Munster and Leinster has not only attracted huge numbers of spectators but has lured many potentially good hurlers and Gaelic footballers into the sport. The lure of making a handsome living from playing professional sport is a huge attraction for talented athletes and will inevitably rob the GAA of some potential stars.

There has been an argument about paying top footballers and hurlers, but it has never really got off the ground. The country is not big enough to support a number of professional teams and, in any case, professionalism would undermine the essential attraction of the sport. The historian Kevin Whelan has argued that community rather than amateurism is the defining characteristic of the GAA. 'The joy and core strength of the GAA is precisely that it is a community game – played by communities, owned by communities, and central to the expression of community in Ireland', says Whelan. The introduction of payment would undermine both.

A feature of the GAA is the behaviour of the fans, particularly at hurling matches. Unlike soccer there is never any segregation among the spectators. Even when there are over 80,000 people in Croke Park, it is assumed that violence among the spectators will not become an issue.

Of course there are rare exceptions, but these, when they happen, are more often at local club matches when local rivalries spill over into unruly behaviour. The GAA undoubtedly faces huge challenges in the years ahead. One of them is the worrying trend since 2010 of the dominance of a small number of teams threatening to undermine the appeal of both codes. The organisation's history inspires confidence that it will be able to overcome this problem. The introduction of the qualifier system (quickly dubbed 'the backdoor') in 2001 showed how the organisation can respond to problems in spite, or maybe because of, its democratic structures. Various suggestions about modernising the championship structure have again emerged and some action will inevitably follow.

An ongoing problem is the lack of an international dimension for top GAA players. An experiment involving an Irish team chosen from the country's top Gaelic footballers playing a test series under compromise rules against an Australian Rules team began in 1984. The series has had its hiccups and rule changes but it was still going in 2015 despite a lot of criticism from sports commentators in both countries. Despite the criticism, it has proved attractive for both players and spectators and has had an influence on rule changes in Gaelic football which have speeded up the game.

An annual competition between Ireland and Scotland involving a cross between hurling and shinty has not attracted anything like the same interest. The attempt by the GAA to introduce an international dimension to the national game is characteristic of the organisation's ability to combine a respect for tradition with the need to change.

Half a century ago the dogmatic pronouncements of the Citizen about the evils of 'shoneen games' and his boasts about the GAA as being 'racy of the soil' were still reflected in the public utterances of the organisation. Today the Citizen's views would strike most GAA people as bigoted and unpleasant. Leopold Bloom was met with a snort of derision when he defined a nation as 'the same people living in the same place' but that definition is now the generally accepted one of Irishness inside and outside the GAA. The real paradox is that the organisation created by Cusack now reflects Bloom's tolerant views every bit as much as his own.

Further Reading:

M. Cronin, W. Murphy and P. Rouse (eds), *The Gaelic Athletic Association 1884–2009* (Dublin, 2009)

T. Humphries, *Green Fields: Gaelic Sport in Ireland* (Dublin, 1996)

S. King, *A History of Hurling* (Dublin, 1996)

L. Ó Caithnia, *Sceal na hIomana* (Dublin, 1980)

B. Ó hEithir, *Over the Bar* (Dublin, 1984)

P. Rouse, *Sport and Ireland: A Short History* (Oxford, 2015)

Notes

1   C. Cruise O'Brien, 'Foreword', *SMI*, p.16.

2   The James Hardiman Library, National University of Ireland Galway, http://nuigarchives. blogspot.ie/2012/10/a-ban-on-ye-small-ball.html

3   M. Cronin, W. Murphy and P. Rouse (eds), *The Gaelic Athletic Association 1884–2009* (Dublin, 2009), p.41.

CHAPTER 7

Michael Collins and Éamon De Valera

MARTIN MANSERGH

1 Introduction

At least from today's perspective, a curious feature of the original *The Shaping of Modern Ireland*, which, though published in 1960, was a product of broadcasts in the late 1950s, was the way that it stopped at the threshold of the Irish revolution. There was a concluding essay on Pearse and Connolly by Dorothy Macardle, previously author of a meticulous but partisan narrative, *The Irish Republic*, which had a foreword by Éamon de Valera. While the ostensible reason that the academic community did not stray further was the unavailability of Irish archival records for events subsequent to 1916, the actual reason was partly political. It had much to do with the very asymmetrical life trajectories of Michael Collins and Éamon de Valera, one cut tragically short in Co Cork on 22 August 1922, and the other destined to hold public office, ultimately as a presidential figurehead, into his tenth decade. By and large, professional historians did not want to take sides, or to write Civil War history that would just be an echo of Civil War politics, preferring to stop at the Rising or the Truce of July 1921.

Since 1960, the whole struggle for independence, and the stories of those involved, has been the subject of innumerable books and articles, both popular and academic. In the last twenty-five years, the Civil War, as well as the darker side of the Irish revolution, has also come under scrutiny. New source material has been provided by the release of the records of the Bureau of Military History as well as the military pension application records of Volunteers. The only taboos left are where decisions have been taken to keep files closed. At this stage, the lives of both de Valera and Collins are well researched and documented, and most of the principal issues concerning them have been highlighted, but further in-depth studies and biographies can be anticipated, as perspective keeps shifting with the passage of time.

If de Valera dominated mid-twentieth century politics in the first generation following independence, allowing the playing-field of academic debate around the Civil War to be both levelled and muted, the Michael Collins narrative, greatly aided by the very popular Neil Jordan film and the Tim Pat Coogan biography, has come to dominate in more recent times. His political intestacy, as argued by John M. Regan on the grounds that his successors quickly discarded his political and conspiratorial methods, is, superficially, no more. The present Taoiseach Enda Kenny has strongly identified with him to a much greater extent than any of his Fine Gael predecessors, with his portrait hung over the fireplace in his personal office. Significantly, the portraits that preceded it in the same room occupied by previous Fianna Fáil Taoisigh were not of de Valera, but of Lemass, then Pearse. One of the highlights of the poignant career of Brian Lenihan as Minister for Finance was to speak at Béal na mBláth in August 2010 in praise of Collins. Enthusiasm for Collins extends beyond any boundary. In the mid-1990s, a prominent loyalist paramilitary had a slightly disconcerting effect when he confided at a bilateral meeting with Bertie Ahern that the one person he admired in Irish history was Michael Collins.

Tim Pat Coogan, on the concluding page of his Collins biography, presents the respective reputations of Collins and de Valera in zero-sum terms. He quotes the elderly President as conceding in the mid-1960s to Joe McGrath, a very prominent businessman who had once been a Free State Minister: 'It's my considered opinion that in the fullness of time history will record the greatness of Collins, and it will be recorded at my expense.' Like many iconic statements attributed to famous individuals, it is second-hand and uncorroborated, but it is an accurate enough prediction of the prevailing mood over the last twenty-five years.

De Valera was someone who gave a great deal of thought to his historical reputation, meeting historians, authorising an official biography by Thomas P. O'Neill and Frank Pakenham, as well as an edition of his speeches and statements that appeared posthumously with background introductions by a former government secretary, who was very close to him, Maurice Moynihan. The period of his life that most preoccupied him and that he felt he had most need to justify was the twelve months from the Truce in July 1921 to the outbreak of the Civil War in June 1922, covering the negotiation of the Treaty, the split over it and the drift into near-anarchy.

History, if it is to be instructive, needs to transcend, rather than simply validate, partisan accounts of the conflicts of the past, particularly as the outcomes that it leaves behind are the result of many different and often opposing forces. It would be unfair to others who played a prominent role in shaping the emergence of an independent Ireland to adopt a dualist approach focused only on the two most prominent leaders. Despite the open confrontation between them in disputes from negotiation of the Treaty to the Civil War, they were close allies for a crucial period, and in a longer perspective their roles were complementary, even if quite different. The split was less ideological than one of tactics and temperament, and it was, of course, what is not always acknowledged, a power struggle. Nevertheless, both made major contributions to the shaping of modern Ireland and to the crossing of the independence threshold.

That is a long way from saying, however, that the actions and decisions of both men in the heat of revolution and state formation were fault free or that the outcome achieved was, in all respects, optimal. The birth of the State was a difficult and troubled one, and by no means inevitable. In particular, the price of consolidating that achievement was an entrenchment of partition with the creation of Northern Ireland and of devolution there based on a crudely-administered majority rule. It was a festering sore that was to erupt fifty years later, leading to a renewed and prolonged, if mainly localised, conflict, before a comprehensive settlement was reached that addressed many of the deficiencies of the 1921 Treaty settlement. These deficiencies mainly concerned Northern Ireland, as the other limitations relating to what was initially called the Irish Free State were able to be remedied politically over time.

While both reasonably stable and solvent, the Irish State itself, for both external and internal reasons, had to wait at least a generation till the 1960s, before it began to prosper and continued emigration and population decline could be staunched. Some of this retardation had to do with the shortcomings of the Sinn Féin philosophy of self-sufficiency shared by both Collins and de Valera. However, an independent

Ireland needed to become part of a wider international organisational network, of which, unlike the British Commonwealth, it could become an enthusiastic member. The United Nations from 1955 and even more the EEC, now EU, membership from 1973 supplied this need. Earlier, the Irish Free State's joining the League of Nations in September 1923, despite British reservations about this escape from tutelage, provides a more positive conclusion to the revolutionary period, than either 6 December 1922, when the State formally came into existence, or the end of the Civil War in April 1923.

2 Farm Boys

Both Éamon de Valera and Michael Collins shared rural farming backgrounds in Munster in the aftermath of the land war during the period when tenant farmers were helped to become the owners of the land. However, de Valera's uncle, by whom he was brought up, was a farm labourer and lower down the social rung. Neither Collins nor de Valera had any political connections or belonged to any emerging professional elite or had relations successful in business at a local level. Both drew sustenance from their rural background, and were steeped in the values, traditions and folklore of the Irish countryside and the attitudes of late nineteenth-century Catholic nationalism. Among de Valera's earliest memories were an eviction, the shooting dead of three protestors in Mitchelstown in 1887 and the Parnell split.

There were important differences also. De Valera was eight years older than Collins. Born in America in 1882 and carrying a Spanish surname, as well as being tall and athletic, he stood out from his peers. Though one should not exaggerate the abnormality of families that had been split by post-famine emigration or the pragmatic arrangements for family care that sometimes resulted, Collins's upbringing was more secure and straightforward, and he had no cause to be defensive about it.

The young de Valera was determined to become more than a farm labourer. Pressurising his mother in America for funding, he managed to climb onto the educational ladder, and eventually to progress practically to the top over a twenty-year period, having briefly contemplated a vocation to the priesthood along the way. He excelled in mathematics, and later liked to think of political problems in mathematical terms, which remained largely a closed book for his colleagues. He was to become one of a limited number of political leaders who were not just inspirational to the public but respected for their intellectual capacity. He just missed out on the chair of mathematical physics at University College Cork in 1913 after a quasi-political campaign that involved extensive lobbying, including his identification as a Home Rule supporter. He had joined the Gaelic League in 1908, where he encountered his future wife in his Irish teacher Sinéad Flanagan, who reinforced his dedication to the cause of the Irish language and who, in all probability, was a radicalising influence.

It was very natural for him to join the Volunteers when they were formed in December 1913, to provide the same backing to Home Rule as the Ulster Volunteers formed in January of that year gave to resistance to Home Rule. His reading of Irish history and of British imperialism convinced him that it would probably be necessary to fight for even limited freedom. He did not support the imposition of Redmondite control over the Volunteers or of putting the freedom of other small nations ahead of Ireland's by participation in the war in advance of Home Rule. Shortly before the Rising, he had advanced to the position of battalion commandant, and, while he was sworn into the Irish Republican Brotherhood (IRB) by Thomas MacDonagh, kept his commitment to it to a minimum. Lifelong, he disliked both secret organisations and guerrilla warfare, which made him the complete opposite of Michael Collins. He was little involved in the politics and the conspiracies leading to the Rising, and concentrated on organisation and training. He was regarded as capable and reliable.

Michael Collins grew up on a reasonably substantial 90-acre farm in West Cork, not too far from the home-place of celebrated Fenian Jeremiah O'Donovan Rossa. His life exemplified O'Donovan Rossa's conviction that the Irish 'needed to show England that she is losing more than she is gaining by holding us'. The sense of dispossession arising from the confiscations of the sixteenth and seventeenth centuries was still strongly felt in West Cork, with the Protestant landowning and farming community, though a minority, being stronger here than almost anywhere outside of Ulster. These tensions were to come periodically to the surface through the period of the war of independence to the Civil War.

Michael Collins would have been influenced by strong nationalist teachers. He obtained a post office job in London in a UK-wide competition, and moved there for six years, taking a succession of jobs in administration and finance, including a brief spell as a British civil servant at the Board of Trade. Socially, he stuck mainly to the London-Irish community. He joined the GAA and the IRB and was active in both.

When he resigned in January 1916, his employer was left with the impression he was leaving to join up. He was, but the theatre of war involved the opening up of a new front in Ireland. In his contributions to the Treaty debate, he referred more than once to having lived and worked in London. He spoke of the prejudice that Irishmen routinely encountered from the plain people of England even more than from the aristocrats, in support of the argument that the British should be given no excuse for arguing that they had to remain. His fellow London Irishman and close follower, Joe Good, believed that the knowledge Collins acquired of the English during this period was the key to his ability to take them on with such confidence in the war of independence.

3 The Rising

Collins participated in and observed the Rising at close quarters in the General Post Office (GPO). His future cabinet colleague, Desmond FitzGerald, described him as 'the most active and efficient officer in the place', exercising authority in a way that brooked no argument. He was subsequently very critical of the conduct of the Rising, and clearly had little time for Pearse-style rhetoric. It could be argued that, while strong on practicalities, he underestimated the long-lasting emotional power of the Proclamation and indeed of Pearse's oration at the graveside of Jeremiah O' Donovan Rossa on 1 August 1915.

Éamon de Valera was in command in the south-east of the city, where one of the most effective military engagements of the week took place, holding up and inflicting heavy casualties on British troops advancing from Kingstown. He only surrendered when he received orders to do so. It has been alleged that, like Thomas MacDonagh, he was overwrought towards the end through lack of sleep. He never took on a military command role subsequently, enlisting symbolically as a private in the anti-Treaty Irish Republican Army (IRA) at the beginning of the Civil War.

He was lucky to be spared execution, as he was next in line after James Connolly. He had not come to political notice previously. When

General Maxwell, under growing British Government pressure to halt the executions, asked if he was important, prosecuting counsel William Wylie famously replied: 'No. He is a schoolteacher who was taken at Boland's Mill.' On the contrary, as the most senior survivor of the Rising with a notable military record, he would be ideally placed for political leadership both in the struggle for independence and subsequently in independent Ireland, as it turned out, for many decades.

It quickly became clear in the aftermath of the Rising that there would not be another long wait for a further opportunity to win freedom. Renewed political efforts to implement Home Rule on any basis stalled. De Valera and Collins were both in prisons in England and Wales, where they exercised leadership roles among the prisoners, as the sea-change in opinion at home began to take shape. On release in December 1916, Collins threw himself energetically into reorganising the Volunteers, making full use of the secretive IRB network which, in a couple of years, he would come to lead. There, as president of a metaphysical Irish Republic 'virtually established' dating back to 1869, he would, in a sense, be on a level with de Valera who, on his visit to America in 1920, had adopted the title of President to enhance his position as head of a renewed shadow government, 'the Government of the Irish Republic'.

De Valera, on his release in mid-1917, was immediately confronted with a decision about whether to stand as Sinn Féin candidate in Clare, and a positive answer catapulted him into a leading political role. The victory was full of historical resonance, as O'Connell's victory in the 1828 Clare by-election had been the prelude to Catholic Emancipation. Soon thereafter, he replaced Arthur Griffith as leader of Sinn Féin, which was the best existing vehicle for a united separatist alliance, once its out-of-date dual monarchist Austro-Hungarian model was replaced by the Republic declared outside the GPO.

While Collins remained a strong supporter of de Valera well into 1921, they had, even at this point in time, a divergent attitude of how independence would be achieved. Establishing a new sovereign independent state requires the fulfilment of two conditions: firstly, gaining the exercise of authority and jurisdiction, initially *de facto*, within its territory, and, secondly, obtaining international recognition. Collins concentrated mainly on the first task, de Valera on the second.

There is a huge paradox, little commented on by historians, in the opposite directions taken by national and international politics in 1918. John Redmond, as leader of the Irish Parliamentary Party (IPP), had, soon after the outset of the war in September 1914, as the price for at least putting Home Rule on the statute book, encouraged Irish enlistment on the side of the British Empire and especially for the sake of another small Catholic country, Belgium, whose neutrality had been violated. When the war ended in November 1918, the allies, joined and latterly led by the Americans, had won, but in the general election of December what had been, at least until the conscription crisis of April 1918, the pro-allied IPP was completely wiped out, outside half a dozen seats retained in the North. Put another way, Sinn Féin triumphed only weeks after the 'gallant allies in Europe', Imperial Germany and the Austro-Hungarian Empire, had quite literally crumbled.

The outcome of the war turned one of the strategic calculations of Sinn Féin on its head. In 1922, Michael Collins candidly told an American journalist, Hayden Talbot:

> In my own estimation the rising and the subsequent revival in Ireland, and the importance of the rising in its international character, were all inseparable from the thought and hope of a German victory. Ireland's position at that time was to look to the Peace Conference for a settlement of the age-long dispute between Britain and herself. [1]

Certainly up to the middle of 1918 and the failure of the March offensive on the Western front, a German victory was plausible, especially after Russia had been knocked out of the war and the nascent Soviet Union subjected to a humiliating peace, the Treaty of Brest-Litovsk.

4 Wilsonian Principles

Arguably, 'the gallant allies in Europe' invoked in the Proclamation played the same role as the notion of 'the French are on the seas' in 1798 in boosting belief in the viability of revolution with a vision of powerful external allies in the wings. It aroused a good deal of scepticism at the time, Joe Good, one of Collins' lieutenants noting, after the phrase was used by Pearse in a morale-boosting speech to an assemblage of Volunteers in March 1916: 'I remember feeling doubtful and taking "our allies" with a certain amount of salt – a doubt more than justified by the later disasters in County Kerry' (a reference to the fate of the *Aud* with its German arms shipment to aid the Easter Rising; the ship was captured and scuttled, two Volunteers were drowned and Roger Casement, who had arranged the shipment, was promptly arrested after being landed by a German submarine). In 1918, the British exploited the previous connection, without any evidence of a fresh 'German plot', to round up and detain much of the Sinn Féin leadership, including de Valera, while aiming to blacken them in American eyes. All this left the electorally victorious Sinn Féin open to the accusation, especially in the anglophile American press, that they had backed the wrong horse. It may be that British influence would always have ensured that Ireland would receive no hearing at the Peace Conference convened by the Americans and their allies, but certainly the previous perceived alignment of Irish separatists with the Kaiser's Germany meant that the Americans could easily brush the demand aside.

After being sprung from Lincoln Jail with Collins' help, and assuming leadership of the Dáil, which was engaged in the task of establishing an alternative administration, de Valera's first priority was to go to America, above all, to internationalise the Irish claim to national self-determination, to raise funds, and to combat Article 10 of the Covenant of the League of Nations, which appeared to protect the integrity of States and therefore preclude independence. As early as 1917, de Valera, with the advantage of his American background, saw opportunities in aligning the Irish cause with American war aims, as definitively set out in President Woodrow Wilson's Fourteen Points in January 1918.

Because Wilson with his Ulster Presbyterian background had no sympathy with Irish separatism, there has been a tendency to downplay the enormous influence of Wilsonian principles not just on de Valera but on the actual achievement of Irish independence. De Valera was, from 1917 to 1921, the undisputed political leader of the Irish independence movement so he ought to be credited with some insight into the factors that made it electorally successful. Throughout his public life, he made reference to Wilson's intervention as a crucial factor. The end of the war was the high point of international enthusiasm for the nation-state. Between the Armistice of 11 November 1918 and the general election of 14 December, new nation states were literally in the process of formation: Poland, Czechoslovakia, Hungary, Iceland, Latvia, Lithuania and the new Kingdom of Serbia, Croatia and Slovenia that would become Yugoslavia.

In April 1919, in a Dáil debate on the League of Nations, de Valera claimed that acceptance of principles in President Wilson's Fourteen Points 'will mean that the long fight for Irish liberty is at an end'. At the other end of his political life, in 1964, in his address as President of Ireland to the US Congress, he recalled:

> President Wilson, during the First World War, had put the rights of people to self-determination as a fundamental basis for peace. We in Ireland took advantage of the fact that that principle had been enunciated by the head of this great nation. There was a general election due at the time, and we took advantage of that election to make it clear that the people wanted independence.[2]

When de Valera toured America in 1919–20, he likened the potential role of America in Ireland's struggle to the role of France in the American War of Independence. The Black and Tans were repeatedly compared in their behaviour to the German occupation forces in Belgium; no hint of 'gallant allies' there. He even went so far as to say that 'Irish labor is heart and hand with American labor in wishing that the ideals for which the war was fought should really be accomplished.' Lloyd George's counter-argument, aimed at American opinion, was to compare Ireland to the secessionist South in the American Civil War. The problem with that comparison was that the position of the Irish was more akin to the slaves than the slave-owners.

Irish sacrifices during the First World War probably did count for something in the public opinion of allied countries. The Mayor of New York John F. Hylan said, when officially greeting Éamon de Valera in City Hall in January 1920: 'The question that must be answered sooner or later is why Ireland, alone among the smaller nations, should be excluded from a just and legitimate share in the triumph of the late war.'[3]

De Valera deserves credit as leader for grasping the opportunity to adapt the national demand to the international context that emerged from the First World War. Related to that, he also articulated in America the crucial, even if highly controversial insight, that Irish freedom would never be won in alliance with Britain's enemies. In the process, he forged an economical Irish foreign and defence policy that continues to serve to this day. The core of this was his assurance on the analogy of Cuba and the Monroe Doctrine that Ireland would never allow itself to be used as a base by Britain's enemies. From the early Middle Ages, Ireland had been a potential springboard for rivals to the throne, then post-Reformation for Britain's continental enemies, Spain, France and Germany. A precondition of Irish independence was that that fear be removed, and that an independent Ireland would not prejudice what would later be described as any British selfish strategic interest. This undertaking was fulfilled by de Valera to unofficial British satisfaction, even if not to Churchill's, during the Second World War.

De Valera's visit to the US in the midst of the struggle for independence has generally been written off as a failure, because of the failure to win recognition for the Irish Republic and because of the rows with Irish-American leaders. The fact of the matter, however, is that what most influenced Lloyd George towards peace moves in late 1920 and early 1921 were worries about American opinion, in a context where Britain needed a favourable settlement of its vast war debt to the United States that had to be approved by Congress, which did happen in 1923.

5 Revolutionary Leaders and Negotiators

All military campaigns and especially liberation struggles benefit from having a charismatic leader. Legends grew up around Michael Collins as the mastermind against the British and the disabling of much of their imported intelligence capacity as well as the far-reaching neutralisation of the regular Royal Irish Constabulary (RIC). Memoirs show that he was often intimately involved in the detailed planning of operations and the choice of Volunteers or units to carry them out. Dubbed by his supporters as 'the man who won the war', which overstated both his role and the result, he was also credited with innumerable feats of escape and deception. There is no doubt that he did lead the war in Dublin, and that he provided support, encouragement and resources to capable commanders initiating actions elsewhere, centralised control being unrealistic. There is little evidence of his personal involvement in armed engagements until the very end. He was in a good position to assess the strengths and weaknesses of the IRA campaign. While he accepted without difficulty that his role had been, to an extent, mythologised, he was left, subsequent to the truce, in a unique bargaining position. Even the British had bought into the myth, Lloyd George's confidant and assistant secretary to the cabinet, Tom Jones, writing to Conservative leader Andrew Bonar Law on 24 April 1921: 'Where was Michael Collins during the Great War? He would have been worth a dozen brass hats.'

However, Collins had a dual role. The war economy had to be financed, and the bones of an alternative administration to counter the one based in Dublin Castle had to be built up. Collins was Minister for Finance from April 1919, and his main job was to raise the Dáil loan and to fend off British efforts to capture Dáil funds. Continuing the role in the parallel Dáil ministry and Provisional Government, in the early months after the Treaty, Collins' prestige helped put the stamp of the new State-to-be on proper administration and financial orthodoxy and on the primacy of the Department of Finance, which, though fluctuating a little from time to time, remains in place to this day. Again, Collins' formative period working in London, briefly even as a civil servant, may have predisposed him to administrative continuity to underpin revolutionary political change.

In complementary respects, both de Valera and Collins, at the time of the Truce, were realists. Collins knew that the IRA had not won the war, but had just about, under increasing pressure, managed to hold their own, while causing Britain serious embarrassment over their security failures and repeated incidents of indefensible behaviour by crown forces, in particular by the specially recruited Black and Tans and Auxiliaries. While he had not wanted a Truce on any terms that implied defeat, afterwards Collins was not amongst those who were keen to resume the war if this could be avoided. He was in favour of taking the gains on offer and building on them to establish a more complete freedom. The most important of these gains was the complete withdrawal of the British army from the twenty-six counties. He was so obviously republican that he did not need to prove it, even after signing the Treaty, but he was never attracted by theoretical or doctrinaire ideological positions.

De Valera was a tenacious negotiator, who set a lot of store on upholding principles, as the exchange of multiple letters with Lloyd George before the opening of negotiations demonstrated. He recognised that the coercion of unionists in Northern Ireland by the rest of nationalist Ireland was not realistic, but also that some compromise on the crown would be necessary. If the context for the Sinn Féin election triumph in 1918 had been American endorsement of the principle of national self-determination, the context for the British in the Treaty negotiations was the reshaping of the British Empire after a war in which the Dominions had come into their own. (To this day, for Australia, the Dardanelles was a defining experience.) The British Government was absolutely determined that a self-governing twenty-six-county Ireland had to fit into this framework, making it, incidentally, the only former British territory to have Commonwealth membership involuntarily thrust upon it. At a later stage, in the 1937 Constitution, de Valera would be able to deliver on his own formula of external association, but in 1949 the Costello-led Interparty Government chose to ignore the option opened up by India to become a republic within the Commonwealth, and cut all ties with it, thrown back instead on a purely bilateral relationship, including, crucially, the Common Travel Area.

De Valera described his external association formula, which was put forward more than once by the Irish negotiators and rejected by the British, as 'a little sentimental thing', and opponents and commentators have argued ever since that the difference with the oath contained in the Treaty and between external association and dominion status was not big enough to justify the split, let alone a civil war. What this leaves out of the account is that it was an attempt by de Valera to bridge the gulf between those, both in the IRA and in politics, who wanted a wholly independent republic, the so-called 'isolated republic', and those prepared, reluctantly in most cases, to accept dominion status, if they had to. Hard-line republicans had little time for de Valera's compromise, and, after he lost power in January 1922, his authority, with the IRA especially, visibly waned.

The negotiators obtained, with the exception of some financial legacy obligations, full economic autonomy, except in currency matters which were not an issue. The defence restrictions and retention of the ports, which seemed to prejudice an independent foreign policy and about which Erskine Childers was so concerned, proved not to be such an issue after 1938, when the British Government of Neville Chamberlain decided that Irish goodwill in a looming war situation was more important than port facilities, though Churchill vehemently disagreed.

There was much argument as to which of de Valera and Collins should go to London or be of the delegation to negotiate for the Treaty and who should stay at home as a final arbiter in case of difficulty or breakdown. In the end it was Collins who went to London as one of the negotiating party. The British exploited the differences in what was, in theory, a united Irish front, apart from the Ulster Unionists, and then expected those who signed the Treaty to impose it, as necessary, on the rest. Most of the public congratulations went to Lloyd George. It was a failure both of leadership and discipline on the Irish side to allow a wedge to be driven between them in this way. There are comparatively few historical instances, certainly in modern times, where plenipotentiaries have signed an important agreement without first securing the backing of the head of government. Even in those days, telephone communication existed, but it was not used. The present Finance Minister Michael Noonan has quipped: 'If Michael Collins had a mobile phone, we would still be under British rule.'[4] It was equally anomalous that there should be a head of government on only one side of the table in such a key negotiation. De Valera should clearly have joined the negotiation in the latter stages, and, if the motive for not doing so was to try and hold the movement and the government together, he failed miserably.

Collins can also be criticised for being headstrong and impulsive, and for being temperamentally unsuited to the subtleties of negotiation. In his defence, his argument in the Treaty debate that it would provide the freedom to achieve freedom was, with qualification, valid, if one ignores Northern Ireland. The qualification is that the Irish Free State faced sanctions in the economic war of the 1930s, when it tried to complete its freedom. During the Second World War, as it maintained its neutrality, Ireland also faced a considerable political and economic squeeze, inspired by Churchill's lingering conviction that Britain had never fully recognised it, juridically speaking, as a sovereign independent state.

De Valera and the TDs who followed him were quite entitled to reject the Treaty. They went on not merely to conduct a political guerrilla campaign against it, which was one thing, but to tolerate the throwing off of civilian authority by the IRA, which was quite another. De Valera was foolish in heightening the spectre of civil war in emotive terms. One of the unfortunate consequences of the whole independence struggle from 1916 to 1921 was the reluctance, which became a refusal, by many on the military side to defer to or obey democratically mandated civilian authority. De Valera felt fundamental questions should not be decided by simple Dáil majority, but be referred to the people. Post-the 1937 constitution, referenda would be held, but in 1922 elections were the only imperfect remedy.

6 Civil Warriors

The first six months of 1922 saw a descent into near-anarchy, as British troops withdrew and the Royal Irish Constabulary (RIC) ceased to function, and the Provisional Government, slow to confront former comrades, was unable to guarantee public safety. It was, nevertheless, during this unpromising period that Collins began to recruit in February

1922 for a new and, in principle, unarmed police force unlike the RIC, An Garda Síochána, a vital institution that began to come into its own after the civil war.

The drawing up of the Free State Constitution on *de facto* republican lines was probably the most hopeful initiative for avoiding civil war, which was always Seán MacBride's belief, and it was the basis of the Collins–de Valera electoral pact which allowed the June 1922 general election to be held. Churchillian belligerence steered by a deeply ideological civil servant, Lionel Curtis, vetoed the draft Constitution, and insisted on the explicit imposition of the Treaty to the letter and even beyond. The pact, of course, fell apart on election-day when the Constitution was published.

Another Collins initiative, which was much less constructive, involved an attempted covert armed destabilisation of Northern Ireland, presumably in the hope that it might unite opposing IRA factions. This was after he had attempted to come to some understanding with the Prime Minister of Northern Ireland, James Craig, in the Craig–Collins pact, about the treatment of nationalists, especially around Belfast; this pact also fell apart. Briefly, Collins was raising individual cases in a way that would not happen again till after the Anglo-Irish Agreement of 1985.

The reverse side of independence was partition, and no Irish leader was able to get a handle on the political phenomenon of Ulster Unionist resistance strongly backed by a substantial section of the British political and military establishment. The crucial power-play occurred before August 1914. At first, in 1912, even separatists like Pearse and Connolly believed Home Rule was going to happen. The foundation of the Irish Labour Party in 1912 was with a view to providing an opposition to conservatism in a Home Rule parliament. The build-up of massive resistance with the signing of the Covenant, the formation of the Ulster Volunteers and clear signs of wavering in British ministerial ranks was, at first, met among nationalists with denial and assurances that it was bluff. The reality then – and ever since – was that the British were not prepared to act as enforcers for Irish nationalism. Because different leaders had always to be against partition in principle, for fear of being accused of abandoning northern nationalists, Ulster Unionists were left largely free to choose the maximum defensible extent of territory to be excluded, including counties Fermanagh and Tyrone, the city of Derry and the town of Newry, where they were in a minority.

James Connolly, the one leader who knew the North well, had the sense, acting with Pearse, to exclude it from countrywide plans for the Rising, saying cryptically that they would deal with unionism when they had won control of the rest of the country. IRA activity in the North in the 1920–22 period tended to be counter-productive, and allowed unionism both to mobilise its militias and entrench itself. Nor did the Belfast boycott undermine resolve. Devolution at arms' length from Dublin, de Valera's preferred solution, had no attractions for unionists. Collins' and Mulcahy's attempts to make Northern Ireland non-viable by guerrilla actions had failed, even before they had to be called off because of the Civil War. The Boundary Commission, which had ambiguous terms of reference, and produced a minimalist report, proved to be a mirage. Lloyd George was quite happy to encourage Collins' wishful thinking. One often has a sense that the primary concern of the Irish negotiators was to preserve a thin façade of unity in the Treaty to defend themselves from being accused by Redmondites of doing no better than them, despite all the political indictments that they had sold the pass.

As far as Northern Ireland was concerned, and both Treatyites and Anti-Treatyites were equally responsible, Ulster Unionism succeeded in protecting its position completely, while nationalism drew a blank, with northern nationalists more vulnerable than they had been under the Union. Denying the justice of partition and the legitimacy of Northern Ireland advanced things very little, until the civil rights campaign of the late 1960s exposed the shortcomings of the 1920–21 settlement and the part of the original problem that had not been resolved.

The final catalyst for the Civil War was the wholly irresponsible assassination of Sir Henry Wilson in London by, in all probability, agents of Collins, even though de Valera was blamed. The critical point is that the Conservative leader, Andrew Bonar Law, on whom the continuation of the Lloyd George-led coalition depended, had had enough. His chief grievance was that those who had signed the Treaty had, up to that point, not shown a willingness to take risks and they were not sincere about the principle of consent. Collins was left with little choice but to take on the Four Courts garrison and then the IRA in other parts including Cork, making use of logistical support from the British.

From the beginning, de Valera had no real conviction when it came to fighting the Civil War, but he had little influence with the IRA leadership.

Many republican-minded IRA officers opted out. Politically speaking, de Valera was not in a position to deliver peace. While de Valera headed up a shadow government from October 1922 without power, it was only after the death of Liam Lynch in April 1923 and the end of the Civil War that he was able to reassert political control. His position then was that political decisions must be taken by a majority of the representatives of the people, subject to the right of referendum, as the democratic alternative to arbitrament by force. He also clearly stated in July 1923 that 'the war, so far as we are concerned, is finished', while continuing to contest the legitimacy of the Irish Free State and its institutions for another few years.

When the Civil War started, Michael Collins repeatedly deferred the summoning of the Third Dáil, so that the actions of the Provisional Government and the forces under their control in the first two months and more of the Civil War were not accountable. While it would be an exaggeration to describe this as a dictatorship, given that there was still a civilian government, it could be said that democracy was suspended. Paradoxically, while Collins was seeking what might be described in modern terms as a relatively soft landing for his opponents and former comrades, whom he aimed to either defeat or persuade to stop, his mainly civilian successors after his death had a much more hard-line approach. While restoring parliamentary democracy, they were quite prepared, as necessary, to operate outside the rule of law, both overtly and covertly, to deter and demoralise the republican forces. The best that can be said for the period is that Irish democracy, at birth, had a difficult passage and the difficulties did not entirely disappear until quite a long time afterwards.

Collins, displaying too much bravado, perished in an ambush, and ever since there has been speculation about what he might have contributed. His successors, who may have mistrusted the maverick side of his nature, were much more mundane, and not in the heroic mould. Actual independence was a hard road and a considerable anti-climax. The first priority was to rebuild and to lay sound foundations with no scope for extravagance.

6 Conclusion

Republican politics, once it began operating within the state's framework, proved much more popular than republican violence. De Valera founded a pragmatic republican party, Fianna Fáil, that astonishingly dominated Irish politics for eighty years, and that was never out of government for long. In the initial period, after it entered the Dáil, it did frighten the horses, the *Church of Ireland Gazette* claiming in 1927 that 'it is Fianna Fáil versus Christendom'. He led the country during difficult decades, and consolidated its independence and sovereignty, and by the 1950s his obvious conservatism would have become much more attractive to many members of the Church of Ireland, particularly after the Costello-led interparty government had removed Ireland from the Commonwealth.

The promised land of greater prosperity did not come until after de Valera had retired from the Taoiseach's office. His most notable legacy was the 1937 Constitution, which, like the draft 1922 one overseen by Collins, omitted the crown. In the negotiations that led to the Anglo-Irish Agreement of 1938 and the return of the ports, and in defence of neutrality throughout the Second World War, he displayed a skill and backbone so far unrivalled since.

Ireland has moved on from the legacy of both men, and operates on a much broader international canvas. In a world that will always contain life-threatening challenges, a small independent country has to strive to sustain itself in each generation, but on balance, depending on its geographical situation, it has opportunities that would be denied it if it had stayed subsumed in a larger country. To this day, political separation from a larger state anywhere in Europe is very difficult, usually impossible, to achieve. Yet it was something that Collins and de Valera as leaders managed to accomplish. It was against an historical background of a relationship with Britain, and previously England, which, though it was not uniformly negative, was punctuated with conquest and disaster and an absence of solidarity. In his foreword to *The Shaping of Modern Ireland*, the editor, Dr Conor Cruise O'Brien, explained: 'There is a common basis in all movements of subject peoples: the reaction of the proud and sensitive, not to oppression – Ireland in the early twentieth century was scarcely oppressed – but to contempt and fear, the mutual memory of *past* oppression.'[5] That explanation certainly fits what we know both of Collins and de Valera and the vast majority of those who participated with them in the making and shaping of an independent Ireland.

Further Reading:

J. Borgonovo, *The Battle for Cork July–August 1922* (Cork, 2011)

P. Canning, *British Policy towards Ireland 1921–1941* (Oxford, 1985)

T.P. Coogan, *Michael Collins: A Biography* (London, 1990)

Dáil Éireann official report, *Debate on the Treaty between Great Britain and Ireland Signed in London on the 6th December, 1921*

C. Dalton, *With the Dublin Brigade. Espionage and Assassination with Michael Collins' Intelligence Unit* (Cork, 2014)

G. Doherty and D. Keogh (eds), *Michael Collins and the Making of the Irish State* (Cork, 1998), including John M. Regan, 'Michael Collins – The Legacy and the Intestacy', pp.117–126

R. Fanning, *The Irish Department of Finance* (Dublin, 1978)

D. Ferriter, *Judging Dev: A Reassessment of the Life and Legacy of Eamon de Valera* (Dublin, 2007)

J. Good, *Enchanted by Dreams: The Journal of a Revolutionary* (Dingle, 1996)

D. Hannigan, *De Valera in America: The Rebel President and the Making of Irish Independence* (New York, 2010)

T. Jones, *Whitehall Diary*, Volume III Ireland 1918–1925 (London, 1971).

D. Macardle, *The Irish Republic*, with a preface by Éamon de Valera (Dublin, 1951)

J. McConnel, *The Irish Parliamentary Party and the Third Home Rule Crisis* (Dublin, 2013)

Michael Collins' Own Story Told to Hayden Talbot, with a Preface by Éamonn de Búrca (Dublin, 2012)

M. Moynihan (ed.), *Speeches and Statements by Eamon De Valera 1917–1973* (Dublin, 1980)

D. Ó Beacháin, 'The Dog that didn't bark: Southern unionism in pre- and post-revolutionary Ireland', *History Ireland*, Volume 23 No.4, July/August 2015, pp.44–7

T. Ryle Dwyer, *Big Fellow, Long Fellow: A Joint Biography of Collins and De Valera* (Dublin, 2006)

The Earl of Longford and Thomas P. O'Neill, *Eamon de Valera* (London, 1970)

M. Walsh, *Bitter Freedom: Ireland in a Revolutionary World 1918–1923* (London, 2015)

Notes

1   *Michael Collins' Own Story Told to Hayden Talbot* With a Preface by Éamonn de Burca (Dublin, 2012), p.38.

2   M. Moynihan (Ed.), *Speeches and Statements by Eamon de Valera 1917–73*, (Dublin, 1980), p.599.

3   D. Hannigan, *De Valera in America: The Rebel President and the Making of Irish Independence* (New York, 2010), p.107.

4   *Irish Times*, 6 March 2015

5   C. Cruise O'Brien, 'Foreword', *SMI*, pp.9–10.

CHAPTER 8

Edward Carson[1]

Eugenio Biagini

1 Introduction

Carson was the driving force behind the 1912–14 Ulster campaign, which killed both Home Rule and parliamentary attempts to accommodate Irish nationalism within the UK constitution. In the process, this movement asserted the sovereignty of 'the people' (defined as the unionist majority of Ulster) against that of parliament, making their claim effectual by organising a volunteer army for the purpose of fighting – if necessary – against the forces of HM the King Emperor. It thus marked a new departure in both political thought and practice, setting an example that southern nationalists admired and emulated and which resonated with wider and more tragic developments throughout the length and breadth of Europe. There, from the 1910s to the 1930s radicals of diverse persuasion exploited what looked like a general collapse of confidence in reasoned argument and resorted to armed insurrection, led by charismatic leaders who claimed the legitimacy of the visionary and the vanguard. Thus, if Ireland led the way, Ulster led Ireland.

In a way, this was not surprising. Heavily industrialised, densely populated and highly urbanised (40 per cent of its 1.6 million inhabitants lived in towns by 1911), the province enjoyed an unprecedented level of self-confidence. Belfast was one of the largest ports in the world and its shipyards the most advanced. Throughout the previous century Ulster's 'exceptionalism' in an otherwise socially conservative and economically backward country had been widely praised by both local observers and foreign visitors. If 'Ireland' (i.e. the South) had a problem with the

Union as it then stood, in the age of the *Titanic*, 'Ulster' did not: in fact, the Union was supposedly the reason for its extraordinary economic development and prosperity. Yet, as Ian McBride has noted, its stance against Home Rule was not that of 'a homogeneous people united against a common enemy', but rather of 'a community deeply divided along lines of ideology, religious denomination and class'.[2] Moreover, the key role in the crisis was not played by some radical Ulster Presbyterian, but by a Dublin unionist, a man of law and order, a former solicitor general for England and Wales and a distinguished member of the Bar. That man, of course, was Edward Carson. Without his inspiring leadership and ability to mediate between the gun-runner and Westminster, the Ulster rebellion would not have acquired the profile and ideological coherence which made it so effective. The present chapter focuses on Carson's ideas and their relevance in what was primarily a 'religious' crisis – not because it was essentially theological, but because it was a religious/national conflict, in which political views were held with the intransigence of a religious creed, while confessional Christianity helped to mobilise the masses and articulate their concerns.

2 Political Religion?

For R.B. McDowell, who authored the relevant chapter in Cruise O'Brien's book, the stance taken by Ulster in 1912 was self-evidently the rational thing to do: 'The Protestants of the north, whose own religious feelings were strong enough to make them aware of the dangers inherent in *odium theologicum*, had no desire to find themselves a religious minority in independent Ireland. They thought it was to Ireland's economic advantage to be closely connected with Great Britain, and above all they did not want to be thrust out of the United Kingdom.'[3]

It is interesting that he reported such views as matters of fact, though each of the points which he made was quite unrelated to what was ostensibly at stake: not 'independent Ireland', but a modest measure of devolution, whose government-in-waiting was led by a loyal imperialist, John Redmond. In fact, at the time, even the more advanced nationalism of Sinn Féin was dominated by men like Arthur Griffith, whose vision was not of a republic but a Habsburg-style Dual Monarchy. In an attempt to conciliate the North, Griffith went as far as to propose that the new Irish parliament should rotate between Dublin and Belfast with Ulster being given near-veto powers over Irish economic policies. The latter would surely have been an option worth contemplating by anyone seriously interested in commercial advantages, as the signatories of the Covenant claimed to be; it was, to say the least, 'better business' than the civil war threatened by Carson. Griffith was not alone in articulating alternatives. Between 1911 and 1914 William O'Brien and his All for Ireland League proposed the creation of a senate elected on a proportional representation weighted in Ulster's favour and urged a conference of all parties. Carson, in June 1912, in his speech during the committee stage of the Home Rule Bill commended O'Brien and his efforts, but believed it was now too late for such accommodation. He declared: 'if they had been made by the majority of them [nationalists] for the last 20 years [they] might, I admit, possibly have had some effect on some of the unionists in Ireland. Their idea was certainly a worthy idea.'[4] However, if it was too late, this was certainly because of Carson's own actions, and particularly his encouragement of the arming of the North.

McDowell did not even consider why such proposals were ignored by the Ulster Unionists. Instead, he wrote as if the outcome which was to emerge by 1937 – a Dublin-centred, Anglo-phobic, protectionist Roman Catholic state – was the only possible result of acquiescing to Home Rule in 1912–14. Neither did he question whether the *odium theologicum* to which he referred was what drove Catholic nationalists at the time or whether, even if this had been the case for some of them, it would not have been possible to restrain such animosity by legal means, as had been done in British Quebec, for example, or, for that matter, in Belgium or Italy.

Whatever the case, McDowell was certainly right in stressing the role of religion in the Ulster Crisis. Indeed, on this point there has always been general agreement among historians. It was religion that provided not only the myths by which the Northern movement lived, but also its radical ideology and perception of the Irish 'other', which was so important to the definition of the Ulster 'self' – including its allegedly superior work ethic and attitude to industrial enterprise. As William McKean – a former moderator of the Presbyterian General Assembly – put it, 'We are plain, blunt men who love peace and industry. The Irish question is at bottom a war against Protestantism.'[5] At the time, ministers of all denominations could be found to assert categorically that 'a Home Rule Parliament would be the domination of Rome. Therefore it followed we would be the slaves of slaves under a Roman Parliament which must be dominated by the Roman Catholic hierarchy'. Sermons drew on alleged parallels with the past, in total disregard of the importance of context and social change: 'Ulster held the pass in 1688 and 1689, and also in 1886 and 1893, and history will yet record that ... in 1912 and 1914 Ulster ... like the brave, unconquerable Spartans at the Thermopylae, held the pass against mighty odds.'[6]

Given the extent to which sectarian issues affected the crisis and informed politics in general, it is remarkable how little we know of Carson's own religious views. This is partly a reflection of the evidence available, which is limited. His spiritual life did not have the intensity displayed by that of some of his collaborators and supporters, including Fred Crawford, the gun runner. The latter's diaries document a classical Puritan providentialism reminiscent of the tradition of John Bunyan, though Crawford was actually a Methodist and, therefore, (confessionally) an Arminian rather than a Calvinist. Carson may not have been a theologian, but he shared in this cultural milieu. His favourite hymn, 'O God our help in ages past', was a classic example of eighteenth-century evangelicalism. Written by Isaac Watts (1674–1748), it emphasised the Almighty's steadfastness and sovereignty throughout history and politics:

> O God, our help in ages past,
> Our hope for years to come,
> Our shelter from the stormy blast,
> And our eternal home.
>
> Within the shadow of thy throne,
> Still may we dwell secure.
> Sufficient is thine arm alone,
> And our defense is sure.
>
> Before the hills in order stood,
> Or earth received her frame,
> From everlasting thou art God,
> To endless years the same.

This hymn must have offered much-needed reassurance to Carson and his followers when they contemplated insurrection and the possibility of a government repression, but its theology was too complex to be interpreted as a mere battle-song for 1912. The same applies to Carson's overall outlook. Though he was often quoted in sectarian contexts and his features are still displayed on loyalist banners and murals, there is evidence that he held rather nuanced religious views. His morality may have been 'Old Testament', as Alvin Jackson has written,[7] but his theology was certainly not – at least, if by 'Old Testament' we mean an unforgiving commitment to enforcing the law and a single-minded and formalistic application of rules. There was certainly a New Testament side to his spirituality. On his deathbed Carson shared his spiritual concerns with the Primate Charles D'Arcy, and admitted: 'I have seen so much to shake my faith', but continued: 'and what remains with me is no more than I learned at my mother's knees: "God so loved the world that He gave His only begotten Son ...".[8] The verse, John 3:16, continues: 'that whosoever believeth in him should not perish, but have everlasting life'. In evangelical circles this is referred to as 'the Gospel in a nutshell'. There was here an awareness of God's love for a fallen world, perhaps also encouraged by Carson's sense of his own mortality and awareness that he, like everyone else, needed forgiveness. This was borne out by his behaviour in both his private and professional life. Whatever his reputation and personal style, in his legal practice and career Carson often displayed compassion for the victims of his own devastating rhetorical skills at the Bar, including Oscar Wilde, in whose prosecution he refused to be involved (he defended Queensbury in the original libel case, which involved attacking Wilde, but he was not involved in the subsequent prosecution case). He opposed capital punishment and, generally speaking, advocated forbearance in retribution, though he insisted on the firm application of the law.

Such moderation should normally have also affected his attitudes to religious *politics*, also because people of his class and education were expected to adopt a detached approach to Orangeism. It was a matter of social prejudice as much as political principle: as the Provost of Trinity College wrote to Carson in 1908, Ulster Unionist leaders deserved contempt for 'pandering to the lowest class of Orangemen instead of instructing them'.[9] Orangeism was privately associated with the lower middle class, while an affectation of liberalism was part of the refinement expected of the elite. Indeed, despite his close connection with the Order, Carson himself – who flirted with Milnerite federalism and had once applied for membership of the National Liberal Club – 'always retained a certain qualified liberal unionist reputation'.[10] So why was he prepared to play the 'Ulster card' so ruthlessly in the crisis of 1912–14?

3 Democracy and Sectarianism

This question is linked to the other, equally important issue, of why the rest of the political elites were similarly ready to embrace sectarianism? Despite the eminence of sectarian warriors like Henry Cooke in nineteenth-century Ulster, middle-class Protestants deprecated open expressions of religious animosity and some ministers went as far as forbidding the flying of flags over churches. This was to change in 1910–14. Though many evangelicals and other 'dissenting voices' remained vocally opposed to sectarianism, the latter's social acceptability increased rapidly. The transformation was driven by two factors. The first was the impression that Catholicism was becoming more aggressive, authoritarian, triumphalist and political. Particularly damaging was the 1910 McCann case – involving the 'stealing' of children from a confessionally-mixed family, and the Roman hierarchy's claim that non-Catholic marriages were tantamount to concubinage. For Joe Lee, the incident 'proved to the Protestant in the street how the papal viper could wriggle its way into the nuptial bed'.[11] Michael Whitley has noted that Protestant fears were compounded by the supremacist language used by some nationalists with reference to Ulster Unionists. Anti-Protestant riots in Limerick and the one at Castledawson (Co Londonderry) – involving a Hibernian band attacking a group of schoolchildren – further increased loyalist anxieties.

To be fair, it is important to bear in mind that, at the time, anti-Catholicism was not limited to Ulster loyalists: on the contrary, as Dan Jackson has shown, Carson's campaign against 'Rome Rule' also attracted widespread support even in England. Moreover, both before and after the First World War rabid anti-clericalism was the mantra of the left throughout Europe, especially in *Catholic* countries, including France, Spain and Italy. There anarchists, radicals, socialists and republicans deplored 'priestcraft', Jesuits, 'superstition' and Catholic piety in general as the hallmarks of all things reactionary and obscurantist. Even in advanced Irish nationalist circles similar views were privately expressed by people like Captain Jack White and Rosamond Jacob. It would be tempting to explore what made Catholicism so repellent to the left at the time, but this would require a separate paper.

In any case, there was a second and more important factor which explains why this mixture of theological and political attitudes became so explosive in Ulster after 1911: in that year the Liberal government enacted the Parliament Act, which removed the veto power of the House of Lords and thus deprived unionists of their most important institutional safeguard against rapid and undesired change. Conservative and unionist leaders denounced the constitutional revolution as a *coup d'état*, and demanded a general election on Home Rule – as the latter remained undoubtedly controversial among the electors. But what they feared more than anything else was a fourth consecutive election defeat. On 15 October 1913, a couple of weeks after Carson indicated that he was ready to negotiate ('I am fully conscious of the duty there is to try and come to some terms'),[12] the Conservative Party leader, Andrew Bonar Law, was moving towards a more intransigent position. A memo of a private conversation with the prime minister, noted that he had provided Asquith with various reasons justifying his reluctance to compromise on Home Rule: the most important of these was '[t]hat if the question of Ulster were removed one of the strongest points in our favour in an Election would be gone and our chance of winning would ... be diminished'. Moreover, if the party compromised on Ireland and then lost an election, it would be in danger of splitting. Exploiting and perpetuating the constitutional crisis generated by Home Rule was the Conservatives' best electoral strategy at a time when the effects of democracy were still difficult to gauge. From 1885, when the parliamentary franchise had been extended to all male householders on a simple residential qualification, there had been major steps towards the redistribution both of land and political power, especially with the creation of county councils in 1898. Though most of the relevant reforms had been introduced by Unionist governments as part of a strategy to 'kill Home Rule by kindness', from 1906, when the Liberals came back into power, it had become clear that there was the potential for more radical social and economic change. The removal of the Lords' veto made such developments apparently inexorable.

In short, the Tories feared that 'democracy' would, at last, bring about the end of the old order, as Lord Salisbury had indeed anticipated as early as 1867 and dreaded for the rest of his career. They were not alone: throughout Europe, as a reaction to the rise of the radical and socialist left, authoritarian conservatism was rearing its head in new ideological garments, involving militarism and mass mobilisation. In the run up to the First World War, in Germany, Austria-Hungary and Italy anti-constitutional plots were continuously being hatched in conservative, court or military circles by elites who had reason to fear that only force – or a major European war – could stop the democratic rot from finally setting in. Bonar Law represented one of the most vocal and able exponents of the United Kingdom version of this last-ditch struggle against democracy coupled with a desire for an aristocratic counter-revolution.

The irony is that he and his party contrived to fight this potential rise of the democratic tide by mobilising the masses both in Britain and in Ulster, where the movement became openly subversive. As Graham Walker has written, 'the [1912] Solemn League and Covenant demonstrated the radical populism defining Ulster Unionism, the notion of "the Sovereign People"'.[13] The latter was the counterpart of the weakness of 'constitutionalism': power reverted to the people – Edmund Burke's 'uncivil state' – 'if the policy of a British government appear[ed] to undermine the rights of the constitutional people', i.e. the basis on which ordinary citizens are prepared to abide by the law.[14] An even greater irony is that such assertion of the people's absolute right to self-determination was comparable to that which inspired the Easter Rising in 1916. Indeed, whether or not the Ulster Volunteer Force (UVF) – with a membership of over 100,000 – was 'the real' people's army of the Irish Revolution, it became a source of inspiration for the militant nationalists who organised the Irish Volunteers.

However, besides the aforementioned parallels there are also important differences. To begin with, the success of the Ulster rebellion depended both on it being *counter*-revolutionary and on the support which the Covenanters enjoyed in British army circles as well as on what Florence O'Donoghue described in 1914 as 'the unseen powers behind them'.[15] The latter had long discovered what Woodrow Wilson and the League of Nations would fail to grasp in the 1920s – namely, that the 'self-determination' of one imperial minority meant oppression and irredentist claims for some other, with smaller groups competing for access to limited resources in the same region. It was of critical importance that Carson was an outsider, a leading lawyer with London connections, someone who was 'instinctively agnostic about the concept of "two nations" in Ireland': this gave him the authority to present the myth of 'the Honest Ulsterman' to English electors persuasively.[16]

It was an opportunity he could not afford to miss, because, for men of Carson's class and culture, sectarianism was a threat, almost as bad as direct democracy: left to its own devices, it might result in people seizing the political initiative. (As J. Smyth has noted, this was a fear which motivated gentry involvement in the Order from as early as the 1790s.[17]) However, if disciplined and controlled from above, sectarianism could help to sway the masses at a stage when democracy made them a force to reckon with. In this context, the key factor was the culture of popular militarism. The Boer War had shown that the lower classes were more responsive to jingoism and the appeal of the flag than to socialist internationalism. In the crisis of 1912–14 '[p]opular militarism was an obvious draw for many of those joining the UVF'.[18] Arming the people was a risky operation, because with the wielding of arms came direct access to sovereignty. Carson was aware of the dangers and 'was at pains to point out in many public speeches that the UVF was under professional military command'[19] – in other words, the Ulster Volunteers were under the control of men like himself, i.e. they were not 'a nation in arms', but 'the army of the nation'. The regular army had abundant experience of handling large numbers of working- and lower middle-class men and turning them into pillars of the establishment, and its methods and structure could be easily adopted to secure similar ends when drilling a volunteer force. Carson, the eminent magistrate, sanctioned the organising of a community militia with the argument that 'if force had to be employed in opposition to the law it would be disciplined and controlled by open and known authority'.[20] His main concern was not to shelter Catholics from undisciplined violence, but rather to prevent the democratic potential of armed working- and lower middle-class power from escalating into something threatening for the establishment. Like Redmond and Griffith, Carson never abandoned the principle of parliamentary sovereignty, '[not] even when reviewing paramilitary forces'.[21]

4 Sorcerer's Apprentice?

In a 1933 letter to his friend and historian John Marriott, Carson stated that, from the moment Gladstone offered Home Rule, it became 'impossible' to make 'any lasting settlement in Ireland', and that 'all the elements that had the real power were not only anti-English but really far from being civilised'. He concluded in similar tones: 'I quite agree that in the end it is a question of nationhood. The Celts have done nothing in Ireland but create trouble and disorder. Irishmen who have turned out successful are not in any case that I know of true Celtic origin ...'[22] These were bold statements for a man who, in his student days, played hurley and who, in one of his last speeches in the Lords, described himself as 'an Irishman born in the Free State'.[23] Granted that he rejected Ireland's claim to be a nation because he feared that this was tantamount to acknowledging her right to independence, the question arises about what it was, in his view, that made 'a nation'. In his set-piece speech at the Balmoral Showgrounds, in April 1912, Carson had explained that '[m]en do not constitute a nation because they happen to live in the same island. Ireland is not and never has been a nation. There are two peoples in Ireland separated from each other by a gulf of religion, of race, and above all, of prejudice far deeper than that which separates Ireland as a whole from the rest of the united Kingdom.'[24] It is a passage curiously reminiscent of the 'Citizen's' argument in *Ulysses*, and suggests that the narrow views satirised by James Joyce were not the exclusive preserve of Gaelic militants like D.P. Moran or Michael Cusack, with whom the 'Citizen' has often been identified. Moran agreed with Carson and indeed Craig about partition: he did not wish to have a Protestant influence in Ireland any more than the Northern unionists wished to have a large Catholic lobby in Ulster – even at the cost of 'sacrificing' their fellow-loyalists in Monaghan, Cavan and Donegal.

It is also interesting that, despite the significance of the Covenant as a founding document for Northern Ireland, in Carson's description of the nation there are no references to factors such as common laws, a shared past and the memory of shared sufferings and successes – so important for liberal nationalists in the tradition of Ernest Renan. Neither is there any reference to the future, to a shared vision, which is crucial for a covenanted – or Habermasian – understanding of what a nation should become. Instead, Carson's reference to 'prejudice' as a component of identity echoed Edmund Burke, another eminent Irishman and a barrister who, like Carson, was ambiguously posed between liberalism and conservatism and opted for the latter under the pressure of revolutionary events in the 1790s.

By the end of his life Carson was far more saddened and embittered by the changes he had witnessed than Burke was even in the darkest hour of the anti-French Coalition in 1797, when he died. In one of his last speeches, surveying De Valera's Ireland, Carson summed up what he then considered to be a life of disappointments – suffered and inflicted: 'I only came into public life because I cared for my fellow Loyalists in Ireland ... and I saw them in the end betrayed ... under the pretext that certain safeguards were provided. Now ... every one of these safeguards [have been] ... set at nought and made useless. That is not a pleasant political career.'[25] On a previous occasion, in 1921, at a dinner with Sir Charles Biron, Metropolitan Magistrate, Carson had gone so far as admitting: 'looking back at politics, I think we made a great mistake in not accepting Mr Gladstone's first Home Rule Bill.'[26] For an arch-unionist a greater admission of political failure would have been hard to conceive. Like a sorcerer's apprentice trying to handle powerful, dark forces, Carson had facilitated and guided fateful changes, but not the ones he would have wanted, and, in the process, compromised much of what he valued most.

But what precisely could have been his alternative plan? In an interview in 1928, Blanche Dugdale, the niece of the former Irish Chief Secretary and Prime Minister A.J.Balfour, , asked him that very question. 'Yes', he answered, 'I should have left Ulster out of it and given Southern Ireland something like Gladstone's Home Rule Bill.' But when Dugdale continued, teasing him about the viability of fighting the Irish Republican Army (IRA) until they accepted Home Rule, and asked him whether 'it was [not] a losing battle all the time', Carson replied: 'Losing battle? never ... Joe [Chamberlain] would *never* have acquiesced. ... I *revered* Joe. He was a very great man.'[27]

Here, perhaps, we have the key to Carson's vision of the nation. Like Chamberlain, he believed in the United Kingdom as an Anglo-Saxon project, an 'Expansion of England' which would have served the interests of all by assimilating the 'Celtic' element into the racially more 'progressive' Germanic element, creating a British equivalent of the (equally Anglo-Saxon-dominated) American melting pot. Again, like Chamberlain, Carson was not prepared to compromise, especially if this involved accepting that Ireland also was 'a nation', and that pluralism was essential to the making of a viable democratic United Kingdom.

Despite his frequent references to Gladstone's strategy as a better option than the one which was eventually followed and of which he had been a stalwart champion, it is commonly believed that Carson remained unrepentant. To the very last he spoke 'fundamentally ... [as] an Irish Unionist, a member of a deserted garrison, a conservative facing defeat and seeing the close of a great tradition'.[28] Both before and after partition, he was to receive many letters from Southern Protestants complaining about ill-treatment at the hands of republican groups, and he did his best to help them, both publicly and in private.[29] His bitterness overwhelmed all his political ambitions. He felt that the Southern unionists had been abandoned by a metropolitan elite which regarded their community as a pawn in a political game.

However, it was disingenuous, to say the least, to blame only London for the abandoning of the Southern loyalists, especially in view of his colleagues – such as Craig – being altogether ruthless in their determination to cut their losses and cast off not only the Southern loyalists, but also those of the Ulster border counties, in order to create their own equivalent of D.P. Moran's dream of a homogeneous country, in their case 'a Protestant state for a Protestant people'. Whatever the case, Carson's view that London should have fought to the bitter end to keep the South was unrealistic, especially if this was with the intent of helping Southern Protestants. As it was, the latter were often targeted by the IRA because of their loyalty (putative or real) to the government. Crown forces had been unable to protect them *before* the Treaty, and indeed throughout the nineteenth century whenever there had been agrarian violence. This situation contributed to the mass exodus of Protestants from the South – as many as half a million by the 1850s, as Brian Jenkins has noted.[30] Those who stayed behind and prospered did so primarily because of the good will and toleration of their Catholic neighbours, not because of the Union. In the meantime, what improved communal relations was land reform (which benefited both Catholic *and* Protestant farmers) and economic growth, not state violence. Had Lloyd George embarked on a fight to the bitter end in 1921, Southern Protestants in rural districts would have had to be evacuated or (more likely) would have spontaneously fled in even larger numbers than actually happened. Even those who wanted to stay, depending – as they did – on the co-operation of their Catholic neighbours and farm labourers, would soon have been forced to join the nationalist side.

Carson died on 22 October 1935. The final words in the obituary of the *Church of Ireland Gazette* noted that he was '[a] son of the south [who] will be laid to rest in a northern Cathedral [St Ann's, Belfast]. May it be an omen of days to come when men of every province may be able to win each other's love, and by mutual respect for each other's opinions forge links which cannot be broken even by death.'[31] Of course, this was mere wishful thinking. In fact, earlier that year, the July marches had been marred by sectarian riots of a violence and intensity which found no parallels until the outbreak of the Troubles in 1968.

Further Reading:

A. Aughey, 'The Character of Ulster Unionism', in P. Shirlow and M. McGovern (eds), *Who are the People? Unionism, Protestantism and Loyalism in Northern Ireland* (London, 1997), pp.16–33

J.V. Bates, *Sir Edward Carson* (London, 1921)

E.F. Biagini, 'The Third Home Rule Bill in British History', in G. Doherty (ed.), *The Home Rule Crisis 1912–1914* (Cork, 2014), pp.412–42

R. Blake, *The Unknown Prime Minister* (London, 1955)

G. Boyce, 'Respectable rebels: Ulster Unionist resistance to the Third Home Rule Bill, 1912–194', in A.F. Parkinson and E. Phoenix (eds), *Conflicts in the North of Ireland 1900–2000* (Dublin, 2010), pp.28–39

G. Dangerfield, *The Damnable Question: A Study in Anglo-Irish Relations* (London, 1976)

R. Gerwarth and J. Horne, *War in Peace: Paramilitary Violence in Europe after the Great War* (Oxford, 2012)

K. Haines, *Fred Crawford: Carson's Gun-runner* (Donaghadee, 2009)

A. Jackson and R. Foster, 'Men for all Seasons? Carson, Parnell and the limits of heroism in modern Ireland', *European History Quarterly*, 39/3 (2009), pp.414–38

D. M. Jackson, *Popular Opposition to Home Rule in Edwardian Britain* (Liverpool, 2009)

N. Mansergh, *The Unresolved Question: The Anglo-Irish Settlement and its Undoing 1912–72* (New Haven, 1991)

A.T.Q. Stewart, *Edward Carson* (Dublin, 1981)

B.M. Walker, *A Political History of the Two Irelands: From Partition to Peace* (London, 2012)

Notes

1   I am grateful to Alvin Jackson, Ian McBride and Brian Walker for their comments on a previous draft of this chapter.

2   I. McBride, *The Siege of Derry in Ulster Protestant Mythology* (Dublin, 1997), p.14.

3   R.B. McDowell, 'Carson', in *SMI*, p.92.

4   G. Boyce and A. O'Day (eds), *The Ulster Crisis, 1885–1921* (Basingstoke, 2006), p.158.

5   Cited in D.G. Boyce, 'The Ulster crisis: Prelude to 1916?', in G. Doherty and D. Keogh (eds), *1916: The Long Revolution* (Dublin, 2006), p.50.

6   Both cited in T. Bowman, *Carson's Army: The Ulster Volunteer Force, 1910–22* (Manchester, 2007), p.122.

7   A. Jackson, *Sir Edward Carson* (Dublin, 1993), p.41.

8   Cited in H. Montgomery Hyde, *Carson: The Life of Sir Edward Carson, Lord Carson of Duncairn* (London, 1953), p.495.

9   Cited in P. Bew, *Ideology and the Irish Question: Ulster Unionism and Irish Nationalism 1912–1916* (Oxford, 1998), , p.42.

10   See Bew, *Ideology*, p.41; Jackson, *Carson*, p.94.

11   J. Lee, *Ireland, 1912–1985: Politics and Society* (Cambridge, 1986), p.11.

12   On 20 September 1913: cited in Jackson, *Carson*, p.32.

13   G. Walker, *A History of the Ulster Unionist Party: Protest, Pragmatism and Pessimism* (Manchester, 2004), p.35.

14   A. Aughey, 'The character of Ulster Unionism', in P. Shirlow and M. McGovern (eds), *Who are the People? Unionism, Protestantism and Loyalism in Northern Ireland* (London, 1997), p.23.

15   D. Ferriter, *A Nation and Not a Rabble: The Irish Revolution 1913–1923* (London, 2015), pp.127, 134.

16   See Walker, *Ulster Unionist Party*, p.36.

17   J. Smyth, 'The men of no Popery: the origins of the Orange Order', *History Ireland*, vol.3, No.3 (Autumn 1995), p.52.

18   T. Bowman, *Carson's Army: The Ulster Volunteer Force, 1910–22* (Manchester, 2007), p.66.

19   Ibid., p.7.

20   See McDowell, 'Carson', p.94.

21   See Bowman, *Carson's Army*, p.77.

22   Carson to Sir John Marriott, 6 November 1933, cited in H. Montgomery Hyde, *Carson: The Life of Sir Edward Carson, Lord Carson of Duncairn* (London, 1953), pp.490–1.

23   *Hansard Parliamentary Debates*, House of Lords, vol.75, 1929–30, p.845.

24   Cited in A.P. Parkinson, *Friends in High Places: Ulster's Resistance to Irish Home Rule, 1912–1914* (Belfast, 2012), p.37.

25   Cited in Hyde, *Carson*, p.491.

26   C. Biron, *Without Prejudice* (1936), cited in Hostettler, *Sir Edward Carson*, p.292.

27   See Hyde, *Carson,* p.487.

28   See McDowell, 'Carson', p.97.

29   PRONI D/1507/A/49/30, William Donovan, from Cork City, to Carson, 18 July 1934.

30   B. Jenkins, *Irish Nationalism and the British State: from Repeal to Revolutionary Nationalism* (Montreal, Kingston, London, 2006), p.135.

31   'Edward Carson', *Church of Ireland Gazette*, 25 October 1935, p.677.

CHAPTER 9

Archbishop William Joseph Walsh[1]

DAITHÍ Ó CORRÁIN

1 Introduction

To contemporaries he appeared more an institution than a man. Though he claimed no inclination towards the episcopate and preferred academic work, he was *the* preeminent Irish Catholic prelate of the late nineteenth and early twentieth century. Archbishop William Joseph Walsh of Dublin was a commanding national figure who helped shape modern Ireland through his powerful advocacy of agrarian reform and Home Rule, tenacious championing of Catholic educational interests, and intuitive understanding of the dangers of alienating the laity. Although Irish historiography has been transformed since Shane Leslie's entertaining and flamboyant depiction of him, in the first *The Shaping of Modern Ireland*, as the ecclesiastical doyen, Walsh's significance in the development of modern Ireland remains undisputed. Historians would, however, object to Leslie's loaded description of Walsh as 'the mitred head of opposition to English government in Ireland'.[2] Rather the pursuit of equality was the archbishop's guiding motivation. On returning to Dublin following his appointment as archbishop, he told a reception: 'you may always turn to me with confidence, not in your spiritual concerns only, but in your temporal troubles and difficulties as well, making me in all things without reserve the partner of your sorrows as well as of your joys'.[3] This essay aims to assess and contextualise Walsh's pivotal role in Irish life during his long episcopacy from 1885 to 1921 through the prism of that telling declaration. Unlike Leslie, the present author can draw on decades of archival-based scholarship on the Catholic Church, land, education, Home Rule and the pursuit of political independence – all defining features of Irish history but not rigorously investigated before the publication of *The Shaping of Modern Ireland*. In particular, the pioneering and voluminous work of the late Emmet Larkin on the interaction of the Church, Irish nationalism and the British state revolutionised the understanding of this crucial nexus. Fortunately, two impressive biographies have charted the life and influence of Archbishop Walsh in far greater detail than this synthesised account permits.

2 Early Life and Career

The future archbishop was born on 30 January 1841 at 11 Essex Quay, the only child of Ralph Walsh, a watchmaker from County Kerry and Mary Pierce of Galway. An intimate of Daniel O'Connell, Ralph had his son enrolled in the Repeal Association at the age of nine months.[4] Walsh was educated first at a private school on Peter Street and then at St Laurence O'Toole's seminary school on Harcourt Street. There he acquired a love of music, mathematics and languages, and his academic prowess brought him to the attention of Cardinal Paul Cullen on prize-giving days. In 1855 he attended the Catholic University, then under the rectorship of John Henry Newman, and three years later entered St Patrick's College, Maynooth. Cullen wished to send Walsh to Rome but he remained in Ireland at the wish of his parents. His scholastic career was exceptional and he advanced rapidly from student to professor of dogmatic and moral theology at the age of twenty-seven in 1867, a year after his ordination. A doctor of divinity degree followed in 1874. Possessed of a methodical and forensic mind, remarkable memory (he later mastered the Pitman script and other methods of aiding recall), diligence and wide-ranging erudition, the intellectual Walsh was a born professor imbued with a passion for minute detail and mastering abstruse subjects. These talents brought him to national prominence in July 1875 when called as an expert witness in canon law in the case of *O'Keeffe v McDonald*. This was the last of a series of much publicised actions initiated in the civil courts by Robert O'Keeffe, parish priest of Callan, against Cardinal Cullen (no less), the bishop of Ossory, and other clergymen. The cogency of Walsh's exposition drew praise from the judge and enhanced his burgeoning reputation. In the same year he acted as secretary to the first synod of Maynooth and theological adviser to several Irish bishops.

Walsh's administrative abilities made him the obvious candidate to fill the vice-presidency of Maynooth in June 1878 following the appointment of Daniel McCarthy as bishop of Kerry. Due to the disablement of Dr Charles Russell, following a fall from a horse, Walsh was also acting president and had to contend with the unsatisfactory state of the college's finances, a destructive fire, fund-raising for a college chapel and improvements to student accommodation. Russell's death opened the way for Walsh's advancement and he was confirmed as president in June 1880. The historian of Maynooth College described Walsh's presidency as 'judicious as well as firm'.[5] He was instrumental in the revival of the *Irish Ecclesiastical Record* in 1879 when its publication was transferred from Dublin to Maynooth. Until his death Walsh was a regular contributor on theological questions. A dread of preaching made the written word his *métier*. He contributed countless letters, interviews and pamphlets to newspapers and journals on a myriad of subjects but, above all, he was a vigilant guardian of his church's interests. As his secretary and first biographer noted, Walsh was a formidable adversary and skilled controversialist, who, on occasion, 'could be aggressive and scathing. He wielded with skill the weapons of his warfare, often selecting the club of mace in preference to the rapier in his controversial combats'.[6] Walsh's writing style was legalistic and occasionally tinged with polemic; he also had a penchant for pithy postscripts.

3 The Tenants' Champion

Although his greatest battles were fought in the sphere of education, Walsh's contribution to the land question was substantial. His national profile and the authority of his name soared following his appearance before the Bessborough Commission to inquire into Irish land tenure at the height of the Land War. He represented the trustees of Maynooth, who had been tenants of the Duke of Leinster on Laraghbryan farm near the college but were evicted for refusing to sign the 'Leinster lease'. This agreement compelled tenants to contract out of the protections afforded by the 1870 land act. Walsh's evidence highlighted the absence of freedom of contract between tenant and landlord and underscored the pressing need to legislate for the 3Fs: fair rent, fixity of tenure and free sale. The report of the commission largely accepted these observations and shaped Gladstone's revolutionary land act of 1881 which introduced the principle of co-partnership in the soil between landlord and tenant by granting the 3Fs. During the framing of the legislation Walsh's views were elicited by Hugh Childers, secretary of state for war and an amenable go-between as he favoured Irish self-government. Ever captivated by legal intricacies, Walsh published a much praised 147-page pamphlet – *A plain exposition of the Irish land act of 1881* – to make the technical and detailed provisions of the legislation intelligible for all. In 1885 he was consulted by Edward Gibson (Lord Ashbourne), whom he knew from the O'Keeffe case, while drafting his land purchase measure. Walsh stressed the necessity for moderate annuities over an extended timeframe, something incorporated in the act. Two years later Walsh suggested a roundtable conference of representatives of landlords and tenants to resolve the issue of land purchase. He was sixteen years ahead of his time; the Wyndham Act of 1903 was the product of such a consultation. Walsh's most famous and widely read pamphlet linked currency theory to the Irish land question: *Bimetallism and monometallism: what they are and how they bear upon the Irish land question* (1893).

4 A Political Archbishop: Appointment, Plan of Campaign, the Fall of Parnell

A firm but strongly constitutional nationalist, Walsh shared the conviction of Archbishop Thomas Croke of Cashel, his mentor and confidante, that the people should not be lost to the church during the upheavals of the Land War. This attitude was not shared by Edward McCabe, who succeeded Cullen as archbishop of Dublin in 1879 and cardinal in 1882. He opposed the Land League, the Parnellite campaign for Home Rule, and the involvement of priests in political agitation. McCabe regularly condemned agrarian outrages, denounced the no rent manifesto in a pastoral letter in October 1881, and criticised the Ladies' Land League. His political stance found favour in Rome, at a time when Anglo-Vatican relations were improving, but not in Ireland where he was deemed to be under the influence of his Whig advisers. The increasingly isolated and unpopular cardinal died suddenly on 11 February 1885. Although Walsh had declined the see of Sydney two years earlier, he was 'both the popular choice and the outstanding candidate' to succeed McCabe.[7]

Walsh's preferment should have been straightforward but occasioned great controversy. Under canon law a vicar capitular is elected on the death of a bishop to administer the diocese until a new prelate is installed. Walsh was elected by a substantial majority of twelve out of twenty votes. On 10 March his name received the recommendation of forty-six out of sixty-three parish priests for the vacant archbishopric. The Irish bishops, then in Rome on their *ad limina* visit, also pressed for Walsh's appointment, none more so than Croke. These efforts were opposed by George Errington, who tried to discredit Walsh and push for the appointment of Patrick Francis Moran, archbishop of Sydney and former bishop of Ossory. As the unofficial agent of the British government at the Vatican between 1880 and 1885, Errington kept the pope and the curia informed of the government's view of the Irish situation and helped secure a papal rescript forbidding priests from involvement in the Parnell testimonial fund in 1883. A strong intercession by Cardinal Manning, archbishop of Westminster, was required to convince Pope Leo XIII to appoint Walsh on 23 June 1885. He was consecrated on 2 August in the church of the Irish College in Rome. The appointment was hailed by Irish nationalists as a triumph against British intrigue.

McCabe's tenure was something of an interlude between those of the ecclesiastical leviathans of Cullen and Walsh. Although Armagh was the primatial see, Dublin was more important given the size of its Catholic population of over 380,000, proximity to the government, and the ecclesiastical seniority of its archbishop – both Cullen and McCabe had been cardinals. Archbishop Walsh's heraldic motto: *fide et labore* (by faith and labour) epitomised his episcopal style. He was the hierarchy's most able spokesman and by disposition 'could lead and unite others, not only by his strength of will and intellect but also by his manifest sincerity'.[8] Walsh's tactful stewardship during the illness of Archbishop Daniel McGettigan of Armagh helped unify the hierarchy. He was more temperate than Croke but, like the archbishop of Cashel, was conscious of the volatile political situation. Under Walsh's energetic leadership by the autumn of 1886 the Catholic bishops had endorsed the Irish Parliamentary Party's position on Home Rule and the system of purchase as a solution to the land question. In return the bishops 'had an explicit undertaking ... that the initiative with regard to the education question on all its levels would rest with them'.[9]

Walsh supported the Plan of Campaign (1886–91) but not its violent excesses. This was an effort at collective bargaining on individual estates. Where rent reductions were not granted, tenants offered what they considered a fair rent. If this was not accepted by the landlord it was paid into an 'estate fund' to support tenants ejected for non-payment of rent. The Plan divided the hierarchy. Bishops O'Dwyer of Limerick and Healy of Clonfert dissented from Walsh's defence of the morality of tenants seeking a fair rent. The archbishop of Dublin was assailed by the Tory press for his alleged justification of illegal activity. The *Tablet*, the leading English Catholic paper, dubbed the policies of the Plan 'the doctrines of anarchy'.[10] The Vatican was alarmed and dispatched Monsignor Ignatius Persico on an investigative mission to Ireland in July 1887. The papal envoy did not grasp the intricacies of the land issue or Walsh's motivations in supporting the tenantry. His report regarded the archbishop of Dublin 'as much too politically-minded, too closely involved in public affairs through his association with the parliamentary party, the National League and Plan of Campaign and less committed to his pastoral work than he should have been'.[11] By contrast, Persico admired the moderate nationalism and prudence of Michael Logue, who had been appointed archbishop of Armagh in December 1887. The hope that Logue might counterbalance Walsh's influence was not realised. Walsh was summoned to Rome and, while there, a papal rescript was issued condemning boycotting and the Plan. This was the product not simply of Persico's report but of the divisions within the Irish hierarchy and strong lobbying by the British government and English Catholics. In Ireland there was intense anger at perceived papal interference in political matters. Stunned and exasperated, Walsh was placed in an invidious position (there was even press speculation that he would resign). He reassured the pope that the decree would be obeyed by all good Catholics. On his return to Ireland Walsh dexterously finessed the distinctions between pronouncements on moral and political matters in an effort to comply with the decree, keep violent agitation in check, preserve nationalist unity (both lay and clerical), and maintain the church's influence (both religious and secular). In a letter to the rector of the Irish College in Rome, Walsh remarked that Irish Catholics 'might easily enough be brought into the same state of mind that now so manifestly prevails throughout the peoples of Italy, France and other so-called "Catholic" countries. The same influence is at work which has wrought such mischief there. We must be careful now lest we incur any share of the responsibility'.[12] The 'state of mind' to which he referred, of course, was the virulent anti-clericalism shared by many liberals, republicans and socialists in southern Europe at the time.

The papal rescript had one further painful humiliation for Walsh. In January 1893 he was denied the red hat despite the tradition of the archbishop of Dublin being so honoured, not to mention his undoubted leadership and administrative talents. Instead the archbishop of Armagh became a cardinal as did Persico. Logue was embarrassed by his unexpected elevation and considered it an honour bestowed on Armagh as primatial see rather than on him personally. By way of consolation, Bishop Patrick O'Donnell of Raphoe stressed the political freedom that Walsh retained by his remaining outside the College of Cardinals. Publicly, Walsh gave no indication of his disappointment and graciously congratulated Logue. Historians have tended to dismiss the dour Logue and depict Walsh as the *de facto* leader of the Irish Catholic Church. In fact, as a recent biography of Logue makes clear, over two decades they maintained a strong friendship and an effective collaboration which held rumbustious colleagues such as O'Dwyer largely in check. Logue valued Walsh's advice above all others. The cardinal generally left the political direction of the hierarchy and the university campaign to Walsh, while he took responsibility for ecclesiastical discipline.

The fallout from the papal rebuke of the Plan of Campaign was overshadowed by the dramas surrounding Parnell. The first concerned the accusations made by *The Times* implicating the Irish Parliamentary Party leader in the Phoenix Park murders. Walsh was called as a witness by the special commission set up in 1888 to inquire into the claims. Famously, he deciphered an encoded cablegram which exposed the forgery of Richard Pigott and vindicated Parnell. The second drama was the bombshell of the O'Shea divorce case and the schism in the Irish Parliamentary Party in late 1890. Between the two episodes Walsh completed the construction of an archiepiscopal residence in Drumcondra, something first mooted by Cullen who had acquired a site in 1861. A substantial, detached, two-storey over basement residence was designed by William Hague, a leading Catholic architect who knew Walsh from the reconstruction of St Mary's wing of Maynooth after it was destroyed by fire in 1878. Building work commenced in early 1889 and the archbishop took up residence in the 'brick palace' in October 1890. It was one of the first homes in the city lit by electric light. Walsh took a keen interest in the design of the library. To this end he visited Gladstone's library at Hawarden and used a modified version of the shelving system. One of the first conferences held in Walsh's library was the meeting of the episcopal standing committee on 3 December

1890 that condemned Parnell as unfit to lead the Irish people on moral grounds. This course was forced on Walsh by Parnell's refusal to stand down. He had initially counselled the hierarchy to hold fire in the hope that the party 'would give Parnell a quick and decent burial without need for episcopal interference'.[13] Privately, through Joseph Edward Kenny MP, the archbishop sought unsuccessfully to persuade Parnell to withdraw and was greatly saddened by the split and the anti-clericalism it provoked.

5 Pastor and Educationalist

Walsh's active concern for the poor and the welfare of workers helped 'to overcome much of the residue of Parnellite hostility in the city's working class'.[14] The archbishop promoted the use of arbitration to resolve land and labour disputes, advocated the establishment of a Board of Conciliation and was often called on to resolve labour disputes. For example, in August 1889, his mediation ended a protracted strike by builders' labourers in Dublin and, in April 1890, he intervened in a bitter row on the Great Southern & Western Railway for which he was honoured with the freedom of Cork city. During the 1913 lockout his sympathies were with the workers and contrasted sharply with those of his secretary, Father Michael Curran, who, in one letter, suggested that the workers were 'not sufficiently starved' to see sense and call off the strike.[15] Through letters and other channels the archbishop pressed without success for a settlement. Walsh intervened decisively when a scheme to send children to England raised the spectre of proselytism. He condemned the seemingly innocuous act of philanthropy in a letter to the press on 21 October 1913. Mothers were warned that they could 'no longer be held worthy of the name of Catholic mothers if they so far forget that duty as to send away their children to be cared for in a strange land, without security of any kind that those to whom the poor children are to be handed over are Catholics, or, indeed, are persons of any faith at all'.[16] That this occasioned little hostility towards Walsh personally was due to his compassion and practical concern for the sick, the homeless, the vulnerable and the poor. His priests also regarded him as just and considerate, albeit rather aloof in temperament. This was due to his obsession with optimising the use of his time. When time could be spared, he enjoyed cycling, photography, music, astronomy and exploring Europe during his annual vacation.

Of his many concerns Walsh was most preoccupied by education and, as archbishop, was the hierarchy's foremost advocate of Catholic rights. He served as commissioner of primary (1895–1901) and intermediate (1892–1909) education and played a decisive role in several important reforms. Under the Intermediate Education Act (1878), secondary education was promoted by holding public examinations, awarding exhibitions and certificates, and payment of fees to school managers based on results. Walsh grasped the immense opportunity this afforded Catholic secondary schools by organising Catholic headmasters to participate in the new system. In primary and university education he sought equality of treatment for Catholics. Typically, he set out grievances in writing in the 421-page *Statement of the chief grievances of Irish Catholics in the matter of education, primary, intermediate and university* (1890) and *The Irish university question* (1897). Walsh was quite progressive and favoured the right of women to enter university and to vote. On the National Board he secured better remuneration for teachers and protection from arbitrary dismissal. The entitlement of Catholic training colleges to equal financial treatment was also won. Walsh refused to countenance the building of a cathedral until there was an adequate provision of schools in his archdiocese. He extended the pastoral infrastructure developed by his predecessors, as the Catholic population expanded to over 430,000 during his tenure, by increasing the number of parishes from sixty-five to seventy-six and building seventy new schools and extending forty others.

The most arduous campaign, in which Walsh was indefatigable, was for a university for Catholics. Although discussions with Michael Hicks-Beach and his successor as Irish chief secretary came to nought, the university question was sparked into life by a series of royal commissions in the opening years of the twentieth century. Walsh favoured the solution proposed by James Bryce of a single federal university containing three branches: Trinity (as a Protestant institution), a Catholic college and the existing queen's colleges. This proved unworkable, however. In 1908 Augustine Birrell oversaw the creation of not one but two new universities alongside Trinity. The National University of Ireland (NUI) accommodated Catholic concerns while Queen's University Belfast catered for Nonconformists. The toil of working on the commission preparing for the new university caused Walsh to have a nervous breakdown. When the first meeting of the senate took place on 17 December 1908 the archbishop of Dublin was fittingly elected chancellor until his work was curtailed by illness in 1915. The establishment of the NUI was the crowning achievement of Walsh's life.

6 Disillusionment with the Reunited Irish Parliamentary Party

During the 1890s the Irish Parliamentary Party was divided into squabbling Redmondite, Dillonite and Healyite factions. Walsh played a conciliatory role in helping to reunite the party in 1900 but by 1905 had withdrawn from politics and confined his public interventions to educational and religious matters. He was a staunch supporter of the language revival and gave the Gaelic League 'financial and moral aid at a time when it was looked at askance by politicians'.[17] In 1905 he encouraged the establishment of the Leinster training college to instruct teachers in the best methods of teaching the language and made an annual subscription of £10. As chancellor of the NUI, he had to contend with the heated Gaelic League campaign to have Irish accepted as a matriculation subject. The hierarchy favoured Irish as an optional rather than a required subject but it was eventually agreed that Irish would be compulsory for matriculation from 1913 onwards. In his final decade Walsh was afflicted by illness and poor health but when well manifested his characteristic tenacity. For instance in 1912 he was embroiled in a public quarrel with James Campbell, prominent barrister and Unionist MP for Trinity, over *Quantavis diligentia*, a papal rescript which forbade Catholics to compel ecclesiastics to attend civil tribunals. In refutation the archbishop produced a 110-page pamphlet: *The motu proprio 'Quantavis Diligentia' and its critics*. This dispute attracted much publicity as it occurred during the Third Home Rule episode.

Walsh shared Logue's ambivalence towards the IPP and silence on the Third Home Rule Bill. Neither had confidence in the party leadership believing it too fond of machine politics and bogus conventions, too secularist, too reliant on the Liberal Party and too willing to accept an attenuated home rule measure even at the price of partition. So chilly were relations between Redmond and Walsh that, in March 1912, the IPP leader appealed to him to send a subscription to the Home Rule fund to arrest the damaging impression that the archbishop was out of favour with the Third Home Rule Bill. Walsh's reply was pointedly curt: 'It is now some years since I made up my mind to have nothing more to do with Irish politics and that nothing in the world could now induce me to change my mind in the matter.'[18] Walsh privately supported the measure but was critical of the provisions governing finance and reserved services. During the First World War he was sceptical of Allied propaganda and was steadfast in his refusal to have his office or church property associated with the war or recruitment. In January 1915, for example, both he and Logue refused to write an introduction to Cardinal Mercier's pastoral 'Patriotism and Endurance' lest propaganda be made of Belgian refugees. Even masses for the war dead were refused but with some exceptions such as the requiem held for Willie Redmond.

7 Final Years: William the not so Silent

Between 1916 and 1921 Walsh's public interventions were rare but spectacular. Like the vast majority of the hierarchy he made no comment on the Rising and accurately judged the public mood following the executions, arrests and internment. The prospect of partition as part of a Home Rule settlement spurred him to break a decade-long silence. In a letter to the *Irish Independent* on 27 July, under the headline 'Ireland being led to disaster', he deplored the IPP's lack of independence in parliament and its branding of all critics as '"factionalist", "wrecker" or "traitor"'.[19] A more devastating salvo followed in May 1917 during the South Longford by-election. An appeal against partition was organised by Bishop McHugh of Derry and signed by sixteen Catholic (including Walsh) and three Church of Ireland bishops. In an explanatory letter to the *Dublin Evening Herald* on 8 May Walsh warned that 'anyone who thinks that partition, whether in its naked deformity, or under the transparent mask of "county option" does not hold a leading place in the practical politics of today, is simply living in a fool's paradise' and, in a postscript, added his belief that 'the country is practically sold'. Leaflets containing Walsh's letter were distributed at the polls and accompanied by the comment: 'this is a clear call from the great and venerated Archbishop of Dublin to vote against the Irish Parliamentary Party traitors and vote for Joe McGuinness!'[20] The timing of the letter had the effect of linking the partition issue to the Sinn Féin cause and contributed to McGuinness's narrow victory. In a letter to the rector of the Irish College, Walsh revealed that he had acted to turn the scale against the IPP 'renegades' who had led Ireland to 'universal shipwreck' and who, since the electoral reverse, assailed him 'up and down through the country, openly as "a liar"'![21] Sensitive to the changing political tide, the archbishop made a further significant gesture in September 1917 when he sent his car to participate in the funeral procession for Thomas Ashe.

Walsh was sceptical about the prospects of the Irish Convention and, like his brother bishops, was fearful that increasing violence would end constitutionalism. In his Lenten pastoral in 1918 he reminded the faithful that the Church was strictly opposed to secret societies, including Fenians, as he had in 1915 and 1916. According to his secretary, the archbishop did not send a message of sympathy on the death of John Redmond in March 1918 and refused a requiem mass. During the conscription crisis Walsh played a pivotal role in persuading Logue to meet de Valera and other representatives of the Mansion House conference and form a clerical–nationalist collaboration against conscription. Walsh was a national trustee of the anti-conscription fund. As he had in the 1880s, he understood the popular will and for this reason, unlike Logue, supported Dáil Éireann as the democratic wish of the Irish people. At the 1918 general election he let it be known that he voted for the first time since becoming archbishop and backed Sinn Féin. During the War of Independence the hierarchy was fearful of lending moral sanction to either side in the deepening conflict. Walsh abjured violence but blamed coercive British policy in Ireland for the disturbed state of the country. In November 1919, through the medium of Cardinal O'Connell in New York, he made a deliberately public donation to the Dáil loan and emphasised the restrictions imposed on Ireland. In 1920 he sought clemency for hunger strikers and Kevin Barry, celebrated a public requiem mass in Dublin for Terence MacSwiney, and condemned the Government of Ireland Act for making partition a reality. He used his last pastoral in 1921 to urge that 'our people may be strengthened to withstand every influence that would drive them … into courses forbidden by the law of God'.[22]

Walsh died on 9 April 1921 at 32 Eccles Street and, even in death, appeared to remain in touch with the people. As his coffin left the pro-cathedral for burial in Glasnevin it was draped with the tricolour. Walsh's combination of extraordinary intellect, industry, indefatigable vigilance, political acumen and deeply-rooted nationalism equipped him to guide the hierarchy adroitly through the political turbulence of the period. Towering above his brother bishops, the very length of his episcopacy engendered a sense of stability and the perception of him as an institution. He was driven by a desire for equality and justice in the spheres of Home Rule, land ownership, education and labour relations.

While Irish historiography has deepened and nuanced our knowledge of each of these areas, it has not diminished Archbishop Walsh's significance in the shaping of modern Ireland.

Further Reading:

P.J. Corish, *The Irish Catholic Experience: A Historical Survey* (Dublin, 1985)

P.J. Corish, *Maynooth College, 1795–1995* (Dublin, 1995)

M.Curran, 'The late archbishop of Dublin', The Dublin Review (July–December 1921) Vol. 169. nos. 338–9, pp.93–107

E. Larkin, *The Roman Catholic Church and the Plan of Campaign in Ireland, 1886–1888* (Cork, 1978)

E. Larkin, *The Roman Catholic Church in Ireland and the Fall of Parnell, 1888–91* (Liverpool, 1979)

D.W. Miller, *Church, State and Nation in Ireland, 1898–1921* (Dublin, 1975)

T.J. Morrissey, *Towards a National University: William Delany SJ (1835–1924): An Era of Initiative in Irish Education* (Dublin, 1983)

T.J. Morrissey, *William J. Walsh, Archbishop of Dublin, 1841–1921: No Uncertain Voice* (Dublin, 2000)

D. Ó Corráin, '"Resigned to take the bill with its defects": the Catholic Church and the third Home Rule bill', in Gabriel Doherty (ed.), *Cork Studies in the Irish Revolution: The Home Rule Crisis 1912–14* (Cork, 2014), pp.185–209

J. Privilege, *Michael Logue and the Catholic Church in Ireland, 1879–1925* (Manchester, 2009)

D.C. Sheehy, 'The "brick palace" at Drumcondra: Archbishop Walsh and the building of Archbishop's House' in James Kelly & Dáire Keogh (eds), *History of the Catholic Diocese of Dublin* (Dublin, 2000), pp.313–30

Notes

1   Obituary comment in the *Freeman's Journal*, 21 April 1921.

2   S. Leslie, 'Archbishop Walsh' in *SMI*, p.100.

3   M. Ronan, *The Most Rev. W. J. Walsh* (Bray, 1927), p.5.

4   P.J. Walsh, *William J. Walsh: Archbishop of Dublin* (London, 1928), p.2.

5   P.J. Corish, *Maynooth College, 1795–1995* (Dublin, 1995), p.231.

6   See Walsh, *William J. Walsh*, p.25.

7   T.J. Morrissey, 'Walsh, William Joseph', *DIB*.

8   See Ronan, *Walsh*, p.10.

9   E. Larkin, *The Roman Catholic Church and the Creation of the Modern Irish State, 1878–1886* (Dublin, 1975), p.395.

10 A. Macaulay, *The Holy See, British Policy and the Plan of Campaign in Ireland, 1885–93* (Dublin, 2002), p.54.

11 Ibid., p.355.

12 Walsh to Tobias Kirby, 3 July 1888 (Irish College Rome, Kirby papers, no. 219) in D. Keogh, *The Vatican, the Bishops and Irish Politics, 1919–39* (Cambridge, 1986), p.8.

13 F.S.L. Lyons, *John Dillon: A Biography* (Chicago, 1968), p.115.

14 See Morrissey, 'Walsh', *DIB*.

15 Curran to Walsh, 26 September 1913 (Dublin Diocesan Archives (DDA), Walsh papers, Bishops File 1913).

16 *Freeman's Journal*, 21 October 1913.

17 See Walsh, *William J. Walsh*, p.524.

18 Walsh to Redmond, 20 March 1912 (DDA, Walsh papers, 377/1).

19 *Irish Independent*, 27 July 1916.

20 M. Laffan, *The Resurrection of Ireland: The Sinn Féin Party, 1916–1923* (Cambridge, 1999), p.102.

21 Walsh to Michael O'Riordan, 16 June 1918 (Irish College Rome, O'Riordan papers, no. 19, letter 41) in J. an de Wiel, *The Catholic Church in Ireland, 1914–1918: War and Politics* (Dublin, 2003), p.175.

22 *Irish Catholic Directory*, 1922, pp.517–18.

CHAPTER 10

George Russell, D.P. Moran and Tom Kettle

DANIEL MULHALL

1 Introduction

In his influential book, *Culture and Anarchy in Ireland, 1890–1939*, the historian F.S.L. Lyons wrote about the struggle between what he called 'Irish Ireland' and 'Anglo-Irish Ireland' which, he argued, had come to a head in the opening decades of the twentieth century. Lyons wrote about 'the collision within a small and intimate island of seemingly irreconcilable cultures, unable to live together or to live apart, caught inextricably in the web of their tragic history'.[1]

There was certainly an abundance of political and cultural debate in the Ireland of that time. It was conducted on the pages of magazines and journals with a variety of causes to advance. Developments in early twentieth-century Ireland reflected wider trends. All over the world, the political pulse quickened with the evolution of the suffragette movement, the strengthening of trade unionism and the development of revolutionary socialism which eventually brought about the downfall of Russia's Tsarist regime in 1917, and this is to mention just some of the political agendas that flared during Europe's *Belle Époque*.

In Ireland, things took their own particular course and it seems to me that most of the ideological action took place within what I would term the broad tradition of Irish nationalism. There was, of course, a deep North–South/unionist–nationalist divide, which ultimately reflected itself in the division of Ireland, but this featured surprisingly little in the prodigious output of writers from the nationalist tradition in the pre-independence era. When W.B. Yeats took up cudgels in the 1920s on behalf of the Anglo-Irish tradition – 'the people of Burke', 'the people of Grattan', 'the people of Swift' – it was already something of an antiquarian affectation on his part, and there were few members of this community willing to mount the rhetorical barricades with him in defence of their tradition. The real focus of dispute throughout this period was the nature of the Ireland to be created in a new century and in the novel environment of looming self-government.

George Russell (Æ), D.P. Moran and Tom Kettle all featured in *The Shaping of Modern Ireland* (1960), Russell alongside Horace Plunkett as advocates of the cooperative movement, Moran in combination with W.P. Ryan, editor of *The Irish Peasant*, and Kettle with Francis Sheehy-Skeffington as representatives of that conspicuously talented generation which came of age in the early years of the twentieth century, one that also included James Joyce, and many of the leaders of the Easter Rising. All three edited political journals; Russell (*The Irish Homestead* and *The Irish Statesman*) and Moran (*The Leader*) continuously for decades, and Kettle (*The Nationist*) for a brief period in 1905. In spite of the many differences that divided them, all three clearly belonged within the bounds of Irish nationalism and sought in their writings to map out the breadth of that tradition. Whereas Moran (viewed by Lyons as a formidable opponent of 'cultural fusion') and Russell are seen in Lyons's book as representative of separate Irish cultures in conflict with each other – it was Moran, indeed, who coined the phrase 'The Battle of Two Civilisations' to refer to Ireland's situation at the turn of the century – I see my three subjects as reflective of diverging trends within Irish nationalism as it approached its moment of truth. They wanted to delineate Ireland's future direction at a time when it had begun to look as if cherished yet ill-defined national ambitions were capable of being realised.

2 Lives

Born in Lurgan in 1867, but brought up partly in Dublin, and now best-known as a friend and artistic collaborator of W.B. Yeats, George Russell (Æ) was, in his own right, a significant figure in the Irish literary revival. Poet, painter and mystic, his life took an unlikely turn when he became involved with Horace Plunkett in 1897 as an organiser in the nascent agricultural cooperation movement. This led him, in 1905, to the editor's chair at the movement's journal, *The Irish Homestead*, and to an energetic immersion in weekly journalism that lasted until its successor, *The Irish Statesman*, folded in 1930. He developed lofty ideals for Ireland and evolved into an advanced, if esoteric, nationalist in the aftermath of the 1913 Lock-out and the Easter Rising. Æ was a significant, occasionally influential commentator during the turbulent years after 1916, and especially in the 1920s as the Irish Free State strove to find its feet. Weighed down by what he saw as the persistent under-performance of his ambitions for his country, a disenchanted Russell left Ireland in 1933 and died in Bournemouth two years later.

Whereas Russell was born into an Ulster Protestant family, David Patrick (D.P.) Moran came from a very different background. Born in Waterford in 1869 and part of the rising Catholic middle class of that period, Moran developed an enthusiasm for the Irish language while working in London during the 1890s. He must have encountered condescending attitudes towards Ireland in late-Victorian England, for his writing is full of resentment at England's aura of success and Ireland's evident failure, having consigned itself to being, as he saw it, a pale imitation of its Imperial neighbour. He returned to Ireland in the closing years of the nineteenth century and, in 1900, launched *The Leader* which he edited until his death in 1936, operating throughout these years as a sworn enemy of anything he considered antipathetic to his vision of an Irish Ireland. In his 1960 essay on Moran, Brian Inglis describes him as a destructive critic, with an aim of making Ireland Irish, Catholic and 'fit for freedom'; though Inglis tempers these observations by noting that he 'always had constructive long-term ends in view'.[2]

Younger than Russell or Moran, Tom Kettle was far more of a political insider than they were. Son of the land war activist and staunch Parnellite, Andrew Kettle, the younger Kettle, who was born in 1880, is representative of an Irish generation that would, most likely, have played an influential role in Ireland had Home Rule become a reality in 1914. A precocious talent at school and university, Kettle was an accomplished orator as well as an active sportsman, keen on athletics, cycling and cricket. After his spell as editor of *The Nationist*, and at the Bar, Kettle was elected MP for East Tyrone in 1906 and seemed destined for an extended and successful political career; in 1910, however, he stepped down to become an economics professor at University College Dublin. Involvement in the Irish Volunteers resulted in Kettle being in

Belgium on an arms-purchasing mission when war broke out in 1914. His experiences there convinced him of the need to resist German aggression and this led to his enlistment and death on the Somme in September 1916.

Russell, Moran and Kettle were all active in public debate for most of their lives. Through the journals they edited, which stood alongside other publications such as *An Claidheamh Soluis*, *The United Irishman*, *The New Ireland Review* and *Sinn Féin*, they helped ensure that when Irish independence arrived in 1922 it came against a backdrop of decades of vigorous, tempestuous debate about the country's future. Why was Ireland so richly endowed with political debate at that particular time? It sprang, I would say, from two sources: disenchantment with Ireland's manifest frailties and failings in the eyes of those who came of age after the death of Charles Stewart Parnell in 1891; and an expectation that fresh opportunities for Ireland were coming within reach.

4 Ideas

Through his involvement in the cooperative movement, George Russell gained a hands-on knowledge of the condition of rural Ireland and he did not like what he saw. This apparently unworldly mystic developed a social philosophy which he thought could guide an emerging Ireland towards momentous national achievement. His ideas were expressed in two significant publications, *Cooperation and Nationality* (1912) and *The National Being* (1916).

His was an idealistic vision of Ireland's future, founded on a damning critique of the social realities he witnessed in rural Ireland. Russell favoured the creation of what he termed a rural civilisation and a cooperative commonwealth. In *Cooperation and Nationality*, he bemoaned the meanness of life in the west of Ireland and attributed this to an excessively individualistic social and economic system that militated against the fulfilment of human potential. As he put it, 'there is beauty of earth, mountain, sky and water, but no beauty in life'. This convinced him that there was a need for an agricultural revolution based on cooperative principles, which would allow for the building up of a new social order. This would provide for 'economic development, for political stability and a desirable social life'.[3]

In *The National Being*, he developed these ideas further. Russell wanted to apply the cooperative principle to urban as well as rural life and to make it the basis of a national civilisation for Ireland. In particular, he wanted to establish proper democratic control of Ireland's economic life. A sceptic about the power of the state, he feared that governments, even democratic ones, were prone to being dominated by what he called the aristocracies of wealth.

His thinking contained a curious mixture of rampant idealism and sober practicality. He wanted to build a democratic body politic for 'the soul of Ireland' and believed that scholars, economists and scientists were needed 'to populate the desert depths of national consciousness with real thought' and thus 'carve an Attica out of Ireland'. For Æ the visionary, Ireland was an 'Isle of Destiny' – 'and when our hour is come we will have something to give to the world'.[4] He wanted to spread national ideals so as 'to create a civilisation worthy of our hopes and our ages of struggle'.[5] It was his view that: 'to quicken the intellect and imagination of Ireland, to coordinate our economic life for the general good, should be the object of national policy'.[6]

Where Russell was reflective and an instinctive consensus-seeker, Moran was an uncompromising advocate of a set of campaigning ideas expressed through the pages of *The Leader*. He called it 'The Philosophy of Irish Ireland' and during his time in journalism he took no prisoners in his pursuit of those he considered enemies of the authentic Gaelic, Catholic Ireland he sought to bring into being. As with Æ, Moran's ideas were influenced by what he witnessed in rural Ireland, in his case during a brief cycling tour of the countryside in 1899, but he drew very different conclusions about the country's malaise and how it could be remedied.

Yeats and Æ were regular targets of Moran's argumentative pen. They were seen as representatives of 'the English mind' in Ireland. Æ was 'the hairy Fairy', a reference to his flowing beard and his interest in fairies, while Yeats was dismissed as a nonentity, or described as 'pensioner Yeats', a reference to the Civil List pension he received from the British Government from 1910 onwards. Uncompromising in his belief that 'the foundation of Ireland is the Gael and the Gael must be the element that absorbs',[7] Moran totally rejected the idea that Irish literature could be written in English. It was 'a mongrel thing' and the writers of the Irish literary revival 'lacked every attribute of genius but perseverance'. Moran dismissed this Yeatsian enterprise as 'one of the most glaring frauds that the credulous Irish people ever swallowed'.[8] For his part, Æ regarded Moran as a malign influence in Irish public life.

Surveying the history of Ireland's struggles, Moran derided Henry Grattan, the outstanding Irish parliamentarian of the eighteenth century and a figure often lionised by constitutional Irish nationalists for having secured added powers for the old Irish Parliament in 1782. Moran also dismissed the founding figure of Irish republicanism, Wolfe Tone, as not Irish, but 'a Frenchman born in Ireland of English parents'. The United Irishmen, whose struggle Tone had inspired, were depicted as 'a colossal failure'.

Nor had Moran any affection for the romantic nationalists of the Young Ireland movement of the 1840s, part of whose sin, as he saw it, was that they had concocted the fallacious idea that Irish literature could be written in English. He was often critical of the Irish Parliamentary Party, which, he maintained, was not composed of 'real Irishmen', and of the more radical nationalists of the emerging Sinn Féin movement, who were described as a 'green Hungarian band' on account of Arthur Griffith's desire to have Ireland follow the Hungarian example in prising concessions from the Austrian Empire. Only the Gaelic League attracted any significant measure of approval from Moran. It was credited with having brought about 'a partial revolution' in Ireland by having let loose constructive energies. But Moran had his differences even with the Gaelic revivalists when he insisted that Gaelic propaganda needed to be conducted through the medium of English. *The Leader* carried just one Irish language article each week and Moran never fully mastered the language.

Moran's 'Philosophy of Irish Ireland', which was based on a series of articles he contributed to the *New Ireland Review* between 1898 and 1900, presents itself as a wake-up call for nationalist Ireland which, in Moran's view, had fallen asleep and become a pale, unsuccessful imitation of Britain. The escape route from this morass was through the Irish language which, for Moran, could become a potent weapon for use in warding off foreign influence. He wanted to isolate Ireland from British influence so that it could develop its own nationality.

In his lively book, Moran was not much concerned with the nature of self-government (although Home Rule was the only option that was conceivable at that time), but wanted 'a separation of national personality, the keeping distinct and clear cut as many things as possible that may mark us off from our neighbours'.[9] Like Russell, Moran was concerned about Ireland's profound economic weakness. He acknowledged that the country could not, at that stage, supply 'the wherewithal for her own civilisation', but gave no indication as to how an Irish Ireland might go about rectifying this failing. Self-sufficiency was his lodestar and he insisted that 'the age of economics' had arrived.

What Moran wanted was 'a self-governing land, living, moving and having its being in its own language, self-reliant, intellectually as well as politically independent, initiating its own reforms, developing its own manners and customs, creating its own literature out of its own distinctive consciousness, working to their fullest capacity the material resources of the country, inventing, criticising, attempting and doing'.[10] Put like this, his platform had much to recommend it, although his bitter barbs directed against Protestants and what he called West Britons show him in a more negative light, 'a great hater' as Conor Cruise O'Brien has described him. O'Brien also saw Moran as someone whose writings 'constitute the only sustained explicit exposition of Catholic nationalism that we have'.[11]

As a member of the Irish Parliamentary Party, Tom Kettle was positioned at the pre-First World War centre of gravity of nationalist Ireland. An opponent of Sinn Féin in its pre-1916 incarnation, he believed that the place for a Home Rule Ireland was firmly within the British Empire. In 1904, Kettle was involved in founding the Young Ireland Branch of the United Irish League, a nationalist organisation supportive of the Irish Parliamentary Party at Westminster. As outlined by Kettle, the organisation's purpose was 'to purify and harden the constitutional movement by bringing into it young, capable and enthusiastic men'.[12] The Irish Parliamentary Party was probably in need of renewal considering that its most prominent figures Redmond, Dillon, O'Brien and Healy, had all been acolytes of Parnell during the 1880s. It is no coincidence that Kettle's closest political ally in the party was Joseph Devlin, the only leading figure to have emerged after the death of Parnell.

With Kettle as editor, *The Nationist*, while clearly an affiliate of the Irish Parliamentary Party, addressed a broad nationalist agenda, supportive of the Gaelic League (although Kettle never made much of an attempt to master the language), the GAA and an industrial revival for Ireland (something Moran also favoured). The paper was even willing to give a hearing to the 'Hungarian' policy advocated by Arthur Griffith. In many ways, its approach was not unlike *The Leader*, except that Kettle wrote from within the broad tent of the Irish Parliamentary Party and without Moran's sharp rhetorical elbows. In fact, the public positions taken by Kettle suggest that the differences between constitutional nationalism and the more radical variants were sometimes a matter of tactics and pragmatism rather than of ultimate ambition. He once wrote, for example, that 'an Irish War of Independence would be today justifiable if it were possible'. There were those who believed that, had things turned out differently, Kettle could have brought the Irish Parliamentary Party more into tune with the emerging forces that eventually displaced it.

Unlike Russell and Moran, Kettle had an insider's faith in politics and in the state. Politics was not 'a mere gabble and squabble of selfish interests', but 'the State in action'; and, he continued, 'the State is the name we call the great human conspiracy against hunger and cold, against loneliness and ignorance; the State is the foster-mother and warden of the arts, of love, of comradeship, of all that redeems from despair that strange adventure which we call human life.'[13] More prosaically, he suggested that: 'The State is you and me and the man around the corner.'[14]

Kettle wrote that the really important history was that 'in which we ourselves are engaged in making'; he wanted to fix attention on 'the living souls and bodies that make up the actual Ireland'. By the standards of his day, he held progressive views and was a supporter of the suffragette movement, although he parted company with the Sheehy-Skeffingtons when they confronted the Irish Parliamentary Party on the issue of votes for women; Kettle was, first and last, a loyal Irish Parliamentary Party man for whom Home Rule had to take precedence over all other causes. As an academic, he concerned himself with the economics of nationalism and the financial aspects of Home Rule. For him, nationalism and national self-direction were among the first principles of national prosperity. His assumption was that economic well-being would flow naturally from political independence. He was a supporter of free trade, but believed in subsidising emerging industries. In the argument between pasture and tillage, he favoured mixed farming because he believed it would produce a higher output and support a larger population. Ireland's economic future, he argued, rested not on the potential of big cities, but on country towns manufacturing products connected with farming.

4 Outcomes

1913 was the year when events in Ireland began to accelerate. Russell was radicalised by what he saw during the 1913 Dublin Lock-out and wrote passionately in defence of the workers. He condemned the Dublin employers, led by William Martin Murphy, for deliberately, 'in cold anger', attempting to 'break the manhood of the men by the sight of the suffering of their wives and the hunger of their children'. Russell went to London to speak at a rally in support of the strikers at the Royal Albert Hall during which he had harsh words for the Irish Parliamentary Party MPs, 'these cacklers about self-government' for their silence in the face of what was happening in Dublin, and for the Catholic Archbishop of Dublin, William Walsh, who had opposed the sending of workers' children to England to be cared for temporarily by sympathetic families there. D.P. Moran agreed with the Archbishop on this point and, although not without sympathy for Dublin's urban poor, he was antagonistic to the workers' leader, James Larkin (someone Russell greatly admired) and to the Irish Transport and General Workers' Union because he feared its activities would harm Irish industry. Kettle was part of a peace committee that tried to bring the dispute to an end and was generally sympathetic to the claims of the Dublin workers, recognising 'the causal bond between want and unrest'.

For Kettle, the establishment of the Irish Volunteers brought him back into active politics. Like many of his nationalist contemporaries, Kettle was dismissive of Ulster unionism and, despite the upheavals of the Ulster crisis of 1912–1914, he insisted that the Home Rule cause would ultimately prevail. The outbreak of the First World War proved to be one of the great watersheds of Irish history and certainly changed the course of what was left of Kettle's life. John Redmond's decision to offer unconditional support to the war effort proved fateful, for it split nationalist Ireland and, as the war dragged on, undermined the standing of parliamentary nationalism while providing a space in which a republican struggle could flourish.

When war broke out, there was no doubt about where Tom Kettle would stand. Indeed, he was probably more committed than his party leader to Irish involvement in the war. Reporting from Belgium as a correspondent for *The Daily News* (London) on the conflict's opening months, he was profoundly shocked by the German treatment of Belgium, a view widely shared within nationalist Ireland. On return from the continent, he threw himself wholeheartedly into recruitment, urging Irish nationalists to rally to a cause that could unite Ireland and Britain, and Irishmen, North and South. As a reflection of the depth of his commitment to the war, he was even willing to consider military conscription in Ireland, something that was a complete non-starter for most Irish nationalists. During the war, Kettle co-edited a collection of battle songs associated with Irish Brigades who had fought with Europe's Catholic powers over the centuries, insisting that Irish soldiers fighting on the Western Front were part of that proud martial tradition. Now, however, they were going out 'to fight for the sake of Ireland and for Ireland's cause'.

For his part, D.P. Moran backed the establishment of the Irish Volunteers in 1913, but declined to participate in the movement's leadership. In a failure to fathom the depth of unionist opposition to Home Rule, he was, like Kettle, dismissive of the Ulster Volunteers. Moran came out against recruitment and broke with John Redmond when he urged his supporters to enlist in the British Army. As Patrick Maume puts it, in Moran's opinion 'the demands of war on such a scale were too high a price to pay for Home Rule'.[15]

Russell viewed with trepidation the emergence of the rival Ulster and Irish Volunteers in 1913, which he saw as a threat to the peaceful cooperative methods he favoured. His firm pacifism made him see any resort to violence as a sign of intellectual failure, but he was opposed to German militarism and generally supported the war effort while refraining from encouraging enlistment. He grew close to James Connolly in the years leading up to the 1916 Rising, seeing trade unionism as a form of cooperation in an urban, industrial setting. Connolly reciprocated by viewing the cooperative movement as a potential ally for urban workers. Although such an alliance never took root in Ireland, it should be recalled that to this day many British Labour MPs are nominees of the Cooperative Movement.

Despite these connections with one of the Rising's leaders, Æ was, like Yeats, taken completely by surprise by the events of Easter week, which he attributed to the deprivation of Dublin's working-class communities. In a poem about the Rising, Russell made it plain that Pearse's dream was not his: 'But yet the thought, for this you fell, turns all life's water into wine'. Connolly was described as 'my man' and the Rising as 'the confluence of dreams/That clashed together in our night'.[16]

The Easter Rising, when his offices were destroyed during the fighting, also caught D.P. Moran unawares and he did not immediately recognise its transformational impact. For a time, he considered the leaders of the Irish Parliamentary Party to be the ones with the requisite experience and ability to steer Ireland's fortunes at the end of the war. In 1916, he initially supported Lloyd George's scheme to grant immediate Home Rule with six counties excluded, and it took time for him to be won over by the claims of the resurgent Sinn Féin movement, which he eventually came to see as an Irish Ireland party. In 1918, he rejoiced in Sinn Féin's electoral triumph and the eclipse of the Irish Parliamentary Party.

The Easter Rising had a huge effect on Tom Kettle, for during the conflict his devoutly pacifist brother-in-law, Francis Sheehy-Skeffington, was murdered by a deranged British officer. Kettle went to the Western Front sensing that the Ireland he had left behind, quite possibly forever, had been remade by the Easter Rising. Those who fought in Dublin would, he suspected, be seen in history as 'heroes and martyrs' while he would be remembered, if at all, as 'a bloody British officer'. Kettle was fundamentally an essayist rather than a poet, but the extremity of his situation, facing very likely death on the Somme, drew from him his finest verse, 'To my daughter, Betty, the gift of God'.

> So here, while the mad guns curse overhead
> And tired men sigh with mud for couch and floor,
> Know that we fools, now with the foolish dead,
> Died not for flag, nor King, nor Emperor,—
> But for a dream, born in a herdsman's shed,
> And for the secret Scripture of the poor.[17]

At this remove, it is astonishing to encounter such dogged idealism about the nature of the First World War almost two years into the conflict and in the midst of the carnage on the Somme. In his last days, Kettle resolved, should he survive, to devote himself to the quest for international peace.

One of Kettle's defining characteristics was that he was, in sharp contrast to Moran, a committed European who considered that his generation needed to dedicate itself not just to 'the recovery of the old Ireland' but also to 'the discovery of the new Europe'. His support for the war effort was conditioned by a belief in the need to resist 'Prussianism' (we would probably now call this 'militarism'), which he saw as the enemy of European civilisation. Kettle's advice to his country was that 'to become deeply Irish, she must become European'.[18] If he were forced to choose between the two, he admitted that, ultimately, he cared more for liberty than he cared for Ireland. He had high hopes that the tears and blood shed in Europe would be a prologue to two reconciliations – between Protestant Ulster and the rest of Ireland and between Britain and Ireland, or as he put it in verse: 'Free we are free to be your friend. ... Closing a battle, not forgetting it.'

George Russell had one brush with active politics when he sat as a member of the Irish Convention that tried to broker a compromise between republicans and unionists. He set out his ideas in *A Memorandum on the State of Ireland* published just before the Convention assembled in which he pointed out that the Home Rule Act, unless 'radically changed' to include 'unfettered control over taxation', would no longer meet the aspirations of nationalist Ireland. His argument was that nothing short of the status enjoyed by the self-governing dominions would suffice to create good relations between Ireland and Britain. The settlement he proposed was close enough to what eventually emerged in the Anglo-Irish Treaty, except for the exclusion of six counties of Ulster, something Russell argued against on economic grounds. Entrenched positions on both sides meant that the Convention, from which Russell resigned in February 1918, failed to reach any agreement. Æ correctly recognised that the new nationalist movement derived its power from 'the growing self-consciousness of nationality' which had all the force of a religion. Reluctantly, he found himself having to take a stand on the national question, concluding that 'a man must be either an Irishman or an Englishman in this matter. I am Irish.'[19]

Russell's main concern after 1916 was that violent conflict would shatter the economic life of Ireland. It seemed to him that the country was suffering 'from a kind of suppressed hysteria'. He responded with bitterness to attacks by British forces on cooperative creameries and feared that the 'wild nightmare of revolution' would shatter any prospect of Irish unity.

Both Russell and Moran supported the Anglo-Irish Treaty and sharply condemned the anti-Treaty republicans. For Russell, the Treaty did not hinder any of Ireland's fundamental aspirations. The key thing was that the country was now free to forge its own economic policy, something that also appealed to Moran, who saw fresh opportunities to pursue his ideal of a Catholic, Irish-speaking state. With this in mind, Moran shed few tears about partition because he felt that the absence from the new state of Protestant-dominated Ulster would facilitate the achievement of his particular ambitions for Ireland. An increasing worry for Russell was that violence was demoralising Ireland and bringing about a decline in the country's intellectual life. Both men were depressed by the Civil War and the damage being done to the potential of the new state.

Moran initially supported the first Free State Government, but subsequently switched allegiance to Fianna Fáil on account of his belief in protectionism; he reverted to Cumann na nGaedhael, however, when de Valera's policies began to alarm him. While he had some leanings towards right-wing ideologies of the 1920s and 1930s, as his biographer puts it, 'he was a pro-business conservative, not a fascist'.[20] Æ took a broadly similar stance, generally supporting the Free State government, but he was never won over by de Valera.

5 Legacies

To what extent can Moran, Russell and Kettle be said to have contributed to the shaping of modern Ireland? What unites all three is their concern for Ireland's economic development. D.P. Moran's influence was most apparent in the Catholic and Gaelic identity that characterised the new state. In his enthusiastic embrace of Catholic values, he was on to a winner in a country with such a large Catholic majority. Yet, Moran never recovered the verve or the influence of his early years at *The Leader*. He was an arch-critic who found it hard to rally contentedly and consistently behind any political creed other than his own. His achievement was to express the values and prejudices of the emerging social class – Catholic, nationalist and conservative – that, for better or worse, dominated the new Irish state during its formative decades.

Æ, with his more radical, inclusive agenda, was up against it, but his role, and of those who followed him like Sean O'Faolain in *The Bell*, was to mount a critique of the values of what he saw as an introverted nationalism that had narrowed its focus with the advent of independence. Unlike Moran, whose star had peaked before 1916, Russell's most influential phase was as editor of *The Irish Statesman*, which offered a perceptive, intelligent commentary on the affairs of new state when it was just finding its feet. In his gradual disenchantment with Ireland, the fork in the road for Russell was the imposition of literary censorship, brought about, he wrote, by 'the din of a strident minority', which certainly included Moran, who had campaigned against 'evil literature' for more than a decade. This shook the foundations of Æ's faith in a distinctively Irish civilisation forged from ancient roots combined with contemporary nationalism.

Tom Kettle would no doubt have been gratified to read Æ's elegy for him, comparing his sacrifice with those of the men of 1916:

You proved by death as true as they,
In mightier conflicts played your part,
Equal your sacrifice may weigh,
Dear Kettle, of the generous heart.

It would surely also please him that his fate as a casualty of the First World War is now widely acknowledged as part of the Irish story of those turbulent years, and that there is a monument to his memory in Dublin's Stephen's Green, which stands near to that of the republican activist and 1916 combatant, Constance Markievicz.

As for the battle between Irish Ireland and Anglo-Irish Ireland, by the time Moran, Russell and Kettle were busy sketching out their aspirations for Ireland's future, Anglo-Ireland was already passing into history, the land acts of the early twentieth century having eroded its economic and social significance. With the advent of independence, Anglo-Ireland had either abandoned the country or made its peace with the new realities.

George Russell had far less of Yeats's emotional affection for the Anglo-Irish tradition, although he insisted that Ireland must avoid shutting itself off from the world in a Gaelic bastion. What he argued for was 'the wedding of Gaelic to world culture', otherwise 'Ireland would not be a nation but a parish.'[21] I suspect that Russell would respond well to the hybrid culture of today's Ireland and its outward-looking face. Russell once wrote that: 'We want a raft which can be constructed in one generation and which will float the next past our pressing dangers into the open sea of the future.'[22] He was part of that raft and so, in their different ways, were D.P. Moran and Tom Kettle.

Further Reading:

N. Allen, *George Russell (AE) and the New Ireland, 1905–1930* (Dublin, 2003)

T. Brown, *Ireland: A Social and Cultural History* (London, 1981)

T.M. Kettle, *The Ways of War* (London, 1917)

D. Kiberd and P.J. Mathews (eds), *Handbook of the Irish Revival: An Anthology of Irish Cultural and Political Writings, 1891–1922* (Dublin, 2015)

P. Kuch, *Yeats and AE: 'The antagonism that unites dear friends'* (Gerrards Cross, 1986)

D. McCartney, 'Hyde, D.P. Moran and Irish Ireland', in F.X. Martin (ed.), *Leaders and Men of the Easter Rising* (London, 1967)

P. Maume, *The Long Gestation: Irish Nationalist Life, 1891–1916* (Dublin, 2000)

S. Pašeta, *Thomas Kettle: A Biography* (Dublin, 2009)

H. Summerfield, *That Myriad-Minded Man: A Biography of George William Russell AE 1867-1935* (Gerrards Cross, 1975)

H. Summerfield (ed.), *Selections from the Contributions to the Irish Homestead*, G.W. Russell – AE, Vols. 1 & 2 (Gerrards Cross, 1978)

Notes

1   F.S.L. Lyons, *Culture and Anarchy in Ireland, 1890-1939* (Oxford, 1982), p.177.

2   B. Inglis, 'Moran of The Leader and Ryan of The Irish Peasant' in *SMI*, p.109.

3   G. Russell (Æ), *Cooperation and Nationality* (Dublin, 1912), p.36.

4   G. Russell (Æ), *The National Being: some thoughts on an Irish polity* (Dublin, 1916), p.157.

5   Ibid., p.3.

6   Ibid.,p.166.

7   D.P. Moran, *The Philosophy of Irish Ireland* (Dublin, 1905), p.37.

8   Ibid., p.22.

9   Ibid., p.26.

10 Moran's statement of principles in *The Leader*, 1 September 1900, reproduced as an Appendix in Patrick Maume (ed.), *The Philosophy of Irish Ireland* (Dublin, 2006), p.115.

11 C.C. O'Brien, *Ancestral Voices: religion and nationalism in Ireland* (Dublin, 1994), p.35.

12 Quoted in J.B. Lyons, *The Enigma of Tom Kettle: Irish Patriot, Essayist, Poet, British Soldier, 1880-1916* (Dublin, 1983), p.62.

13 T. Kettle, *The Day's Burden: Studies, Literary and Political and Miscellaneous Essays* (Dublin, 1918), p.16.

14 Quoted in Donal Lowry, 'Kettle, Thomas Michael ("Tom")' in *DIB*, Vol. 5, p.165.

15 P. Maume, *D.P. Moran* (Dublin, 1995), p.35.

16 G. Russell, 'To the memory of some who are dead and who loved Ireland' in D. Kiberd and P.J. Mathews (eds), *Handbook of the Irish Revival: an Anthology of Irish Cultural and Political Writings, 1891-1922* (Dublin, 2015), pp. 455-6.

17 T. Kettle, 'To My Daughter Betty, The Gift of God' in N. MacMonagle (ed.), *Windharp: Poems of Ireland since 1916* (London, 2015), pp. 8-9.

18 See Kettle, *The Day's Burden*, p.xii.

19 Quoted R.M. Kain & J.H. O'Brien, *George Russell (A.E.)* (London, 1976), p.43.

20 See Maume, *D.P. Moran*, p.51.

21 *The Irish Statesman*, 19 January 1924.

22 Quoted in J.J. Byrne, 'AE and Horace Plunkett', in O'Brien (ed.), *SMI, p.*163.

CHAPTER 11

Daughters of Ireland: Maud Gonne MacBride, Dr Kathleen Lynn and Dorothy Macardle

ELISABETH KEHOE

1 Introduction

For many of the Irish revolutionary women who played a leading role in overthrowing British rule, one woman embodied the instrument of their repression. Victoria, the 'Famine Queen' whose government was so slow to cope with the disasters of the potato blights and resulting famines of 1845–1848, had, in Irish revolutionary circles, gained the reputation of an at best naïve, and at worst cruel, ruler of her Irish subjects. And as the monarch's fear of Fenians escalated through the fifty years of her reign, and demands for Irish independence grew – with concomitant violent acts and reprisals – she insisted on the imposition of harsh measures to make an unruly people 'behave'.[1]

The three women of this chapter represent the antithesis of Victorian ideals of feminine behaviour. Fuelled by a passion for independence, both for Ireland and for women, and infuriated by injustice, they fought with the same weapons – rhetoric, protest and violence – as did their male counterparts. Like the suffragettes in Britain, and indeed in Ireland, these rebellious women stood out from the crowd, and it is important to grasp within the historical context how daring was their behaviour. Each of the three – whose lives neatly inhabit successive and overlapping periods leading up to and following the Rising – came to the cause of Irish independence of their own volition and often against the will of their families and friends. Their aspirations and demands placed them well outside the mainstream of society and, indeed, they were perceived, outside of their limited revolutionary circles, as unfeminine enemies of the established order.

The men who challenged British authority, whether through political or violent means (or a combination of both), were frequently viewed as troublemakers, but the women who led demands for change had the added disadvantage of being mocked and isolated for their beliefs. This enforced isolation drew them together, and one of the first female organisations to establish its own revolutionary identity was that of the Inghinidhe na hÉireann, Daughters of Ireland. Founded in 1900 by Maud Gonne, this society was of huge significance – although most of its members placed nationalist objectives above feminist ones, and the Inghinidhe was a manifestation of the emerging new version of Irish nationalism post-1898. The society, interestingly, co-existed and overlapped with the growing feminist movement in early twentieth-century Ireland.[2]

2 Justice for All

Maud Gonne (1866–1953) was a charismatic and successful leader, although assessments of her legacy have fluctuated. A strikingly beautiful woman – tall and elegant – she was a gifted actress and the lifelong muse of W.B. Yeats (who asked her to marry him no fewer than four times). Gonne attracted, during her lifetime and after her death, a range of polemic opinions about her role in the shaping of Ireland. There was always much to criticise, for she had no sense of moderation, and her life reads – to even the most fervent admirer – as a melodramatic soap opera.

Gonne was born in England to prosperous English Protestant parents, and her father was a captain of the Seventeenth Lancers. Following the early death of her mother from tuberculosis, Gonne experienced a rackety childhood, travelling with her father on his various military postings and then as a military attaché. Gonne grew up with family members or her father in London, throughout Europe, and particularly in France and in Ireland where he was posted at various points. Despite a socialite existence that included making her debut at the vice-regal court in Dublin, Gonne was increasingly drawn to the plight of those less fortunate, and was particularly distressed at the injustice of the evictions in Ireland. Her hatred for Britain grew as did her identification with the cause of Irish nationalism.

Her father died before her twenty-first birthday, leaving her a sophisticated, well-travelled heiress. In the summer of 1897, while recuperating from lung disease in the French Auvergne, Gonne met the vehemently anti-British right-wing French politician Lucien Millevoye, who encouraged her to fight for a free Ireland. She and the much-older married man also became lovers, and their son Georges was born in secret, in 1889. Gonne kept quiet about this alliance – which lasted, on and off for thirteen years – and when Georges died of meningitis in 1891 at the age of just two, she hid her deep grief by pretending publicly to be mourning the tragic death of the Irish nationalist leader Charles Stewart Parnell. Privately, she used some of her inheritance to build a memorial chapel for her baby in France.

Gonne now spent a great deal of time in Ireland, where she had already gained a reputation for melodramatic flair – and continued to make quite a splash in Dublin, openly courting nationalists. In 1889, just before conceiving her child, she famously met Yeats. Like Yeats, and his friend the nationalist writer, artist and theosophist George Russell (known as Æ), Gonne was an avid believer in the spirit world, and, on informing them of the tragedy of the loss of her 'adopted' son, Russell shared his belief that a soul could be reborn if another was conceived near his body. Gonne convinced Millevoye to join her in Georges's memorial chapel, where their daughter Iseult was conceived, and born in 1895 – another 'adopted' child.

Of these dramatic developments Yeats knew little. Gonne lived a double life after 1889, spending part of her time in Dublin with a growing circle of Irish nationalists, backed by Yeats' support. She also travelled frequently to the poorest areas of the country, using her talents as an actress to rally crowds during speaking tours on behalf of evicted tenants. In France, where her cousin May resided with Iseult and their large menagerie of pets, Gonne worked ceaselessly to raise the profile of Irish independence, publishing *L'Irlande Libre* at her own cost, writing articles for the French, American and Irish press, as well as lecturing and fundraising in Europe and the United States.

Such was Gonne's disgust at Victoria's visit to Ireland in the spring of 1900 that she and other like-minded women organised the Ladies' Committee for the Patriotic Children's Treat (LCPCT), which provided tea and games in July to those children who had not been 'bribed' to attend the event organised for Queen Victoria during her visit. This was a great success, and the LCPCT was succeeded by the formation of the Inghinidhe, of which Gonne was elected president, with Jennie Wyse Power (a stalwart from Ladies' Land League days and later the first woman to sit in the Irish Senate), Anna Johnson and Mrs James Egan as vice presidents. One of its main objectives was to support the study of Ireland's native language, its literature, history, music and art, so as to combat pernicious English influences.

Reviving the ancient arts of Ireland was perceived as a powerful weapon with which to combat British rule, and Gonne relished the opportunity to use theatre and literature to highlight the cause of Irish independence. She firmly believed that the children of Ireland needed to learn Irish, and be taught about the proud artistic and creative legacy of their country: she herself taught classes in drama. The inspiration that she provided to Yeats was of critical importance to his astonishing work in furthering the Literary Revival, which had such enormous significance in the development of the cause. Indeed, he created her most famous role, that of Cathleen ni Houlihan, in his first openly nationalist play, written with Lady Gregory in 1902. In leading the Inghinidhe, Gonne eagerly engaged in high-profile, public attacks on the establishment, and was sometimes referred to as Ireland's Joan of Arc. She was enormously talented at motivating and inspiring others, writing to Yeats in 1903: 'I am the voice, the soul of the *crowd*.'[3]

Unlike Yeats, his mentor Lady Gregory, and others who embraced a brand of a rather high-minded, Anglo-Irish nationalism by means of a cultural revival, Gonne was increasingly drawn to the violent discourse and actions of men such as Major John ('Foxy Jack') MacBride, whom she met in Paris on his return from South Africa, fighting with the Boers against the British. Exiled Irishmen had for years found a safe haven in Paris – and secure banking – and Gonne, with her considerable funds and dynamic spirit, provided a meeting place for Irish nationalists. Raising funds was, as ever, a major preoccupation for the nationalists, who made frequent trips to the United States for this purpose and

Gonne travelled with MacBride to America to speak to sympathisers and address crowds. On their return, she decided to accept his marriage proposal.

Gonne converted to Catholicism and married MacBride in Paris. Because MacBride was a wanted man, the ceremony, held in February 1903 at the British consulate, had the predictable elements of high drama with which Gonne was associated. She worried that MacBride would be arrested before the completion of the ceremony, but was determined to make political capital of the event. The best man bore the green flag of the Irish brigade, and the bridesmaid the blue flag presented to Gonne some years previous by the Inghinidhe. The chaplain of the Irish brigade celebrated the marriage, and at the celebratory breakfast toast upon toast referred to the struggle – with the bride raising her glass: 'To the complete independence of Ireland'.[4]

The marriage of two strong, independent individuals, aged 36 and 35, was predicted by family and friends to end in disaster, and it rapidly did so. Gonne's relationship with Yeats took much effort to retrieve its closeness, though it was helped by the fact that the marriage union was so patently a disaster, even from the early days of the honeymoon. MacBride was a drinker, and could not be trusted near the female members of the household. There was, however, an outcome of enormous consequence: in January 1904, Seagan (later Sean) MacBride was born. His birth was greeted with great fanfare by nationalists; he was perceived as the product of two great revolutionaries and a certain future leader of the struggle.

Everything about Sean was used as political theatre. An early photograph portrays the boy in his mother's arms, draped with the flag of Inghinidhe. The Major is standing beside his wife and child, behind a table on which is displayed the sword of honour presented to him on behalf of the nationalists by John O'Leary, along with his gun belt, holster and two pistols. When Gonne brought Sean to Ireland to be baptised, MacBride, still in exile, had to stay behind and O'Leary stood as godfather. The inevitable split between the two, however, which was soon made public, caused huge consternation in Ireland where Gonne was blamed for traducing a national hero – and accused of splitting the movement in as heinous a way as had Parnell. Men who disliked her drive and spirited feminist views called her 'Mad Gone'.

Gonne's concern during the marital split was to protect the movement from any negative associations, and to keep her children from MacBride, a delicate undertaking since to do so she would have to make facts public that would harm his – and the cause's – reputation. But she took on the legal challenge of suing for separation in France (divorce was not recognised in Ireland) and Sean remained with her in Paris, where he spoke French as his mother tongue, and English with a French accent he retained the rest of his life. As was usual with Gonne, her home was a theatrical madhouse, lavishly yet carelessly decorated, with animals everywhere: dogs large and small, cats, dozens of caged birds, everyone speaking in French. Here Sean remained until he was 12, drinking in his mother's passionate views about Ireland. He and Iseult referred to her as *La Grande Patriote*, or GP for short.

After the split with MacBride was made final by the French courts, Gonne remained primarily in France and, over the ensuing ten years, strove to remain above the political fray, for fear of splitting the nationalists. She remained closely in touch with developments through her many political friends though and, by frequent travels to Ireland, continued to lead (and fund) the Inghinidhe. In 1908 the Society founded a monthly magazine, *Bean na hÉireann* – 'The Irishwoman', with her good friend Helena Molony as editor and for which Gonne provided funds, leadership and articles. At Gonne's initiative, and under her direction, in 1910 the Society created a scheme to provide the poor schoolchildren of Dublin with free food. The city had the highest mortality rate in the United Kingdom, and Gonne was convinced that it was not charity but a right for starving children to be fed. Members of the committee to run the scheme included the militant suffragist Hanna Sheehy-Skeffington (founder of the Irish Women's Franchise League), Constance Markievicz, Helena Molony, Helen Laird, Madeleine ffrench-Mullen, Kathleen Clarke and Muriel, Grace and Sydney Gifford.

With the backing of trade unionist James Connolly, the committee sought support for an amendment to the School Meals Act, in addition to providing the meals themselves, serving and cleaning up. Gonne was dismayed to discover 'secret opposition' from 'some of the clergy in Ireland', who seemed 'to think it dangerous & subversive & socialistic to feed hungry children'.[5] Three years later she was still hard at work on the scheme. There could be no doubt about her commitment and priorities. One of young Sean's first memories was of a St Patrick Society's annual celebration, when the three-year-old was dressed in a white suit and kitted with his mother's membership cross around his neck, and sent round the members with a collecting box while distributing shamrock that had been sent from Ireland by the Inghinidhe.

Gonne also provided many opportunities for other women to become politically engaged, including organising, for example, a number of trips to Paris to attend functions under the auspices of the Franco-Irish society, a group in which Gonne was prominent. Yet although she supplied major financial as well as intellectual and moral support, her increased absence from Ireland coincided with developments within the republican movement that led to a reduced role and relevance for her. As a wealthy Protestant convert who had sullied the name of a hero – and as criticism continued over her personal life – Gonne remained something of an outsider, despite the enormous loyalty she unfailingly inspired in those who worked with her.

Multiple nationalist organisations sought to consolidate through the early years of the century, often at the expense of feminist objectives. The Inghinidhe was absorbed by the newly formed Cumann na mBan (Irishwomen's Council) in 1914. This Irish republican paramilitary women's organisation became an auxiliary in 1916 of the Irish Volunteers. Although independent, its executive was subordinate to that of the Volunteers. Connolly set up his Irish Citizens Army (ICA) after the famous Lock-out of 1913, and the ICA was, in some ways, in competition with the Irish Volunteers (who later became the Irish Republican Army, or IRA). Labour, feminist and nationalist preoccupations were realigning during this period before the Rising, and Gonne, away for long periods in France, was not an important player.

News of the events of Easter 1916 trickled into Paris, and of the executions of MacBride and also of men she had known and admired. Her friends and colleagues from the Inghinidhe, Markievicz, Molony, Dr Kathleen Lynn, Helen Laird, Madeleine ffrench-Mullen, Máire nic Shiubhlaigh, Muriel and Grace Gifford were all involved and acquitted themselves with great courage. Now that MacBride had died – an Irish hero, fully redeemed – Gonne wanted to return to Ireland with Sean. She was furious to be told by the British authorities that she would not be permitted to enter Ireland. She disguised herself and took Sean to Dublin – and was soon arrested in 1918 for an alleged involvement in the 'German plot'. She was imprisoned alongside Markievicz and the Easter Rising widow, Kathleen Clarke, in Holloway prison. Sean, aged 14, ran after the van carrying his mother away, and by the end of the year had lied about his age and joined the IRA. Gonne was released on grounds of ill health six months later and once again put her nursing skills to use, concentrating primarily on humanitarian work.

Although initially supportive of the Treaty, she turned against the government when they began to conduct executions without trial. She was further appalled by the violence of the Civil War, and founded the Women Prisoners' Defence League (WPDL) – mainly made up of prisoners' mothers – to defend the rights of republican prisoners. Gonne indefatigably led marches, meetings and public protests, as well as collecting for the relatives, and providing meals and parcels for those imprisoned. She was arrested for her disruptive activities and even her old friend Yeats – now married and a Senator in the Free State – could do little for her when she was imprisoned in Kilmainham Gaol. She went on hunger strike and was released after twenty days.

Her later years were spent as a committed republican, ceaselessly battling, for some time at the side of the remarkable socialist and suffragist Charlotte Despard, sister of a former viceroy of Ireland. Her campaign for political prisoners continued for decades. Sean followed in his mother and father's republican footsteps and rose swiftly within the ranks of the IRA, within which he remained a prominent member. He served prison terms and was on the run and in exile for a number of years, returning to Dublin in 1936 as the IRA chief of staff. MacBride abandoned the IRA following the adoption of the constitution in 1937 to become a successful politician, also shining as a talented lawyer and human rights activist. He famously built on his mother's human rights legacy, and co-founded Amnesty International for which he was awarded the Nobel Peace Prize in 1974.

3 A Fair Society

Dr Kathleen Lynn (1874–1955) was also a Protestant of means, daughter of an Anglican rector, born and mostly raised in Co Mayo. Her family was middle-class and the Lynns were comfortable members of the county set; Lynn was educated by a governess, before spending time in Manchester and Dusseldorf. She then attended the prestigious Alexandra College in Dublin, an academically ambitious institution attended for the most part by Protestant women – many of whom went on to careers in education, law, journalism and medicine. Inspired by the example of her local doctor, Lynn was determined to study medicine and, in 1894, at the age of twenty, began her medical studies at the Catholic University Medical School – as a female student a rarity (in fact, until 1896 when the organisation formally accepted women, she was only allowed to take classes).

Although legislation introduced in 1876 provided for medical institutions to grant qualifications to men and women, in reality the medical field did not welcome women. Thus even though Lynn proved to be an exceptional student – winning a number of recognitions and being awarded degrees in medicine, surgery and obstetrics in 1899 – she experienced difficulty in finding a residency, and was finally accepted as the first female resident at the Royal Victoria Eye and Ear Hospital. She was a gifted doctor, interning at a number of institutions and winning prizes and she established her home and general practice in the leafy, prosperous Dublin suburb of Rathmines in 1904.

Having, from an early age, shown unmistakable signs of independence, Lynn was also reinforced in her career ambitions by Alexandra College, which encouraged students to become achievers, and also to collectively assume responsibility for social action. The Alexandra College Guild was typical of this ethos: established in 1897, it was intended to promote links between alumni of the school (some of whom were already teaching there) and to encourage good works amongst Dublin's poorest inhabitants. This concern for community service – and in particular for society's most vulnerable – was instilled in Lynn, who used her intellectual ability, medical skill and drive to improve life for others less fortunate.

Like many Irish female activists, Lynn was first inspired by feminism, and she became a member of the executive committee of the Irish Women's Suffrage and Local Government Association from 1903, and remained on the executive until 1916. She became a member of the radical British Women's Social and Political Union (WSPU) from 1908. A mass meeting held in Dublin in June 1912 to promote the demand that female suffrage be included in the Home Rule Bill currently being discussed, included on its podium the vice-president of Sinn Féin, Jennie Wyse Power, Delia Larkin of the Irish Women Workers' Union as well as Lynn.

It was Helena Molony, however, whose influence proved pivotal: Lynn befriended the activist through her distant cousin Constance Markievicz. Molony, an actress and trade unionist, was active in Inghinidhe and she encouraged Lynn to learn more about the national movement. As Lynn later commented, she was 'converted to republicanism through suffrage. I saw that people got the wrong impression about suffrage and that led me to examine the Irish question'. The ICA attracted Lynn for its gender neutrality (hence the 'citizen' army) and Connolly's well-known support for suffrage and social equality. She agreed to teach first aid to the ICA and became a captain and chief medical officer. Lynn and Markievicz worked in the soup kitchens during the 1913 Dublin Lock-out.

Lynn met her professional and life partner Madeleine ffrench-Mullen during their militant periods at the ICA before the Rising, and both were active during the Rising itself. Lynn served as a captain with the City Hall garrison and was later imprisoned in Richmond Barracks, Kilmainham Gaol – where she shared a tiny cell with ffrench-Mullen and Molony – and Mountjoy Prison before being deported to England – returning to Ireland in August 1916. In 1917 she was elected to the Sinn Féin executive, where she pushed for high-level positions for women in the reformed party. She also tended the wounded during the periods of conflict that followed, and her home was frequently raided. After the 'German Plot' arrests of 1918 she was on the run but was soon released as doctors were needed at the height of the Spanish flu epidemic.

Lynn and ffrench-Mullen were, at heart, concerned for a fair and equal society, and one where the disadvantaged could receive decent social and medical care. This applied especially to children and, along with a committee of other women, they set up St Ultan's Infant Hospital in Charlement Street in Dublin in 1919. Lynn was appointed Director of Public Health under Dáil Éireann in January 1919, and in 1920 was elected to Rathmines Council, where she served on committees on Public Health, Housing and Milk. Like Gonne, she was a member of the White Cross, and this group, established in 1920 to fund the victims of the War of Independence, included Kathleen Clarke as honorary secretary, as well as the future historian of the republic, Dorothy Macardle.

Sinn Féin remained Lynn's main political focus and, in May 1919, she was elected to the fourteen-person Sinn Féin Standing Committee. When military action seemed necessary, Lynn did not shirk: her home was often ransacked throughout the War of Independence, and she assisted anti-Treaty forces with first aid. Because of her anti-Treaty stance, her home and St Ultan's were at risk. Lynn stood for Sinn Féin in the general election of 1923 but, although she won in Dublin North, she refused, like all the anti-Treaty republicans, to take her seat. Lynn did not support de Valera's determination to enter Parliament and feared that his supporters were not sufficiently republican; she did not join his Fianna Fáil party when it was formed in 1926, and lost her seat in the general election the following year.

The Civil War was a catastrophe on every level – and it set back equality for women as well. In January 1922, twenty-six members of the Cumann na mBan executive voted twenty-four to two against accepting the Treaty. Wyse Power had been one of those in support, and resigned from the executive forthwith – and there was further disagreement among the rank and file throughout the counties, pitting activist and committed Irishwomen against one another. The national organisation split into factions. The real problem was that Lynn had no taste for the wheeling and dealing of politics. She had a staunch, straightforward understanding of what she believed to be right and wrong: the British should leave Ireland, and no compromise in the form of a treaty should be tolerated. Within that context, however, she was willing to set aside political argument to get an important job done. As she saw it, the wellbeing of the poorest – and especially children – was critical from a point of view of human decency, and for the future of Ireland. Petty rivalries and political manoeuvring had no place in her life, and this was, to a large extent, her undoing on the larger stage. Revolutionaries who failed to adapt to the post-Civil War landscape were demoted and marginalised. Lynn was not sufficiently canny to see this, and she also could not understand why the Catholic establishment, led by the autocratic and controlling Archbishop John Charles McQuaid, should object to her as a Protestant in a position of power at St Ultan's.

Lynn was a militant but not a political tactician and her focus was on action. Furthermore, she was disappointed at the dilution of republican aims by de Valera, and appalled at the regression of hard-fought women's rights. The Irish Free State of the 1930s saw a period of traditional, paternalist values emerge, reinforced by the dominant Catholic Church. Although the first Dáil of 1919 had proclaimed that the care of children was 'the first duty of the republic', the Catholic Church perceived government interference in social and healthcare as undermining their own position. A key concern of the Church was to prevent interference by the state in social programmes and to this end it promoted the ideal of an Irish nation morally governed by two spheres of influence: that of the Church and that of the Family, highly indoctrinated by the Church.

Lynn, a Protestant radical committed to improving healthcare and social conditions for women and children, was vulnerable to suspicion by certain Catholics. Her fierce determination to improve Ireland's infant mortality (one of the highest in the world) led her to pioneer the use of BCG vaccination and to promote the methods of Dr Maria Montessori, who visited St Ultan's in 1934. Archbishop McQuaid, an extremely close ally of de Valera, fought her at every juncture. She could no longer rely on de Valera; by 1937, she recorded in her diary that she had 'nothing but contempt for him and his party'.[6]

Catholic medical interests were of great concern to McQuaid, and he frequently made his views known to de Valera, writing to him on a number of occasions to persuade him that to follow plans by Protestant medical interests would be of great danger. Aided by the Knights of Columbanus, who spied and reported back on the activities of the Protestant medical body, McQuaid sought to diminish the influence of non-Catholics in the profession. It was difficult for Lynn to grasp that she was in any way considered undesirable for sectarian reasons. She saw no reason to bring religion into the medical world, and was astonished (somewhat naïvely) that anyone would.

She was also considered undesirable because of the ambiguity of her thirty-year personal and professional partnership with ffrench-Mullen. Whilst we can never know the exact nature of the relationship, the self-supporting, independent Lynn considered ffrench-Mullen her intimate partner and clearly did not fit the stereotypical mould of a mother surrounded by her many children, an ideal promoted by de Valera and by the Church. (De Valera was, famously, the only leader to exclude women from his unit during the Rising.)

St Ultan's became Lynn's main focus for the rest of her working life, and, although her political career gradually faded, she used her republican political links to raise funds for the hospital, and remained fully committed to the republican cause. She could see – as indeed could many others – that the political administrations of the 1920s and 30s were more focused on pro- and anti-treaty positions and factional power consolidation than on addressing the social conditions for Ireland's poorest. So, while infant mortality ranged between 66 per 1,000 births and 72 per 1,000,[7] the Irish Free State continued to rely primarily on voluntary groups (including religious orders) to provide welfare facilities. Lynn and her colleagues pushed hard for improvements, and she and others travelled abroad to visit other hospital facilities and to improve their practices in Ireland.

Although St Ultan's promoted Lynn's view of a republican Ireland – many of its activities were advertised in Irish, for example – she and ffrench-Mullen were determined to serve the community with no religious bias. ffrench-Mullen wrote to a newspaper in 1922 to assert that St Ultan's had 'no association, direct or indirect, with any political party or organisation. Any person making statements to the contrary will be proceeded against'.[8] Lynn was gaining a reputation as a medical pioneer, and a champion of the care of sick infants. In Dublin especially, there was a desperate need for a large children's hospital, and Lynn was determined to increase the small number of beds available by amalgamating St Ultan's with Harcourt Children's Hospital; she and others committed to fundraising (with great success).

Unfortunately, Lynn was entering a political minefield. The hospital community divided along sectarian lines, with institutions dominated by Protestants, and those dominated by Catholics. In fact, any hospital not under Catholic control was considered Protestant. The historical tendency for Protestants to be over-represented in the medical field – for reasons attributable to patronage and socio-economics – was addressed in the 1930s by a government keen to overturn the situation. In this they were much aided and abetted by Dr Edward Byrne, the Roman Catholic Archbishop of Dublin, and McQuaid, who used his fervent followers in the Knights of Columbanus – in which Dr Stafford Johnson was a major figure – to conduct sectarian audits of hospitals, and to provide opportunities for Catholic professionals. McQuaid specifically warned de Valera that the plan to amalgamate St Ultan's would, 'for generations to come, hand over the Catholic children to an almost exclusively non-Catholic control'.[9] By 1939 the scheme was ultimately abandoned.

Lynn, however, never abandoned her patients and her determination to care for children remained undimmed. She continued working at St Ultan's, where she attended her last clinic in the spring of 1955 aged eighty, becoming a well-known figure who was dedicated to the principle of decent housing, social and medical care for all. She died the following September, and was buried with full military honours. When not working, Lynn had perhaps been happiest in the countryside, where she bought the cottage in County Wicklow that had belonged to Maud

Gonne. It was here that Dorothy Macardle wrote her famous Republican epic, *The Irish Republic*.

4 Freedom and Free Speech

Dorothy Macardle (1889–1958) was born in Dundalk, Co Louth, to Thomas Macardle, the wealthy chairman of the Macardle & Co brewery and to Minnie, the daughter of a British army officer. Thomas Macardle was Catholic and a supporter of Home Rule, while Minnie, although having converted from Anglicanism to Catholicism, was a committed unionist. Dorothy was the eldest of five children, and, like Lynn, was educated at Alexandra College. A clever student, she earned an Honours BA in English at University College Dublin in 1912 and achieved a teaching diploma two years later. She became great friends with Maud Gonne and lived as a tenant in Gonne's home on St Stephen's Green. Macardle was an accomplished writer, and published a series of plays, articles, poems and stories between 1918 and 1922, while also teaching English at Alexandra College.

Macardle became politically active during the War of Independence, and supported the republican side. She put her writing skills to use by becoming a publicist associated with the Sinn Féin Department of Publicity. Macardle also worked on the Management Committee of the White Cross, the organisation in which both Gonne and Lynn were involved. Although the White Cross attempted to portray itself as neutral, it was, in reality, a republican human rights and relief organisation.

During the Civil War, Macardle supported Éamon de Valera and the IRA, continuing her work on their behalf as a propagandist, writing for the republican journal *Eire*. With Gonne, she also worked for the Women's Prisoners Defence League; this organisation vigorously protested against the treatment meted out by the Free State forces to IRA prisoners. Like Gonne and Lynn, Macardle was herself arrested and imprisoned. At Mountjoy she shared a cell with Rosamund Jacob, a leftist nationalist and feminist. The two writers became friends and later flatmates. At Kilmainham Macardle taught a class on 'Revolutionary Irish History' to her fellow prisoners.

Macardle was released in May 1923 and was not welcomed back to the college. She turned to journalism and writing, and supported de Valera's decision to enter constitutional politics in 1926, becoming a member of the Fianna Fáil executive. She continued to work as a journalist, for the

Nation and the *Irish Press*, and worked, too, on writing plays and, in the 1930s, began researching and writing the book which made her famous, *The Irish Republic*. This history of Ireland, written from the republican viewpoint, firmly portrayed de Valera as the talented and dedicated politician with the vision to create a republican nation.

Macardle had many advantages: an experienced writer and propagandist, she had been on the republican side for years, and knew many of the revolutionaries well. She had personal experience of imprisonment and had begun collecting eyewitness accounts of those involved in the War of Independence and the Civil War. With the training of a journalist, she was determined to construct a narrative of the creation of the republic – from the anti-Treaty side – by carefully and meticulously using evidence-based argument. She also employed contemporary documents to build her case. *The Irish Republic*, published in 1937, was an immediate success, and served as a refutation of many previous works that had represented the anti-republican side.

The book was well written, accessible and proved immensely popular. There were those who criticised its obvious eulogy of de Valera, and it is clear that, despite Macardle's protests, he directed her efforts and saw her as a loyal tactician who would serve his political interests. The hagiographic element notwithstanding, *The Irish Republic* was and remains a seminal text. It has been a critical element in transforming a series of events into an inevitable historical consequence: a highly satisfactory example of re-constructing the past to make a compelling narrative of the present. That Macardle chose to use evidence, documentation and carefully substantiated argument added to the strength of the propaganda and was quite a coup for de Valera and Fianna Fáil. It was also a courageous act, for Macardle was one of 'the few Irish historians to reject her family's political affiliation'.[10]

Macardle, although a de Valera supporter, was less and less happy as the party became ever closer to the Catholic Church; McQuaid, in particular, worked hand in glove with the devout de Valera in amending and creating a constitution. The first sign of trouble for activist women came with the proposal of Section 16 of the Conditions of Employment Bill of 1935, which allowed Seán Lemass, Minister for Industry and Commerce, to intervene in the employment of women, giving him power to prohibit altogether the employment of women in industry, to fix the proportion of male to female workers, and to forbid employers from employing a greater number of women than men in any specific industry where the ministry dictated. The Irish Women Workers' Union (IWWU) objected straight away, and planned protests, at which they were joined by other women's organisations and some women of Fianna Fáil, including Macardle. She had become a strong internationalist and frequent traveller, and she argued that the section needed to be deleted from the bill, insisting that to do so was necessary as part of a worldwide campaign for women's rights.

Lemass ignored the arguments, and, in response, the National Council of Women in Ireland announced that it was forming a committee to study the question and to monitor women's interests and rights. Macardle, determined to continue the campaign, became vice-chairwoman. She travelled to Geneva more than once, meeting fellow feminists, and in 1937 she attended a conference there as well as lectures on internationalism and met with League of Nations societies from around the world. Her internationalist humanitarianism was becoming an ever more important part of her life, and she travelled to lecture on civil liberties and against censorship. She was also involved in the Irish branch of the International PEN club, an organisation that defended the rights of writers. Macardle and others became increasingly worried about these issues after 1938. She increased her involvement with humanitarian associations after the war, travelling to France, the Low Countries, Czechoslovakia and Switzerland, where she conducted research on child welfare. She strongly supported UN organisations such as UNICEF and UNESCO.

Macardle was a founding member of the Irish Association of Civil Liberties in 1948. In the early 1950s she campaigned for legal adoption in Ireland. She was disenchanted by de Valera, and her increasingly dark novels during the 1930s and 1940s contained pointed allegorical references to evil masquerading as good. She confided to Rosamund Jacob (an agnostic from a Protestant family) that although de Valera 'had the finest character she knew, she always felt half its capabilities were smothered & kept from functioning by being a Catholic'.[11]

The construction of the republic was based on establishing a return to 'family' and 'traditional' values, as evidenced by a series of legislative measures, such as the 1925 Civil Service Regulations Act, the Juries Act of 1927 and the Conditions of Employment Act of 1936 – all of which set back women's rights. It was the wording of sections of the 1937 Constitution, however, that caused outrage for many of Ireland's revolutionary women. The most objectionable clause was 41, that proclaimed that the state recognised that by a women's life in the home, she was giving the state support; thus the state would strive to produce conditions whereby a woman should not, of economic necessity, have to work outside the domestic sphere and neglect her duties in that realm.

Although it is true that many women did not object to de Valera's paternalist views, those who did, did so publicly and with vehemence. These included Gonne, Lynn and Macardle, all of whom were very angry, and felt that these clauses were moving away from the republican – and egalitarian – ideals of 1916. It was a losing battle, however, and the move towards so-called family and traditional values alienated women from power. Over the following decades, their revolutionary contributions were marginalised and barely visible. The original *The Shaping of Modern Ireland*, does not feature a single woman. Macardle was graciously allowed to contribute a chapter. It was as though the women of the revolution had been erased. Having said that, it was, possibly, an accurate reflection of their perceived impact in the shaping of the Ireland of the late-1950s.

5 Conclusion

What, though, can we learn, through these three subjects, of their legacy more than fifty years later, in 2016? Interestingly, these three women – like a number of other female activists – had turned their attentions and focus outside Ireland after the state became established and had less use for them. They became increasingly alienated from the corridors of power and relegated by the Church to a supporting role. All three had believed, however, through the course of their careers, in the power of internationalism, and at a time that the establishment sought to constrain and limit external contact and influence, Gonne, Lynn and Macardle looked outwards.

Gonne, through her networks in France, was pivotal in internationalising Inghinidhe. Lynn was a radical medical pioneer, who reached outside Ireland to fellow professionals such as Montessori, travelled extensively to learn from other countries and championed the BCG vaccination 1937 at St Ultan's as part of an international campaign to eradicate tuberculosis. Macardle reached out to international constituencies for ideas and to inspire. Horrified by the increasing censorship and closed-mindedness that started engulfing Ireland from the 1930s, she fought for her beliefs within Ireland, but also insisted on keeping her mind open.

A further hugely important legacy of these three women is in the collaborative nature of their work. Not for them the 'Queen Bee' syndrome of which many successful women are accused. It may have taken many decades, but the historians, writers and thinkers of the Ireland of 2016 have benefited from generous women; not just from these three, but from the many more who could not be included in this chapter for reasons of space, and who worked tirelessly and sacrificed themselves without thought for personal gain or self-aggrandisement. This is one of the most significant reasons why they are not remembered by name, though their work has endured and has shaped today's generation.

Modern Ireland is a country that leads the world in ideas and freedom of thought, expression and behaviour. Lynn (and possibly Macardle) would not have had to hide her sexuality after the May referendum of 2015. Ireland continues be a global leader in the battle for human rights, a legacy of Gonne and those such as her son who followed her, and a legacy which has been upheld by the nation's presidents. The challenge of religious dominance in medical and social affairs for which Lynn campaigned is – belatedly but forcefully – taking place. Her ideas on vaccination, and on providing a better life for the poorest in the country and, in particular, its children have now become integral to Ireland's sense of fairness and social justice, however imperfectly it may at times be practiced. Ireland is also a nation that is in the first rank of democracies in terms of civil liberties, for which one of the criteria is a free and independent media and freedom in literature and other cultural expression, which Macardle fought so hard to achieve.[12] Gonne, Lynn and Macardle's contributions are a proud legacy in the shaping of 2016 Ireland indeed.

Further Reading:

M. Cullen and M. Luddy (eds), *Female Activists: Irish Women and Change, 1900–1960* (Dublin, 2007)

L. Gillis, *Women of the Irish Revolution* (Cork, 2014)

M. Gonne MacBride, *A Servant of the Queen: Reminiscences* (London, 1938)

A. Matthews, *Renegades: Irish Republican Women 1900–1922* (Cork, 2010)

A. Matthews, *Dissidents: Irish Republican Women 1923–1941* (Cork, 2012)

C. McCarthy, *Cumann na mBan and the Irish Revolution* (Cork, 2014)

S. McCoole, *Guns and Chiffon: Women Revolutionaries and Kilmainhan Gaol, 1916–1923* (Dublin, 1997)

S. McCoole, *No Ordinary Women: Irish Female Activists in the Revolutionary Years 1900–1923* (Dublin, 2003)

S. McCoole, *Easter Widows: Seven Irish Women Who Lived in the Shadow of the 1916 Rising* (Dublin, 2014)

N.C. Smith, *Dorothy Macardle: A Life* (Dublin, 2007)

Notes

1   M. Kenny, *Crown and Shamrock: Love and Hate Between Ireland and the British Monarchy* (Dublin, 2009), p. 17

2   S. Pašeta, *Irish Nationalist Women, 1900–1918* (Cambridge, 2013), pp.33–45.

3   M.Gonne to W.B. Yeats, 10 February 1903, in *The Gonne–Yeats Letters 1893–1938: Always Your Friend*, edited by A. MacBride White and A.N. Jeffares (London, 1992), p.166.

4   '*United Irishman*', 28 February 1903; cited in M. Ward, *Maud Gonne: A Life* (London, 1990), p.78.

5   M.Gonne to J.Quinn, 17 June 1911, in J. Londraville and R. Londraville (eds), *Too Long a Sacrifice: the Letters of Maud Gonne and John Quinn* (London, 1999), p.77.

6   Cited in M. Mulholland, *The Politics and Relationships of Kathleen Lynn* (Dublin, 2002), p.77.

7   It would not fall below fifty until 1950: M. Ó hÓgartaigh, *Kathleen Lynn: Irishwoman, Patriot, Doctor* (Dublin, 2006), p.85.

8   ffrench-Mullen scrapbook, 1922; cited in obituary of Lynn, *Irish Times*, 15 Sept. 1955 in M ÓhOgartaigh, *Kathleen Lynn: Irishwoman, Patriot, Doctor* (Dublin, 2006) p 20.

9   J. Cooney, *John Charles McQuaid: Ruler of Catholic Ireland* (Dublin, 1999), p.89.

10 N.C. Smith, *A 'Manly' Study? Irish Women Historians, 1868–1949* (Basingstoke, 2006), p.131.

11 R.F. Foster, *Vivid Faces: The Revolutionary Generation in Ireland, 1890–1923* (London and New York, 2015), p.330.

12 Democracy Index 2013 in the Economist Intelligence Unit (2014), available from www.worldaudit.org/.

CHAPTER 12

W. B. Yeats

THEO DORGAN

1 Introduction

If we mean anything by 'independence' now, in the western democracies, we mean probably no more than the limited ability of a nation state, acting from within its self-defined borders, to shape the economic and political sovereignty of the state with a minimum of external influence or coercion. In countries defining themselves as democratic, the idea of the independent state is itself shaped, at least in theory, by the a-priori autonomy of the people on whose authority and with whose consent the institutions of state are brought into existence and maintained in being.

In nineteenth-century Ireland, the uneasy collection of forces notionally committed to achieving Irish independence shared a relatively unformed idea of what it would mean for Ireland to be independent. For the most part, 'independence' meant little more than 'independence from England'.

Until the foreclosure of the Irish parliament triggered by the 1801 Act of Union, Ireland had enjoyed, at best, a limited version of independence as a co-dependent kingdom inside the United Kingdom of Britain and Ireland. Though their formal political loyalty was to crown and parliament in London, the press of day-to-day reality, the relative isolation imposed by distance from the quotidian exercise of power and its perquisites, had the effect of establishing in the powerful landlord class a sense of Ireland's distinctiveness if not at that point a formed idea of independence. When the Act of Union shifted the locus of power decisively to London, many of the major landowners closed down their great townhouses in Dublin and decamped to London; they became absentee landlords, thus breaking the human as well as the geographical connection.

The departure of the bigger landlords allowed the emergence of second-tier landowners as a leading social class, consolidating their interests with those of the bigger figures who had chosen to remain in Ireland. While this process was unfolding, industry and commerce were expanding, and hence a mercantile and manufacturing bourgeoisie was coming into being. As was happening across much of Europe, the accommodations of necessity were breaking down the traditional antipathy of aristocracy towards trade, and a pragmatic rapprochement was well under way in Ireland.

One consequence of industrial development was, of course, the creation not just of an industrial proletariat, but of the *petit bourgeoisie* necessary to manage the lower stages of business, the clerks and administrators who would augment the growing army of clerks and administrators already in the service of the crown in Ireland. As in other parts of Europe, industrialisation and the growth of commercial ventures made it necessary to provide at least for the rudimentary education of the poor, with all the political consequences that inevitably follow from educating the powerless and creating a new class of impoverished and disenfranchised teachers.

These were among the principal political forces in play at the moment when W.B. Yeats was born in 1865, the forces that would play themselves out in all their cross currents and eddies in the course of his lifetime, forces that would, in part, shape him, and to whose uneven unfolding he would himself contribute. There were three other, external, forces that shaped the Ireland into which Yeats was born. In the wake of the Romantic revolution, a profound interest in folklore as a wellspring of high cultural endeavour had embedded itself in the European artistic *milieu* by the mid-nineteenth century. In music and literature especially, great artists and great scholars had turned their attention to these rich and deep repositories of meaning, often suborning theme and image to personal purposes, to be sure, but seeking also to ground more generally in their individual cultures a key proposition of nationalist politics – that it was possible and necessary to define a people, a distinct nation, in terms of its particular imagination, its particular and inalienable cultural expression. In Ireland this impulse took a number of forms: driven by the landowner Douglas Hyde, the Gaelic League sought to bring before the public the rich and neglected poetry of the Irish language, in the original and in translation, as a good in itself, of course, but also as a spur to national pride; at the same time, the patriotic songs of Moore, the patriotic ballads and verse of Davis and Ferguson, were being bent into the service of an emerging distinctiveness of identity. In short, developments in the cultural sphere, seen as, at once, modernising and antiquarian, as acts of advancement as well as acts of repossession, were potent drivers in the emerging politics of the moment.

Next, and this too had its parallels across Europe, the tradition of physical force in opposition to tyranny, however one chose to define tyranny, was very much alive. The Fenian uprising of 1867, quixotic and amateurish as it may have been compared to, say, Garibaldi's revolution in arms, had sown a seed. Deep underground forces of insurrection were marshalling themselves, while agrarian terror organisations flickered, flamed and died out across the landscape alongside more professional political ventures such as the Land League.

Finally, from Daniel O'Connell to Charles Stuart Parnell, Irish representation in the Westminster Parliament had been steadily and inexorably building up a considerable political experience and practice, the long-term aim of which was Home Rule, some kind of limited self-determination under the crown.

2 Enter a Titan

Taken all together, these convergent and overlapping spheres of reality created the milieu into which, on 13 June 1865, William Butler Yeats was born. The family at the time was living in Sandymount, a suburb on the south shore of Dublin Bay, but soon moved to County Sligo, the ancestral home of Yeats' mother, whose people were, in a relatively prosperous way, millers and ship-owners. In 1867 the family moved to London, for the benefit of Yeats' father John, that he might pursue his studies as a painter, and the young poet had his early education there.

From the start, then, the margins of Yeats' life were set; he would spend that life largely inside the triangle defined by Sligo, Dublin and London, between deep country, his nation's capital and the seat of empire. 'At the deep heart's core' of his imaginative life, he would always say, was Sligo – the wellspring of his imagination. The 'smiling public man' would conduct his affairs of the nation in both Dublin and London, spending roughly the same amount of time in each city. Indeed, it is one of the many paradoxes that animate our national poet's life that he passed so much of that life in London, and in other parts of England.

The Sligo countryside gave him the fairies and that sense of the supernatural that flashes and glints through all his early work. With his friend and patron Lady Gregory, he became intimately familiar with a great body of folklore, preserved over centuries in the oral culture of the landed and landless poor. At the same time, as he grew into his twenties, he was conscious that his family and class were experiencing a gradual leaching away of power, or at least of access to power. The Protestant Ascendancy to which he belonged by virtue of family, was gradually being supplanted in power and prestige by powerful Catholic figures and interests. By the 1880s, when the family returned to Ireland, the towering figure in Irish nationalist politics was Parnell who, although a Protestant landowner, represented the objective interests of an increasingly separatist-minded Catholic people.

The Yeats family was broadly in sympathy with the aspirations of nationalism, even though it meant a growing separation from their class and its interests, but Yeats would remain deeply conscious of the part, in particular, that had been played by progressive Protestant intellectuals and political leaders and this, notwithstanding his great affection and respect for the Fenian leader John O'Leary, would make of him always a man divided in his heart, if not in his loyalty to his own idiosyncratic idea of an independent Ireland.

His early commitment to what we might call the cause of Ireland finds a telling expression in his *Autobiographies*:

A Royal Commission, its members drawn from all parties, appointed by a Conservative Government, presided over by Gladstone's Lord Chancellor, had reported that the over-taxation of Ireland for the last fifty years amounted to some three hundred millions. The Irish Landlord Party, which based its politics on the conviction that Ireland had gained by the Union, had a revulsion of conscience. Lord Castletown made a famous speech declaring that Ireland must imitate the colonists who flung the tea into Boston Harbour. Landlord committees were established in every county. Then Lord Salisbury appointed a second Royal Commission to consider the wrongs of landlords, and not one of those committees met again. There was deep disappointment. Protestant Ireland had immense prestige, Burke, Swift, Grattan, Emmet, Fitzgerald, Parnell, almost every name sung in modern song had been Protestant; Dublin's dignity depended upon the gaunt magnificence of buildings founded under the old Parliament; but wherever it attempted some corporate action, wherein Ireland stood against England, the show, however gallant it seemed, was soon over. It sold its Parliament for solid money, and now it sold this cause for a phantom.[1]

It was shrewd of Yeats to observe this, and his analysis is compelling, but what gave me pause when first I read this short paragraph was the unresolved ambiguity of his invoking these great Protestant patriots. Their names ring out like bell strokes, each charged with some freight of history, and more than history – he invests them with the weight and portentousness of dramatic heroes. And yet their class as a whole shows no loyalty to either the memory or the example of these great men, being in the main venal, opportunistic and timid.

Decades later, in a speech to that Senate of the Free State in which he was such an anomalous presence, Yeats would evoke this litany of names again, in the somewhat reduced circumstances of a debate on a bill to provide for divorce:

> We, against whom you have done this thing, are no petty people. We are one of the great stocks of Europe. We are the people of Burke; we are the people of Grattan; we are the people of Swift, the people of Emmet, the people of Parnell. We have created the most of the modern literature of this country. We have created the best of its political intelligence.[2]

He is, of course, inscribing himself, on both occasions, in a lineage of great men, great minds, great men of action and of literature. He is, as certain ambitious minds are sometimes drawn to do, creating a world of peers, of still-living ancestors who are, like himself by imputation, heroic, noble and immortal.

I observe that the Protestant republican, Theobald Wolfe Tone is missing from his list on both occasions, and I observe that the anti-republican orator Burke has crept modestly into the second iteration of this Protestant pantheon.

The fact is that Yeats, no aristocrat himself, had an undying passion for both aristocracy and autocracy. His imagination was caste-formed in part, drawn to those formed by nature and history, as he saw it, to exercise power. I grant him, and it is both an important qualification and a point very much in his favour, that he had an aversion to arbitrary power, to tyranny as we used to call it. His use of the phrase 'one of the great stocks of Europe' is telling in this regard. He believed in what used to be called 'breeding', he admired the sturdy peasant and the 'hard riding' country gentleman, the noblewoman and the refined scholar. He believed, and here is a telling phrase if ever there was one, in rule by the best.

The independent Ireland he dreamed of was never, would never be, politically attainable, not least because the teleology of political evolution embedded in the best of his class and kind would be roughly and inevitably shunted into the margins of history by the brute reality of things as they actually happened.

The fact is that the acceleration of a Catholic politics of independence on the parliamentary front, signalled by the sidelining of Parnell and driven by an emerging Catholic commercial class in the South, together with a hardening of unionist politics in the North, was being shadowed in both parts of the island by an increasingly powerful sector devoted to achieving political ends by means of physical force.

In the gap between these two realities, Yeats spent his life attempting to articulate a vision of Ireland that was part cultural and part mystical. For all his aspirations as a cultural revolutionary though, in his politics – objectively considered – Yeats was a profound reactionary.

Whatever of that, by the time the new century dawned Yeats was a powerful figure in the cultural politics of Ireland, a presence – if a less powerful presence – in the cultural politics of England, and almost wholly divorced from the forces that would shape the island of Ireland in the near and the far futures.

True – if only because Dublin is in essence a village – he had a personal acquaintance with some of those who would make the coming revolution – if revolution it was. Too – not least because he lived to some extent in the heroic penumbra of the Fenian John O'Leary – he was reasonably well regarded by these young cadres, even by the politically sophisticated workers' leader, James Connolly. Even so, Yeats had little or no idea of how serious these men were in their patient planning of an armed uprising. He seems to have been equally oblivious to what was happening in the north of the island.

The grand project of Irish parliamentary politics was, and had always been, Home Rule. By the end of the first decade of the twentieth century, all the signs seemed to suggest that this form of limited self-rule under the crown was, at last, in sight. In the south of the island, while the Protestant Ascendancy was politically opposed to the prospect, there was every prospect that, were Home Rule introduced, they would bend to the new dispensation. Not so in the North. The Ulster Volunteers, with Sir Edward Carson as their figurehead and guiding spirit, were building an armed force to resist Home Rule that would, at its peak, number 150,000 men. It is difficult to believe now that the British authorities were prepared to countenance such blatant preparations for sedition under arms. In the South, though numerically far fewer, the Irish Volunteers were also arming and drilling. Again, to our contemporary way of thinking, it seems peculiar indeed that the government of the day was not prepared to deal with such a blatant challenge to its authority.

Meanwhile, the secret Irish Republican Brotherhood (IRB), which had seized most of the commanding heights in the Irish Volunteers, was preparing an armed rising. In August 1913, a coalition of some 300 employers locked out around 20,000 Dublin workers in an attempt to break the growing power of the trade union movement. Politically reactionary, many of them Catholic nationalists, they may have appeared to Yeats an uncouth, uncultured and ignorant bunch by and large, of a kind Wilde might have had in mind when he spoke of men who knew 'the price of everything and the value of nothing'. Yeats despised them, but not, or not necessarily, because they in turn despised, feared and perhaps even hated the working poor; he hated them because their souls could not catch romantic fire, more prosaically because they had refused to make possible the building of a gallery to house the art collection Hugh Lane wished to bequeath to the Irish people.

There are no grounds for thinking Yeats had any sympathy for the strikers *per se*, but when he published his great public poem 'September 1913' in *The Irish Times*, one month into this bitter labour dispute, if he was not identifying with the workers, he was most certainly attacking their oppressors.

If Yeats in this poem is setting himself firmly against the ascendant new bourgeoisie, it is of more than passing interest that he has now added Wolfe Tone to his Protestant pantheon, and fused their struggle and its intelligence with that of the unrepentant Fenian, John O'Leary. For all that the poem is ostensibly saying that such generosity and selflessness of spirit is in the grave, for all that the poem is a contemptuous dismissal of the petty inheritors of great men, he was surely aware that he was publishing his poem into an incendiary situation, into a context in which, if he was unaware of what the IRB had in mind, he can hardly have been blind to the regular presence on Dublin's streets of armed men drilling as a separatist militia, and the implications of this. Whatever of that, the whiplash of scorn that the poem carries would not have been lost on those militant republican cadres necessarily bent on marginalising this comprador bourgeoisie.

If, by 1913, Yeats had some sense, as he must have had, that the forces by then in play were coming to some forced conclusion, some inescapable contest of will at the very least, neither by temperament nor by analysis could he have sensed or known that, against all historical precedent, the coming War of Independence would be a war led, fought and prosecuted from below. By and large, the separatist forces of Sinn Féin and, more importantly the IRB, were not led by or recruited from the privileged classes. With few exceptions, the leadership cadres were clerks, shopkeepers, teachers, industrial workers or labourers on the land. Some came with military experience in the lower ranks of the British Army, some came from a background of labour activism, most of these in the ranks of the Irish Citizen Army – but almost all came from that large class described memorably by Wolfe Tone as 'the men of no property'. With their world, their hopes and aspirations, Yeats could have had no sympathy, in the strict traditional sense of that word.

3 The Man Who Feared the *Demos*

That he feared the organised political forces of the poor, there is no doubt. He was, as many scholars have pointed out, acutely aware of the armed workers' uprisings in Germany, and later of the Bolshevik revolution. The idea of mass democracy was anathema to him; both his aesthetic and his politics revolved around the central idea that the good could only ever be delivered by the best. There is not much evidence that Yeats understood the class composition of the armed forces preparing to strike for Irish independence, but had he done so it seems perfectly clear he would have been much disturbed at the prospect.

His antipathy to revolution from below is powerfully illustrated, if I may jump forward a moment to 1919, in his extraordinary and much quoted 'The Second Coming' in which, in prophetic vein, he warns *inter alia* that 'Mere anarchy is loosed upon the world' and tells us 'The best lack all conviction, while the worst /Are full of passionate intensity.'[3] That those animated by passionate intensity might be the best, that those who lacked conviction might be the worst does not seem to have occurred to him.

If Yeats regretted in Maud Gonne her willingness to set the little streets upon the great, it was the poor and the powerless *en masse* whom he despised and feared. I should stress that this antipathy was political only, by which I mean that he did not despise the poor and powerless in themselves, although he feared their coming together as a determining political power. In his comings and goings about Sligo and Coole Park, and latterly in the environs of his tower near Gort, he was well-liked as a man by the landless poor; they saw in him a gentleman, neither a snob nor an enemy.

The Easter Rising, that consciously, calculatedly doomed but effective gesture, would eventually draw his reluctant admiration – but neither then nor after would he offer his support, much less his allegiance, to anything resembling a true revolutionary project. I should perhaps say, in passing, that there was never any real prospect that the War of Independence would become a revolutionary war; that prospect, if it ever existed, died in the volley that took James Connolly's life – but then and after, all the evidence is that had it become so, Yeats would have been its implacable opponent.

Nevertheless, there is something very touching, beautifully and endearingly human, about the element of graceful apology in his magnificent 'Easter 1916'. To grant the dead leaders, as he does, that they acted from excess of love, speaks well and more than well of their humanity and his; yet, even now, Yeats clearly does not understand what has really happened, the tectonic shift that the Rising has caused, the irrevocable consequences of the Rising and its suppression.

He had waited long enough to publish his poem on the Rising, and he seemed to consider the gesture complete in itself, seemed unaware that those forces whose participation in the planned rebellion had been countermanded at the last minute were still in existence, still waiting in the wings. To be fair, he was not alone in that, and even now there are those who consider, or choose to claim, that the War of Independence would not have begun had not the British made the fatal mistake of executing the leaders of the Rising. This seems to me unlikely, even a-historical. The IRB's plans, despite the setback in Dublin, were still intact; their training programme had been aimed at a nationwide insurrection and there were many ready to take the place of the executed leaders. The overwhelming vote for Sinn Féin candidates in the 1918 election was taken by the insurrectionists as tacit complicity in, when not explicit support for, the War of Independence on which they were now embarked. Of all this, Yeats was unaware.

All through this period, Yeats' central preoccupation was with understanding the import and meaning of what was being conveyed to him from his instructors in the spirit world. For many years he had been transcribing, with the mediumistic assistance of his wife George, a series of hermetic, not to say bafflingly obscure communications from entities with whom he, at least, was convinced they were in communion.

The general import of these received communications was indeed that the centre could not hold. Yeats understood this to mean, or chose to understand this to mean, that a time of chaos was at hand, and he identified this chaos with democracy, in the sense of the empowering of the *demos*. Outside Ireland, the Versailles terms were being hammered out, the Spartacist uprising in Germany was being brutally suppressed and the Bolshevik uprising was fighting for its life against internal reaction and external blockade by British and French forces.

I have referred above to the poem 'The Second Coming'. According to Terence Brown, Yeats thought or believed that he was receiving metaphors and ideas from his spirit instructor that would be the basis for this poem. Brown also says that the poem was composed in January 1919, but was not published until November 1920. This time delay is, at first, puzzling – especially when we consider that Yeats' great broadside against the philistine employers of Dublin, 'September 1913' was published a month into the Lockout. Again, according to Brown, implicit references in the drafts and notes for the poem make it likely if not plain that the spectre of anarchy, of 'the blooddimmed tide' that haunted Yeats, was external to Ireland. Yet the poem has long since, and perhaps misleadingly, been absorbed into the discourse about the Irish War of Independence.

In the time between the composition of the poem and its eventual publication, a period of some twenty-two months, the war in Ireland had become bloody indeed, not least because Britain had introduced into the conflict a quasimilitary force, colloquially dubbed the Black and Tans, whose habitual atrocities, taken together with certain brutalities on the insurrectionary side, had brought the violence of the war spiralling downward toward horror.

Yeats was afraid, as we see in his letters, that the violence in Ireland – revolutionary violence as it appeared to him – might follow in the wake of the Russian Revolution. It is a mark of his political sophistication that he understood this as a possibility in the abstract, and of his general cluelessness about the real nature of the Irish insurrection that he should have thought it even a remote possibility:

> What I want is that Ireland be kept from giving itself (under the influence of its lunatic faculty of going against everything which it believes England to affirm) to Marxian revolution or Marxian definitions of value in any form. I consider the Marxian criterion of values as in this age the spearhead of materialism and leading to inevitable murder.[4]

He seemed oblivious to the obvious rejoinder that much the same charge could be made against organised capital, no slouch itself, when its interests are threatened, in resorting to murder.

In any case, by the time the Treaty had been negotiated, and the Free State established, Yeats had found it possible to reconcile himself, at least for a time, to those elements of the former insurrectionary forces that were quickly settling into such political power as had been gained. When a minority of the insurrectionists, essentially romantic republicans, seceded from the authority of the newly established parliament and plunged the country into civil war, Yeats was in no doubt where he stood. He became, in fact, a senator of the new Free State, thereby, for the first time in his life, stepping over the line from cultural politics into politics as the profession and exercise of governance.

Yeats, a realist in his own way, but also one deeply attracted to authority, saw in the infant Free State an opportunity to exercise some of the power he felt was the prerogative of his class, but more importantly, given its inherently autocratic nature, a tendency reinforced in its ruthless prosecution of the Civil War, he saw in the new state a vehicle for the implementation of his vision of rule by the best.

The new government was largely composed of men, and a few women, who had an unsophisticated grasp of politics. For the most part, in truth, they had not given much thought, if any, either before or during the bitter War of Independence, to what kind of free Ireland they proposed to establish. Now, suddenly handed power, they simply appropriated the apparatus of governance established by the departing colonial power; they took over, almost in its entirety, the corpus of civil and criminal law, the departmental system by which the civil service was organised, much of the judiciary and all of the Revenue Commissioners. They found, waiting to hand, an established system of government, and were content to make it work.

The Civil War proved a bitter business, more bitter and bloody than the War of Independence that had preceded it. There were atrocities on both sides, leading to a lasting and vicious polarisation in the country, and if Yeats' position as senator identified him as hostile to one side in the struggle, he was destined to find little in common with his fellow senators on the 'other' side, largely committed as they were to defending the economic and political interests of their own class.

4 Conclusion

Perhaps, when all is said and done, it was as well for Ireland that Yeats should have proved incapable of exerting his thought and such influence as he had in the sphere of formal politics. He was a senator appointed by a government that executed seventy-seven prisoners of war without trial in reprisal for murders committed by the republican forces. He was a friend of Kevin O'Higgins, the man who signed those execution orders, a man who could summon the coldness of heart to order the execution of Rory O'Connor, who had been best man at O'Higgins' own wedding. About this barbarism, he made no complaint that we know of. Always there was this naïvety in thrall to his governing idea that the nation, any nation it seems, should be 'controlled by highly trained intellects'. It is difficult if not downright impossible to imagine a modern republic subscribing to such a proposition. Yeats was an admirer of Mussolini, in whom he recognised neither the buffoonish nor the malign characteristics of that bombastic man, and he would go on to write marching songs for O'Duffy's Blueshirts, Ireland's comic opera imitators of the Italian Blackshirts, the German Brownshirts.

More seriously, perhaps, and more culpably, he wrote in 1921: 'One thing I did not foresee, not having the courage of my own thought: the growing murderousness of the world.' After the mass carnage and slaughter of the First World War, how could anyone not have been aware of the growing murderousness of the world?

That he was brave, in his way, none can deny. To have published 'Sixteen Dead Men', when he did, and 'The Rose Tree', and even 'Easter

1916', was to risk the attention and even the wrath of the British military authorities at a time when their control over their own forces, especially over the hated Auxiliaries and the Black and Tans, was imperfect to say the least. And it took real courage to publish 'Nineteen Hundred and Nineteen' which marks, in part, the callous murder by the Black and Tans of a young pregnant woman from Co Galway:

> Now days are dragon-ridden, the nightmare Rides upon sleep:
> a drunken soldiery Can leave the mother, murdered at her door,
> To crawl in her own blood, and go scot-free.[5]

For all that courage, though, and for all the generosity of spirit and selflessness he displayed in helping to shape the cultural revolution which was both precursor and spur to the republican insurrection, Yeats could not bring himself to believe in the democratic principle at the heart of what was now the proposed republic: government of the people, by the people, for the people.

Perhaps, in its way, this lack of belief, his profound reluctance to trust in the wisdom of the common people, was a kind of prophetic fatalism. No government since that first Free State government has ever, really, trusted the people. We are, even in the eyes of our own native government, still not to be trusted to exercise our independence.

In 1938, the year before he died, Yeats published 'The Great Day' in *The London Mercury*:

> Hurrah for revolution and more cannon-shot!
> A beggar on horseback lashes a beggar on foot.
> Hurrah for revolution and cannon come again!
> The beggars have changed places, but the lash goes on.[6]

Indeed. The lash goes on.

Further Reading:

T. Brown, *The Life of W.B. Yeats* (Dublin, 1999)

T. Brown, *Ireland: A Social and Cultural History, 1922–2002* (London, 2004)

E. Cullingford, *Yeats, Ireland and Fascism* (London & Basingstoke, 1981)

R. Ellman, *The Identity of Yeats* (London, 1964)

D. Ferriter, *A Nation and Not a Rabble: The Irish Revolution 1913–23* (London, 2015)

R.F. Foster, *W. B. Yeats, A Life, Vol. I: The Apprentice Mage, 1865–1914* (Oxford, 1997)

R.F.Foster, *W. B. Yeats - A Life, II: The Arch-Poet 1915–1939* (Oxford, 2003)

Notes

1 W.B. Yeats, *Autobiographies* (London 1955), p.310.

2 Cited in B. Arkins, *The Thought of W.B. Yeats* (Bern 2010), p.77.

3 W.B. Yeats, *The Poems*, edited and introduced by D. Albright (London 1992), p.235.

4 D. Kiberd, *Inventing Ireland* (London 1995), p.319.

5 See Yeats, *The Poems*, p.252.

6 See Yeats, *The Poems*, p.358.

CHAPTER 13

Pirrie and Plunkett

MARY E. DALY

1 Introduction

William Pirrie and Sir Horace Plunkett made their contribution to 'shaping' modern Ireland primarily, though not exclusively, in the realm of economics, but their actions and their aspirations were heavily influenced by politics. Both men were born into privileged backgrounds; Plunkett was the younger son of an Irish peer and although Pirrie's biographer described him as 'a self-made man',[1] through birth and through marriage he was connected with Belfast's leading industrial and commercial families. Plunkett is credited with introducing agricultural co-operatives to Ireland; he was also the instigator of proposals for an Irish Department of Agriculture and Technical Instruction, and its first vice-president/minister. Under Pirrie's leadership Belfast shipbuilders Harland and Wolff was transformed into 'the most important shipbuilding and shipping company in the world'.[2] Plunkett and Pirrie were members of two distinct elites: the British and Anglo-Irish landed gentry, and Belfast's industrial/commercial elite. The Plunkett family had played a prominent role in Ireland from the fourteenth century and, through his mother – a daughter of Lord Sherborne – Plunkett was connected with prominent English landed families. Pirrie's grandfather, a member of the Belfast Ballast Board and of the first Belfast Harbour Commissioners, was responsible for cutting the first channel in Belfast harbour that launched Belfast's shipbuilding industry. Through the Barbour family – manufacturers of linen thread – he was connected with the other major Belfast industry, linen. Two brothers of his wife, Margaret Carlisle – who was also his cousin

– founded the Blue Star Shipping Line; another became managing-director of Harland and Wolff.

Plunkett and Pirrie's respective focuses on agriculture and manufacturing industry reflect the binary representations of nationalist Ireland and Ulster, as rural/agrarian and urban/industrial societies. Plunkett was very conscious of this duality. In *Ireland in the New Century* he wrote of 'two Irelands, differing in race, in creed, in political aspiration and in what I regard as a more potent factor than all the others put together – economic interest and industrial pursuit'.[3] Their contrasting backgrounds are reflected in their education – Plunkett was educated at Eton and Oxford, whereas Pirrie attended Belfast Academicals before joining Harland and Wolff at the age of fifteen as a 'gentleman apprentice'. During his training Pirrie gained a comprehensive knowledge of all branches of the business – including marine engineering, ship design and book-keeping. This combination of technical and financial expertise enabled him to control all aspects of the firm's business in later years.

2 Plunkett

As the younger son of a landed family, Plunkett had no obvious career path. For a time he managed the family estate, and for ten years he was a rancher in Wyoming. When he was born in 1854 the Irish landed gentry continued to exercise considerable political and economic influence. In 1892 he was elected as a Unionist MP for South Dublin. By then, the influence of the landed gentry was withering, through the combined impact of falling agricultural prices, legislation transferring ownership and control of land to tenant farmers, the expansion of the parliamentary suffrage and secret ballot and the emergence of a strong Irish Parliamentary Party under Parnell. Dublin South was one of only two Unionist seats outside Ulster, excluding Trinity College. The 1898 Local Government Act, which established county councils, and the 1903 Wyndham Land Act further weakened landed influence over key aspects of Irish government and society. Plunkett's career is best seen as a reaction to this loss of influence; an attempt to recreate a role for landed families in Irish public life. Gailey suggests that Plunkett was afraid of populism, 'staunchly opposed to the extension of the democratic principles in Ireland'.[4] His underlying philosophy is captured in the title of his 1908 book, *Noblesse Oblige*, which Gailey describes as 'the plaintive cry' – a call to the Irish landed elite to re-establish a leadership role. The apparent political vacuum, created by the Parnell split and by the Lords veto on Home Rule, created an opportunity for doing this despite the 1898 Local Government Act.

Plunkett's first project was to establish a network of agricultural co-operatives. He opened a co-operative shop in Dunsany on his family estate, and his original plan was to extend these stores throughout Ireland, following the English model of consumer co-operatives. By 1895, however, the Irish Agricultural Organisation Society (IAOS) – the umbrella group for Irish co-operatives, which he founded – was dominated by producer co-operatives, mainly co-operative creameries. Liam Kennedy claims that 'the co-operative movement represented a disruptive force which exposed latent contradictions in the rural social structure'.[5] Co-operative stores would have competed with provincial shopkeepers, whose influence and wealth had grown significantly in the decades after the famine. Rural families increasingly relied on shop-bought meal or flour, tea and sugar supplied on credit, paying off their debt, in whole or in part, from emigrant remittances, selling livestock, or in exchange for eggs. The economic power of local shopkeepers was matched by political influence; they had become the backbone of the Irish Parliamentary Party and a key force in local government as elected Poor Law Guardians, and after 1898 as local councillors. Shopkeepers were often closely connected with the Catholic clergy – another major source of influence in rural Ireland. Plunkett enlisted the support of local landowners and Catholic clergy in establishing co-operatives, with patchy results in both cases. Some landowners, notably Lord Monteagle, were supportive, likewise the Rev Thomas Finlay, SJ, a professor at University College Dublin. Plunkett claimed that, in 1902, 331 co-operative societies had a priest as chairman, and 50,000 people were brought to the Department of Agriculture and Technical Instruction (DATI) stand at the Cork Exhibition by their local priest. However, Kennedy suggests that the response of the Catholic Church to co-operatives was mixed. He concluded that the clergy used their influence to channel the co-operative movement along 'more acceptable lines' – co-operative creameries, which did not present a direct challenge to local shopkeepers. In the 1890s there was an urgent need to establish creameries if Ireland's long-established butter exports were to continue in the face of technological inventions which had mechanised butter production, wiping out sales of farm-produced butter. Creameries produced butter that was consistent in quality and hygienically produced, and British grocery chains and urban housewives were demanding creamery butter. In Ireland, in contrast to Denmark, the earliest creameries were established as proprietary businesses – not as co-operatives – and proprietary creameries remained important, despite the expansion of co-operative creameries. In addition to developing creameries, the IAOS supplied members with cheaper fertiliser and seed, and tried, without success, to establish co-operative banks which could have undermined the power of local shopkeepers by providing cheaper credit. But while Irish farmers were enthusiastic about creameries there is little evidence that they embraced the principle of co-operation. Ó Gráda concluded that 'as a force of rural regeneration, the Irish co-operative movement was a failure, though the IAOS played an important role in educating farmers and acting as a lobby for the Irish dairying industry'.[6]

In 1895 Plunkett, determined to build on the momentum of the IAOS by issuing an open invitation to a cross-section of Irish society to join a committee to examine the feasibility of establishing an Irish board of agriculture (a British board of agriculture was created in 1889). His invitation had a mixed reception – the most hostile response came from the *Belfast Newsletter*, which suggested that the matter should be left to the Conservative government; the nationalist *Freeman's Journal* expressed the hope that 'it might do no harm'. The Committee became known as the Recess Committee, because it met during the parliamentary recess. The membership included nationalist and unionist politicians, clergymen, prominent businessmen and lawyers. The twelve-person Parnellite wing of the Irish parliamentary Party accepted Plunkett's invitation, but the leader of the Irish Unionist Party, Colonel Saunderson, declined, as did John Dillon, leader of the anti-Parnellite wing. Dillon regarded the Recess Committee as a threat to Home Rule. Their report recommended establishing a department of agriculture and industries for Ireland, whose policies and structures would be similar to ministries operating in other European countries. But when the DATI was established in 1899, its industrial remit was restricted to rural industries, though proposals for developing technical education survived. The DATI continued the emphasis of the IAOS on agricultural education and quality improvements – with a network of itinerant instructors, model farms, measures to improve the quality of seed and livestock and schemes designed to promote the marketing of Irish farm produce and rural industries internationally.

Plunkett's undoubted wish to promote agriculture and raise farmers' incomes was handicapped by his politics. The DATI was, in theory, governed by a council of one hundred, which was described as 'the farmer's parliament'. One-third of the members was nominated (mainly landlords), and two-thirds was elected; two smaller boards oversaw agriculture and technical instruction respectively. The council and boards were complemented by committees of agriculture in every county, which were closely associated with the new county councils. Gailey claimed that Plunkett had been forced to include an elected element to secure parliamentary support for the DATI; evidence suggests that the council and boards had little power. Plunkett appears to have controlled all aspects of the department; he was a strong believer in executive authority, and he duly exercised it. The legislation establishing the DATI provided that the vice-president, which was Plunkett's title, (the Irish Chief Secretary was the ex-officio, largely symbolic president), should be an MP. Although Plunkett lost his parliamentary seat in 1900, and never returned to Westminster, he continued to hold the office of vice-president until he was forced to resign in 1907. The hostility of the Dillonite majority of the Irish Parliamentary Party towards Plunkett was long-standing but, in 1903, Plunkett published *Ireland in the New Century*, in which he appeared to go out of his way to alienate the Catholic clergy, attributing the backward Irish economy to the 'non-economic, if not actually anti-economic' tendencies of Roman Catholicism. Plunkett's biographer, Trevor West, commented that 'for a member of the Ascendancy (however lukewarm his own religious affiliation) to cast aspersions on Irish Catholicism was, at all times, a delicate task; for one in the exposed position of a minister without a seat in parliament it was an unforgivable sin'.[7] Plunkett's strictures were not confined to the Catholic Church. He ascribed Ireland's social and economic failings to the character of the people; the malign influence of the Nationalist Party 'upon the Irish mind', and 'the deplorable effects upon national life by the exclusion of representatives of the landlord and the industrial classes from positions of leadership and trust over four-fifths of the country'. He believed that Irish prosperity would only be possible if landlord and business leaders assumed a greater role. [8] In a public letter published in the influential Irish American newspaper, the *Irish World*, John Redmond, leader of the united Irish Parliamentary Party confessed that he had 'at one time, entertained some belief in the good intensions of Sir Horace Plunkett and his friends', but the evidence of his 'undisguised contempt for Irish race makes it plain to me that the real object of the movement in question is to undermine the National Party and divert the minds of our people from Home Rule'. [9]

Gailey describes *Ireland in the New Century* as 'more than just a *cri de coeur*; it was also a cry of panic, of powerlessness'.[10] Plunkett had also alienated Irish unionists by his public support for issues such as a Catholic university and land reform. His expressions of qualified sympathy for the Boers, and his appointment of T.P. Gill, a Catholic and nationalist as secretary of the DATI, plus his evasive replies when asked about Home Rule added to their distrust, while failing to gain him the support of nationalists. Having failed to be adopted again as the Unionist candidate for South Dublin in 1900, by standing for election he ensured that the seat went to the nationalists. In 1901 he was defeated at a by-election for a former Unionist seat in Galway; in these two by-elections Plunkett was responsible for Unionists losing their only seats outside Ulster, except Trinity College. Plunkett was not the only southern unionist who favoured a more conciliatory approach towards unresolved questions such as land reform and a Catholic university. Galway landlord, Captain John Shawe-Taylor, followed Plunkett's example with a public appeal for a conference of landlord and tenant representatives to devise a final solution to the land question. The resulting 1903 Land Act gave generous land purchase terms to tenant farmers; it also gave financial incentives to landlords to buy their demesnes and remain in Ireland as farmers and landholders. Following the success of the 1903 Act, Lord Dunraven, who chaired the land conference and, like Plunkett, supported a Catholic university, launched an unsuccessful effort to reach agreement with nationalists on some lesser form of devolution than Home Rule. But these constructive unionists failed to work as a team, and the return of a Liberal government in 1906 ended the prospects of further constructive unionist initiatives relating to Ireland.

3 Pirrie

William Pirrie was made a partner in Harland and Wolff in 1875. When Sir Edward Harland died in 1895 Pirrie became chairman, retaining that role until his death. Pirrie's leadership of Harland and Wolff was marked by continuing expansion and innovation. He invested in new plant and new manufacturing techniques, and was among the first to realise the potential of oil-powered ships. Under his leadership Harland and Wolff built larger, more efficient ocean liners with facilities that rivalled luxury hotels. Shipbuilding was a notoriously cyclical industry, but

Pirrie overcame this by negotiating agreements with regular customers guaranteeing them an available berth if they gave a commitment to use Harland and Wolff to repair and refit their vessels. Ships were built on a cost-plus basis, and companies were given loans to cover construction costs. With long-distance shipping increasingly controlled by a small number of shipping lines, Pirrie extended his business interests into shipping – most significantly with the formation of the International Marine Syndicate in 1902. This was a trans-Atlantic syndicate, whose members included J. Pierpoint Morgan, which set out to control the Atlantic shipping business. Pirrie's motive was to secure orders for Harland and Wolff, at a time when shipbuilding was depressed, but membership of this consortium involved an investment of $3.75m. – more than twice the ordinary share capital of Harland and Wolff and its wholly-owned shipping company. Pirrie's business strategy in the years before the First World War involved constant expansion and investment, with Harland and Wolff building a steadily growing number of ships at a modest profit margin. A high and increasing turnover was essential to the firm's profitability, indeed its survival, but this expansion was dependent on ever-increasing borrowings. By the eve of the First World War some bankers were expressing fears that 'time would come when the profits would all come tumbling down'. By 1914, according to Moss and Hume, Pirrie, 'had become a business dictator on a gigantic scale, and no-one within the Company was able to challenge his authority and skill. He would not countenance any failure. Consequently his staff were terrified of him'. Pirrie 'had learned more quickly than most of his British contemporaries how to manage large enterprises employing many thousands of people by using financial information and other statistics fed to him by his chief accountant, and Managing-Director', though he kept this information very much to himself – no other member of the firm had access to the full picture.[11]

The expansion of Harland and Wolff under Pirrie's leadership, to become the most important shipbuilding firm in the world, took place against the background of recurrent crises over Irish Home Rule. As Belfast's most important employer, Harland and Wolff could not escape the political consequences. In 1886 Sir Edward Harland used his position as Lord Mayor of Belfast to co-ordinate Ulster opposition to Home Rule, and Pirrie announced that the firm would move to Liverpool if Home Rule was introduced. In 1887 Harland was elected as Unionist member for North Belfast; in 1892 G.W. Wolff joined him as MP for East Belfast.

When Gladstone's second Home Rule Bill threatened in 1893, Pirrie became treasurer of the Ulster Defence Union, which was chaired by his brother-in-law, Thomas Andrews, who was also a senior member of the firm. When Pirrie, now chairman of Harland and Wolff, became Lord Mayor of Belfast in 1896, a familiar progression to Westminster as a Unionist MP might have been predicted, but Pirrie renounced all party political affiliation and used his years in office to expand nationalist and labour representation on Belfast City Council. He and his wife actively supported a variety of civic and philanthropic causes both Catholic and Protestant, most notably in a major fundraising campaign for the new Royal Victoria Hospital, and it was while he was mayor that plans for a new city hall were launched.

When his three-year term as Lord Mayor ended in 1898, Pirrie and his wife moved to London. Although they retained a large house in Belfast, England was their home for the remainder of their lives. Pirrie's removal to London was primarily motivated by business interests. In many respects Pirrie and Harland and Wolff had outgrown Belfast. As a leading figure in international shipping and shipbuilding circles, it was essential that he should be based in London, and the opulent lifestyle that Pirrie and his wife adopted in England would have been impossible in Belfast. Pirrie had also become alienated from local Belfast interests – notably the Belfast Harbour Commissioners – partly because they did not automatically meet his demands for additional space for the yard (the Commissioners had to consider the requirements of Workman Clark and Co – Belfast's other yard), partly because of his weakening unionist sentiment. In 1902 Pirrie, a Liberal Unionist, agreed to allow his name to be proposed as Unionist candidate for South Belfast, but the Conservative Association selected an alternative candidate. The seat was won by Belfast Protestant Association candidate, Thomas Sloan, who worked in Harland and Wolff, a populist candidate who was strongly anti-Catholic. Unionists accused Pirrie of supporting Sloan, though there is no evidence of this.

In the 1906 general election, which returned a Liberal government with a large majority, Pirrie gave financial support to the party both in Ulster and in London. He was made a peer in the 1906 Birthday Honours. Critics accused him of selling his principles for a seat in the House of Lords. There were also suggestions that supporting the Liberals would open doors for the Pirries in London Society. But Pirrie and his wife both came from a liberal political tradition, and his business interests depended on a liberal economic regime of free trade and free capital flows. By 1906 the Conservatives were flirting with tariff reform, so Pirrie's support for the Liberals is not a surprise; he had also expressed support for some form of Home Rule as early as 1902. Collison Black concluded that Pirrie 'was simply a moderate man, to whom politics did not appear as a matter of primary concern. He was interested only in having a stable political system within which he and other people could get on with their jobs', who came to believe that 'continued government of Ireland from Westminster could be neither stable nor economical'.[12] Pirrie showed little sympathy for sectarianism; in 1913, he threatened to close the shipyard if the Catholic workers, who had recently been expelled by protesting unionist workers, were not permitted to return. He was a benevolent, if paternalistic employer. Harland and Wolff avoided the labour disputes that were common to the shipbuilding industry by negotiating separate plant agreements.

Home Rule was not on the agenda of the Liberal government until the 1910 general election left the Irish Parliamentary Party holding the balance of power at Westminster, and they demanded an end to the House of Lords veto as their price for maintaining the Liberals in government. Pirrie's open support for Home Rule put him at odds with other Ulster business leaders. His primary goal, as ever, was to secure the continuing success of Harland and Wolff – and he felt that by supporting Home Rule he could protect the interests of industrial Ulster in any settlement. Ulster's opposition was the Unionist's strongest card against Home Rule, so the Irish Parliamentary Party viewed the support for Home Rule of Pirrie – chairman of Ulster's most important business – as significant. In 1911 Pirrie used a visit by the postmaster general, Herbert Samuel, to make a public expression of support for Home Rule, and attack the unionist views expressed by the Belfast Harbour Board. In January 1912 shortly before the Home Rule Bill came before parliament, he hired the Ulster Hall for a Home Rule meeting to be addressed by Winston Churchill, First Lord of the Admiralty, and John Redmond. Ulster Unionists retaliated by hiring the hall for the previous night and refusing to vacate it, so the Churchill/Redmond gathering had to be held in a marquee. When Pirrie and his wife were boarding a ship to return to Britain some days later, they were pelted with eggs by an angry mob.

When war broke out in 1914 Pirrie and Plunkett both supported Home Rule, views that left both men out of line with their social and family networks. The war proved highly beneficial to Harland and Wolff. Once again they embarked on a major expansion, this time to meet military needs. Pirrie achieved new influence when Lloyd George appointed him as controller of merchant shipping in 1918 – he was made a viscount in recognition of his service. Plunkett busied himself as an intermediary between political leaders in both Britain and the USA – where he was now spending part of every year – but his war was less successful. In 1917, however, he became chairman of the Irish Convention – the final attempt to reach agreement on an Irish Home Rule settlement. Redmond pressed for Pirrie to be appointed to the Convention, but Lloyd George regarded Pirrie's contribution to war-time shipping as more important. O'Brien describes the Convention as 'a piece of Lloyd George window-dressing for transatlantic display'.[13] It may have served the useful purpose of postponing a British decision on the future of Ireland, but the delay ended any prospect of a Home Rule settlement. Southern and Ulster unionists were divided on the question of fiscal autonomy, but it was the threatened introduction of conscription in Ireland in the spring of 1918 that made the Convention irrelevant. Sinn Féin, which had absented itself from the Convention, became the political voice of nationalist Ireland. It was little consolation to Plunkett that his old nemesis, John Dillon, was a major casualty. In 1919 Plunkett launched the Irish Dominion Party to campaign for a Dominion settlement, but this was a futile exercise.

By 1918 Pirrie had abandoned Home Rule, and reverted to unionism. His appointment as a member of the first Northern Ireland Senate suggests that he and Ulster Unionism had made their peace. But despite this honour and other honours, Pirrie's world was collapsing. In the immediate aftermath of the war, Pirrie squandered the wartime profits made by Harland and Wolff by purchasing shipyards, steel yards, machine works and related industries in order to expand the firm's reach yet again. By 1920 they had plants in seven different locations, six of them in Scotland or England. But 1920 marked the onset of a serious crisis for shipping and shipbuilding; there was serious overcapacity; prices collapsed and unemployment soared. This crisis did not ease in Britain until the outbreak of the Second World War. Pirrie died in 1924.

Plunkett's fate was arguably sadder. To quote Conor Cruise O'Brien: 'Having devoted his life's work to the economic improvement of Ireland and to gradual political reconciliation with England he lived to see his creameries burned by the English and his house by the Irish.'[14] Plunkett too became a senator – of the Irish Free State. The large representation in that senate of Anglo-Irish gentry could be seen as providing an opportunity to realise Plunkett's ideal of giving landed and business leaders a more prominent role in public life, and the agricultural policies pursued by Patrick Hogan, the first minister for agriculture in the Irish Free State were very much a continuation of the work of Plunkett's DATI, with an emphasis on improving the quality and marketing of produce and agricultural education. But Plunkett took no formal part in the new Ireland; he resigned his senate seat and settled in England.

4 Conclusion

At the turn of the twentieth century Pirrie and Plunkett could both be described as liberal unionists – a philosophy that combined support for the union with Britain, with a genuine wish to promote reforms that would benefit the majority of Irish people. But this was a position that became increasingly untenable as the fault lines between unionism and nationalism widened. Both men can be described as political mavericks. They broke with established party lines, changed their views, and adopted positions that were viewed as betraying their family and class. But for Pirrie, business came first; Black determined that 'political activity. . . was but a small part in Pirrie's career'.[15] Did Pirrie's unorthodox politics damage his business or his reputation? Moss and Hume suggest that he was unwilling to open up partnership in the firm to his nephew, John Andrews, (who perished on the Titanic) and others who disagreed with him over Home Rule. When Pirrie died his temporary support for Home Rule did not figure in the encomia, which concentrated on his business achievements. Although Plunkett often decried the dominance of politics over economics in Irish life, West noted that 'all his life Plunkett was lured to politics as a moth to a flame, with consequences which were as regularly fraught with disaster'.[16] While O'Brien claims that 'people who look back on his [Plunkett's] career are more apt to be more interested in how far he had got than in what his motives were', it is impossible to divorce Plunkett's politics from his work for Irish agriculture. A more diplomatic, less overtly-politicised approach could potentially have secured the support of a Catholic church which shared Plunkett's belief in the importance of rural life – as the contribution made by Canon Michael Hayes' Muintir na Tíre, in later decades, suggests.

The impact and influence of Pirrie and Plunkett stretched well beyond Ireland. Plunkett was at ease among political leaders in both

London and Washington. US President Theodore Roosevelt adopted Plunkett's slogan – 'Better Farming, Better Business and Better Living' and appointed him a member of his Commission on Country Life. Black correctly brackets Pirrie with Carnegie, Roosevelt and Morgan – men whose vision and business acumen were recognised internationally. The luxury liners built by Harland and Wolff made crossing the Atlantic a much swifter and more pleasurable experience, and this helped to create an elite trans-Atlantic business community to which Pirrie belonged. His impact on British and American shipping and shipbuilding was much greater than his impact within Ireland outside Belfast, where his most significant contribution was his support for Home Rule, a stance that may have helped to lull the Irish Parliamentary Party into the fantasy that Ulster opposition to Home Rule could be overcome. Pirrie would have been uncomfortable in the introverted Northern Ireland state, despite the fact that a nephew, John Andrews, became Prime Minister. Plunkett too needed a larger stage than the Irish Free State, though an Ireland that was an active member of the British Commonwealth – as happened in the 1920s – should have appealed to him. Both men wished for a united Ireland, that would be part of the British empire/commonwealth, closely linked with Britain; the outcome, whether in Belfast or in Dublin, was not what either wished for. Yet, while they shared a common wish for a united Ireland, each was very much part of a different Ireland – north/south, industrial/agrarian – and Pirrie's contribution to making Belfast a major industrial centre, served to enhance the difference between Ulster and the rest of Ireland.

Pirrie has featured much less than Plunkett in Irish history. He is remembered as the chairman of Harland and Wolff when it was the world's most successful shipbuilding firm. The Harland and Wolff shipyard is now the site of 'The Titanic Quarter' and 'The Titanic Experience'. Plunkett has attracted more attention from historians, perhaps because his writings provide ample material for analysis. The Department of Agriculture, uniquely among Irish government departments, happily dates its foundation to the year 1900 and recognises Plunkett as the first minister for agriculture – all other government departments date their origins to Dáil Éireann and/or the Irish Free State. The county committees of agriculture established by the DATI and county-based advisory services remained a core element of the government's agricultural programme until the late-twentieth century. Many of the co-operatives founded by the IAOS survive today as significant producers of dairy produce, though they have been transformed into major commercial firms, with plants far removed from Ireland.

Further Reading:

E. Biagini, *British Democracy and Irish Nationalism, 1876–1906* (Cambridge, 2007)

S. Connolly (ed.), *Belfast 400: People, Place and History* (Liverpool, 2012)

M.E. Daly, *The First Department: A History of the Department of Agriculture* (Dublin, 2002)

A. Gailey, *Ireland and the Death of Kindness. The Experience of Constructive Unionism 1890–1905* (Cork, 1987)

H. Jefferson, *Viscount Pirrie of Belfast* (Belfast, 1948)

L. Kennedy, 'The early response of the Irish Catholic clergy to the co-operative movement', in *Colonialism, Religion and Nationalism in Ireland* (Belfast, 1996)

R.B. McDowell, *The Irish Convention, 1917–18* (London, 1970)

M. Moss and J. Hume, *Shipbuilders to the World. 125 years of Harland and Wolff, Belfast, 1861–1986* (Belfast, 1986)

C. Ó Gráda, 'The beginnings of the Irish creamery system 1880–1914', *Economic History Review*, xxx, (1977), pp.284–305

T. West, *Horace Plunkett, Co-operation and Politics. An Irish Biography* (Gerrard's Cross, 1986)

Notes

1   H. Jefferson, *Viscount Pirrie of Belfast* (Belfast, 1948), p.ix.

2   M. Moss and John Hume, *Shipbuilders to the World. 125 years of Harland and Wolff, Belfast, 1861–1986* (Belfast, 1986), p.173.

3   H. Plunkett, *Ireland in the New Century* (London, 1905), p.36.

4   A. Gailey, *Ireland and the Death of Kindness. The Experience of Constructive Unionism 1890–1905* (Cork, 1987), p.59.

5   L. Kennedy, 'The early response of the Irish Catholic clergy to the co-operative movement', in *Colonialism, Religion and Nationalism in Ireland* (Belfast, 1996), p.124.

6   C. Ó Gráda, 'The beginnings of the Irish creamery system 1880–1914', *Economic History Review*, xxx, (1977), p.301.

7   T. West, *Horace Plunkett: Co-operation and Politics, an Irish Biography* (Gerrards Cross, 1986), p.75.

8   See Plunkett, *Ireland in the New Century*, pp.62–3.

9   See West, *Horace Plunkett*, p.76.

10   See Gailey, *Ireland and the Death of Kindness*, p.214.

11   See Moss and Hume, *Shipbuilders to the World*, p.173.

12   R.D.C. Black, 'William James Pirrie', in *SMI*, pp.182–3.

13   C. Cruise O'Brien, 'Foreword', *SMI*, p.7.

14   Ibid., p.5

15   See Black, *Pirrie*, p.184.

16   See West, *Horace Plunkett*, p.179.

CHAPTER 14

Countess Markievicz and Eva Gore-Booth

SONJA TIERNAN

1 Introduction

In his foreword to the 1960 publication, *The Shaping of Modern Ireland,* Conor Cruise O'Brien unashamedly notes that the volume examines how significant *men* 'played a part in … shaping modern Ireland'.[1] The contributions to that volume focus on twenty men, without a dedicated chapter to a woman. In considering their subject matter for a series of Thomas Davis Lectures broadcast by Radio Éireann in 1955, the contributors exclusively examined male activity in the focus period (1891–1916). The index of the book confirms that even references to women or to female-led organisations are lacking. The almost total exclusion of one gender from any analysis in this publication does not mean that women did not actively participate in the events leading up to the Easter Rising or indeed in shaping a Free State Republic. The content of the book does, however, suggest that the activities of women during this key period in Irish history were undervalued and, therefore, often overlooked. The publication was, without doubt, a product of its time and reflects the position of women in Irish society in 1960.

In twenty-first century Ireland, women are accepted as contributing towards the political, social and economic structure of the country. In order to re-evaluate the topic, the shaping of modern Ireland, it is now essential to include women in a contemporary analysis. This chapter primarily examines the contributions of Countess Markievicz with a secondary focus on the legacy of her sister, Eva Gore-Booth, both key players in Irish social movements during the period prior to 1916. The advancement of women's equality in modern Ireland has been shaped, in part, by the activities of the two sisters. The decade of centenaries, currently being commemorated in Ireland, has witnessed a concerted effort to include the contributions made by women during the revolutionary decade. One woman who appears at the forefront in these commemorations is the republican activist, Countess Markievicz, who played a central role in affairs leading up to the Easter Rising and in the rebellion itself. To a lesser extent her younger sister, Eva Gore-Booth, is now recalled as a successful and radical political activist during this period.

2 The Gore-Booth Sisters

Markievicz played a key role in nationalist organisations including Sinn Féin, Inghinidhe na hÉireann, the Irish Citizen Army (ICA) and Cumann na mBan. She founded and contributed to the women's nationalist journal *Bean na hÉireann* and helped establish the national youth organisation, Na Fianna Éireann. Patrick Pearse recognised the founding of the Fianna as an intrinsic element in the formation of a viable army, describing them as the 'pioneers' of the Irish Volunteers.[2] Markievicz is perhaps best remembered in Irish history for her leading role in the Easter Rising, acting as second in command of a battalion of Citizen Army troops first in St Stephens Green and later in the Royal College of Surgeons. Markievicz faced a court-martial trial at Kilmainham Gaol on 4 May for her part in the Rising. In her statement to the closed court she did not plead for mercy, instead she remained defiant stating clearly that, 'I went out to fight for Ireland's freedom, and it doesn't matter what happens to me. I did what I thought was right and I stand by it.'[3]

Markievicz was sentenced to death by firing squad. Her sentence was later commuted to life imprisonment on account of her sex, after appeals from Gore-Booth amongst others. There is no evidence to support assertions later made by the prosecuting counsel, William Wylie, that Markievicz begged for her life at the court-martial. However, commentators have cited this account in order to discredit her and deny the importance of her legacy. Thus, Ruth Dudley Edwards has claimed that Markievicz 'lacked the moral courage to admit her failure of nerve when she was faced with the prospect of execution in 1916'.[4] Dudley Edwards did not acknowledge that Wylie's unsupported recollection may have offered a biased account. After all, Wylie had fought with the Trinity College Officers' Training Corps to quash the Rising. Moreover, Markievicz was not the only person to receive a death sentence reprieve. A number of those similarly sentenced during the Easter Rising trials later had their punishment commuted to life imprisonment: these included Thomas Ashe and Éamon de Valera, the latter on account of his American birth. Such attempts to discredit Markievicz have been successfully challenged and her involvement in the nationalist struggle is now well documented, most recently as part of a wider study on *Irish Nationalist Women, 1900–1918* by Senia Paseta.

However, the importance of Markievicz as a pioneer female politician has received rather less attention. Yet, it is perhaps in her role as a politician and labour activist that Markievicz made the greatest impact on the shaping of modern Ireland, especially in relation to gender equality. At the height of Markievicz's republican activities in 1916, women under British rule had little equality with their male counterparts. Legislation to ensure gender equality in labour, equal access to education or even women's equality within marriage was virtually non-existent, though significant steps in this direction had been made from 1882. Many believed that at the core of this inequity there was women's exclusion from the vote in general elections (by contrast, they had been actively involved in local elections since 1870). Without a political franchise women possessed little real power when lobbying politicians for change. Moreover, women were not eligible to stand for election, ensuring that the government of the day was an entirely male body, placed there by an exclusively male electorate. This was a disability of which Markievicz was most aware. In her address at the foundation meeting of the Irish Women Workers' Union she implored women to join the union, stressing that 'as you are all aware, women have at present no vote, but a union such as has now been formed will not alone help you obtain better wages, but will also be a great means of helping you to get votes . . . and thus make men of you all'.[5]

Markievicz understood from her sister Eva Gore-Booth that *economic and political reform, were intrinsically linked*. Gore-Booth stressed that improvements in the working conditions of women would only be achieved if they were entitled to an equal say in the running of their country; which was only possible through a political franchise.

As early as 1896, Gore-Booth established the Sligo branch of the Irish Women's Suffrage and Local Government Association to advocate for votes for women. Markievicz was appointed president, with Gore-Booth acting as secretary of the Association. The issue of women's suffrage would remain a key focus for both sisters for years to come and was soon coupled with trade union activism. Gore-Booth went on to prove herself as a noteworthy trade unionist in Manchester, working amongst a large working-class community, many of whom were Irish female emigrants. Her labour campaigns were often highly successful. Gore-Booth helped secure better working conditions for women in occupations thought to be morally precarious such as pit-brow girls, factory workers, barmaids and circus performers.

Gore-Booth influenced her sister on trade union activism and invited Markievicz to work with her on many campaigns in England. Markievicz would use this experience in her later activities in Ireland. The sisters' followed in the footsteps of a long line of activists campaigning, through constitutional means, for the introduction of women's suffrage in England. Numerous attempts to extend the franchise to women were made since the first petition was presented by MP Henry Hunt in 1832. Related bills and petitions to the House of Commons were repeatedly rejected over the coming decades. The lack of any compromise forced a group of women to become militant from 1905. The militant suffragettes were led by Gore-Booth's protégé and friend, Christabel Pankhurst. Ireland followed suit and a militant suffrage organisation, the Irish Women's Franchise League (IWFL), was founded by Hanna Sheehy-Skeffington and Margaret Cousins in 1908. The question of female suffrage was even more contentious in Ireland than in Britain. Many nationalists argued that it was necessary to achieve independence before seeking women's suffrage; after all, what was the use of a vote for a foreign government? Irish journalists often belittled Irish suffragettes for aligning themselves with English activists. An article published in 1910 in the Irish weekly paper *The Leader* typifies this view noting how 'the movement in Ireland smacks rather of imitation of the English, and we do not regard it as a native and spontaneous growth'.[6] The British government responded harshly to suffragette militancy. Women were arrested and imprisoned across Britain in their hundreds, though less frequently in Ireland. When those imprisoned demanded political status by hunger striking the authorities responded by introducing a horrifying and physically dangerous system of force-feeding. Markievicz realised how the public sympathised with the hunger strikers and this tactic would later greatly influence Irish republican activists imprisoned for their cause. Markievicz herself went on hunger strike while in prison during the civil war for her anti-treaty undertakings.

After campaigning in England, Markievicz returned to Ireland with an agenda to include suffrage for women in the nationalist cause and to advance the position of women in the labour force. When the Parliamentary Franchise (Women) Bill was re-introduced to the House of Commons in February 1912, suffrage became a pervasive issue also in Ireland, which was then the midst of the Home Rule crisis. Irish suffragettes demanded that female suffrage be included in the terms of any Home Rule bill sought. The leader of the Irish Parliamentary Party, John Redmond, refused to support the bill. Redmond met with members of the IWFL in April and made it clear that he would not support the enfranchisement of women, either in the House of Commons or in the event that Ireland received Home Rule. Markievicz found support for women's suffrage elsewhere. The main orchestrators of the Easter Rising promised gender equality in an Ireland free from British oppression, and indeed, as Pašeta has noted, the subjection of women became a vital concern to the signatories of the Proclamation. Indeed, Markievicz's close ally, James Connolly, viewed the 're-establishment of the Irish State' as useless unless it embodied the 'emancipation of womanhood'.[7]

3 Building Democracy

The Proclamation, first read by Pearse outside the General Post Office on Easter Monday in 1916, guaranteed 'religious and civil liberty, equal rights and equal opportunities to all its citizens'. The provisional government distinctly acknowledged Irishmen and Irishwomen as equal citizens vowing that a future 'permanent National Government [of Ireland] . . . would be elected by the suffrages of all her men and women'. Numerous women, including Markievicz, took active roles in the fight for the ideals expressed in the Proclamation during the Rising. Markievicz fought at the rank of lieutenant with the ICA. Female workers, most notably those employed by Jacobs Factory, had played a significant part in the Dublin Lock-out of 1913 and it is not surprising that women were admitted on equal terms with men into the ICA. Many women fought under the auspices of the ICA and the female organisation, Cumann na mBan.

During the final surrender Pearse ultimately chose a member of Cumann na mBan, nurse Elizabeth O'Farrell, to deliver the surrender notice to the insurgents in the outposts around Dublin city. O'Farrell humbly stood beside Pearse during the final surrender to Brigadier General William Lowe. O'Farrell was later airbrushed out of a photograph taken at the moment of the surrender. This altered image illustrates how women's contribution towards advancing the cause of Irish independence was literally airbrushed out of history books in the past.[8]

Those imprisoned for their parts in the Rising were released gradually over the following months. Markievicz was one of the final prisoners to be released in June 1917 as part of a general amnesty. However, she would spend numerous periods incarcerated over the next few years. In April 1918, Markievicz was arrested and imprisoned in Holloway as part of a supposed Sinn Féin plot with Germany. While she was in prison the Representation of the People Act was passed. The act vastly reformed the British electoral system by removing virtually all property qualifications, enabling men over twenty-one years of age to vote. The act also granted women over thirty years of age, who adhered to some qualifications, a vote at general elections. These two reform measures vastly increased the size of the Irish electorate and enabled some women to vote in general elections for the first time. Moreover, the Parliament (Qualification of Women) Act, also introduced in 1918, enabled women to become candidates. Seventeen of them stood for election in 1918, including Markievicz (for Sinn Féin). Her election campaign was run equally by her suffrage and republican supporters. Sinn Féin secured a landslide victory, securing 73 seats out of a possible 105. Markievicz was the only female candidate to be elected, returned for St Patrick's Division of Dublin: she was the first woman ever to be elected to the British House of Commons. In line with Sinn Féin policy, Markievicz refused to take up her seat. She did, however, receive a letter from Prime Minister Lloyd George inviting her to the House for the opening day of Sessions. Letters had been sent to each elected MP indiscriminately and Markievicz thoroughly enjoyed replying to it.[9]

Instead of taking up their seats at Westminster, the elected members of Sinn Féin formed the first Dáil Éireann, which opened on 21 January 1919 in the Mansion House, Dublin. When she was released from prison in March of that year, Markievicz returned to Ireland and to her first sitting at the Dáil. At the meeting in April she was nominated as Minister for Labour, becoming the first woman to serve as a government minister in Ireland. Irish nationalists celebrated Markievicz's cabinet position as proof that a future republic would be based on equality between all citizens. It also exemplified the democratic potential of nationalist Ireland, if independence from Britain was achieved. By contrast, it would take another ten years for a British government to appoint their first female minister: it was only in 1929 that the Labour Premier James Ramsay MacDonald put Margaret Bondfield in charge of the Department for Employment.

Markievicz opposed the Anglo-Irish treaty signed in December 1921 and appeared in the Dáil in her Cumann na mBan uniform to express her objection; she had been re-elected as president of the anti-treaty organisation. As an opponent of the treaty, Markievicz refused to take her seat in the Dáil and spent much of the Civil War on the run or in prison. With the Anglo-Irish Treaty in place, the sitting TDs moved to draw up the Irish Free State Constitution in 1922, setting out the basic laws of the new state. This document includes articles related to the treaty itself and items which the British government insisted on including such as the oath of faithfulness to the King. However, the constitution attempted to address the promises of the provisional government in 1916, as set out in the Proclamation. The focus on deriving power from the people equally is embedded in the document. While Markievicz was not a sitting TD during this time, it can easily be argued that it was thanks to her influence and the energetic lobbying of other women in Ireland that the constitution formalised gender equality. Article 3 stipulated that 'every person, without distinction of sex' shall be treated as an equal citizen and that they shall 'enjoy the privileges and be subject to the obligations of such citizenship'.[10] Indeed, Article 14 granted equal voting rights to all citizens, without 'distinction of sex'.[11] This voting entitlement was significant, bearing in mind that it was adopted by the Irish Free State six years before women in Britain were granted equal voting rights with men.

Markievicz was to have an immediate impact on gender equality in politics in Ireland. She had gained the support of the Irish public and was again elected in the 1923 general election. According to Article 17 of the constitution then in place, TDs were obliged to swear allegiance to the British king. When Markievicz refused to do so, she forfeited her seat. In an attempt to re-engage with parliamentary politics, she joined Fianna Fáil upon its establishment in 1926. She was elected as a Fianna Fáil candidate for Dublin South in the June 1927 general election. Markievicz died five weeks later at the age of 59, never having endorsed the oath of allegiance which the remaining Fianna Fáil members signed on 11 August. She was not replaced by another female cabinet minister for decades to come. Gender equality did not appear to be a central concern for de Valera, the leader of the political party soon to be in charge of Ireland's destiny. After all, the garrison he commanded during the Rising, at Boland's Mill, was one of only two outposts that refused to accept female insurgents. Arguably de Valera included Markievicz as a Fianna Fáil candidate not out of concern for gender balance, but because he was dependent on public support and she, 'the people's Countess', was an intrinsic element of Fianna Fáil's popular appeal. When Markievicz died in a public ward of Sir Patrick Dun's hospital, her legacy quickly began to unravel. Due to ongoing hostilities with the Free State government, Markievicz was denied a state funeral. Five days before her death Kevin O'Higgins, then Minister for Justice, had been assassinated by anti-treaty forces. O'Higgins received a state funeral and his body lay in state at the Mansion House. In contrast, Markievicz's body lay in the Pillar Room of the Rotunda hospital and she received a public funeral. However, she proved to have earned the respect of the people of Dublin who lined the streets in their tens of thousands to honour her funeral cortege.

An attempt to honour Markievicz was made in 1932 when a bust of her was unveiled in St Stephens Green, where she had fought during the Rising. At the unveiling ceremony de Valera gave a speech which shows his effort to recreate her memory. Yet it was a re-visioning which her biographer, Lauren Arrington, believes led to Markievicz's life and work being misinterpreted.[12] De Valera's speech certainly infuriated Hanna Sheehy-Skeffington who retaliated in the pages of *An Phoblacht* stating how:

> Monuments to the dead are often misused – sometimes, no doubt, unconsciously – by the living to misinterpret what those whose memorial is unveiled truly stood for … Constance Markievicz was primarily and essentially a revolutionary, an iconoclast, with the direct vision, the divine discontent of a Joan of Arc … The picture painted by Éamon de Valera of labour's revolutionary heroine is conventionalised beyond recognition … It is an apologia where none is needed. In the speech at the unveiling, Constance Markievicz is thus described: 'To many she was simply a strange

figure, following a path of her own, not following accustomed paths, but the friends who knew her knew that she did that because she was truly a woman.'[13]

4 Legacies

The true legacy of Markievicz remained glossed over until recently. When O'Brien first published the *Shaping of Modern Ireland*, Markievicz's work had not only been forgotten but it had actually been undone. By 1960 no other female politician had held a cabinet position in an Irish government since her. The next woman to hold office was Máire Geoghegan-Quinn, appointed in 1979 as Minister for the Gaeltacht. It would take until 1987 for a woman to succeed Markievicz as Minister for Labour, when Gemma Hussey served for a mere two and a half months in that ministry.

De Valera wiped out the record of successes made by Markievicz and Gore-Booth in a very real way. When he oversaw the redrafting of the Irish constitution in 1937, women were positioned as citizens with a specific social role, primarily defined by their family duties. Article 3 of the 1922 Irish Free State constitution, which promised the equality of all citizens regardless of gender, was simply removed. Instead articles were inserted into the 1937 document declaring that women's ultimate place was in the domestic sphere. Article 41, which still remains unchanged, includes a section declaring that 'the State recognises that by her life within the home, woman gives to the State a support without which the common good cannot be achieved'.[14] The release of the draft version inspired Sheehy-Skeffington to write to the *Irish Independent* asserting that the constitution is 'a Fascist Model, in which women would be relegated to permanent inferiority, their avocations and choice of callings limited because of an implied invalidism as the weaker sex'.[15] The implications of the 1937 constitution were far-reaching, coupled with the lack of a strong female replacement for Markievicz in Irish politics. By 1960, gender inequality in the country could be described as extreme. The marriage bar ensured that women had to resign from civil service positions and many other occupations upon marriage, excluding the vast majority of Irish women from rising to the ranks of senior management and often removing women from public life more generally. In the event that a woman was afforded the opportunity to work, employers could legally pay her less than her male colleagues doing the same job. Within marriage women had no legal protection, even from a violent husband. They had no automatic rights to ownership of the family home, and, as under the 1927 Juries Act non rate-payers could not serve on juries, many married women were thus excluded (by contrast, a man who was not a rate-payer could become qualified if his wife was 'rated for the relief of the poor' in the same jury district). The inequalities were vast and it was only through the dedicated campaigning of second wave feminists that these laws began to change from the 1970s.

Legislation is now in place to protect the rights of women in Ireland; unfortunately this does not ensure that Irish society operates fully on a gender equality basis. There is recent concern that Irish politics is still male dominated. In efforts to improve gender balance it is Markievicz who appears as the icon for change. A full-length painting of the Countess hangs on the stairs to the Seanad. The painting was removed during renovations to the building and, during a Seanad debate, Senator Mary Henry noted the importance of ensuring that the painting was returned to its rightful position. Her speech highlights the importance not only of Markievicz's work in shaping a modern Ireland but as a symbol to inspire future generations. Henry insisted that, 'it is of great importance to show women were involved in our past. It is essential that women are put before all children, particularly girls, so there is some sort of role model for them in political life and so that they understand the importance of everyone in the founding of our State.'[16] In March 2014, in an attempt to rectify the gender imbalance of their party, Fianna Fáil launched an inquiry to ascertain how they could increase the numbers of female candidates at future general elections. Significantly this project was undertaken by a group which the party named the Markievicz Commission and a gender equality document was published in January 2015.

There are now a number of Markievicz statues and places named in her honour, mainly in Dublin and Sligo. No such honours have yet been granted to Eva Gore-Booth. Perhaps her greatest influence in Ireland was as an advisor to Markievicz, certainly she was the greatest inspiration for her sister. Gore-Booth is remembered more for her social reform activism in England. In this way she made a considerable impact, improving the living conditions for Irish emigrants, during a time when more Irish people lived in the city of Manchester than in Gore-Booth's home county of Sligo. Significantly, during the first official state visit of an Irish president to Britain, President Higgins, in his address to the Houses of Parliament, noted how 'Eva Gore-Booth, who is buried in Hampstead, had been making, and would continue to make, her own distinctive contribution to history – not only in the Irish nationalist struggle, but as part of the suffragette and labour movements in Britain'.[17] In 2015, a campaign was launched to erect a blue plaque outside the Manchester house she shared with her partner Esther Roper. In July 2015, the Minister for Diaspora Affairs, Jimmy Deenihan, launched a project to restore Gore-Booth and Roper's joint grave in Hampstead, London.[18]

Gore-Booth's legacy is only recently being recognised in Ireland and her impact is most evident in relation to her sexuality. As well as her labour and suffrage work Gore-Booth established the journal *Urania* in 1916. Through the pages of the journal, Gore-Booth advocated for the social acceptance of gay relationships. That same year she launched an international campaign for the reprieve of Roger Casement's death sentence and refused to refute rumours regarding his homosexuality. In modern Ireland, Gore-Booth is held in high esteem as an early Lesbian, Gay, Bisexual and Transgender (LGBT) rights activist. In 2013, at the Workers' Memorial Day organised by the Irish Congress of Trade Unions, a focus on LGBT workers included a public talk on the legacy of Gore-Booth.[19] In this respect, Gore-Booth's writing is also being remembered and she is being celebrated as an Irish lesbian poet and playwright. An annual award for the best female performance at the International Dublin Gay Theatre Festival has been named in her honour since 2008. At the launch of the festival in 2012, Senator Katherine Zappone applauded the inclusion of the Gore-Booth award as a fitting honour. Zappone and her partner, Ann Louise Gilligan, initiated the debate in Ireland relating to civil marriage equality. It was particularly apt that the referendum on the issue took place in 2015 on 22 May, the date of Gore-Booth's birthday. Gore-Booth was writing and campaigning for LGBT equality one hundred years before the people of Ireland voted in favour of extending marriage to all. In the same way that Senator Henry argued for the importance of female role models, it is also particularly important that young people are presented with gay and lesbian role models, which have been sadly lacking in Irish history.

It is now time to question the legacy of the Gore-Booth sisters as presented by W.B. Yeats in his poem 'In Memory of Eva Gore-Booth and Con Markievicz'.[20] In it, Yeats' reference to both Constance and Eva suggests that they were unfocused and unsuccessful political activists, as he attests:

> . . . The older is condemned to death,
> Pardoned, drags out lonely years
> Conspiring among the ignorant.
> I know not what the younger dreams –
> Some vague Utopia – and she seems,
> When withered old and skeleton-gaunt,
> An image of such politics . . .[21]

This poem is undoubtedly one of Yeats' most admired and has contributed to him being associated with Lissadell House, the sisters' childhood home in Sligo. On 22 July 2015, in an unusual move, the Irish cabinet meeting was held at Lissadell House, the venue was chosen to celebrate the 150th anniversary of Yeats' birth. Possibly for the first time, the legacy of Constance and Eva overshadowed the memory of Yeats. The owners of Lissadell House posted on their web site to remind the Irish public how the Gore-Booth sisters' 'achievement was the legislative change allowing women both to stand for election and to vote'.[22] It was 'one hundred and nineteen years ago [that] Constance and Eva stood on a platform in Drumcliff, Sligo, campaigning for women's rights. For this they were mocked and derided. Constance and Eva would be so proud to see four women ministers at Lissadell, sitting in cabinet, with a female Attorney-General in attendance. They would be so proud that one such minister holds the office of Tánaiste.'[23] While women's participation in Irish politics remains below the European average, the situation is improving and the legacy of Markievicz and Gore-Booth is a central inspiration for change.

Further Reading:

R.M. Fox, *Rebel Irishwomen* (Cork & Dublin 1935)

M. Jones, *Those Obstreperous Lassies: A History of the Irish Women's Workers' Union* (Dublin, 1988)

M. Luddy, *Hanna Sheehy Skeffington* (Dublin, 1995)

S. Ó Tuama, 'Revisiting the Irish Constitution and De Valera's Grand Vision', *Irish Journal of Legal Studies*, Vol 2(2), 2011, pp.54–87

S. Pašeta, *Nationalist Women in Ireland, 1900–1918* (Cambridge, 2013)

E. Roper (ed.), *Prison Letters of Countess Markievicz* (London, 1987)

L. Ryan and M. Ward (eds), *Women and Irish Nationalism: Soldiers, New Women and Wicked Hags* (Dublin, 2004)

S. Tiernan, *Eva Gore-Booth: An Image of Such Politics* (Manchester, 2012)

M.G. Valiulis, 'Power, Gender and Identity in the Irish Free State', *Journal of Women's History*, 6/7:4/1 (Winter/Spring 1995), pp.117–36

Notes

1   C. Cruise O'Brien, 'Foreword', *SMI*, p.1.

2   P. Pearse, *Irish Freedom*, February 1914.

3   E. Roper (ed.), *Prison Letters of Countess Markievicz* (London, 1987), p.24.

4   R. Dudley Edwards, 'Countess Markievicz', *Speaking Ill of the Dead* (RTE Radio, 8 February 2007).

5   Constance Markievicz as quoted in M. Jones, *Those Obstreperous Lassies: A History of the Irish Women's Workers' Union* (Dublin, 1988), p.1.

6   *The Leader*, 19 March 1910.

7   J. Connolly, *The Re-Conquest of Ireland* (Dublin, 1917), p.243.

8   A project by M. McAuliffe and L. Gillis entitled '77 Women' will document the lives of seventy-seven women arrested and imprisoned in Richmond barracks for their parts in the Rising.

9   See Roper, *Prison Letters*, p.88.

10   Constitution of the Irish Free State (Saorstát Eireann) Act, 1922.

11   Ibid

12   L. Arrington, 'Constance Markievicz and the Idea of Ireland', 37th Annual Constance Markievicz Lecture: Irish Association of Industrial Relations, 29 November 2013.

13   H. Sheehy-Skeffington, 'Constance Markievicz: What she Stood for', *An Phoblacht*, 16 July 1932.

14   'The Family, Article 41', *Bunreacht na hÉireann: Constitution of Ireland* (1937) (Dublin: Government Publications, 2012), p. 162.

15   *The Irish Independent*, 11 May 1937.

16   Senator Dr Mary E. F. Henry, 'Adjournment Matter: Portrait of Countess Markievicz', Seanad debate, 13 December 2000.

17   Address by Michael D. Higgins, President of Ireland to the Houses of Parliament, Westminster (8 April 2014), Áras an Uachtaráin speeches.

18   Instigated by Lucy Keaveney, founder member of the Countess Markievicz School.

19   B. Merriman, 'Workers Memorial Day Reflection', ICTU, 27 April 2013.

20   W.B. Yeats, 'In Memory of Eva Gore-Booth and Con Markievicz', Augustine Martin (ed.), *Collected Poems* (London, 1990), p.241.

21   Ibid.

22   Lissadell House and Gardens website, accessed 2 November 2015. http://lissadellhouse.com/index.php/the-cabinet-at-lissad1ll/

23   Ibid.

CHAPTER 15

Patrick Pearse and James Connolly

DIARMAID FERRITER

1 Introduction

Dorothy Macardle was best known for her 1937 book *The Irish Republic*, a history of the revolutionary period that was devoutly anti-Treaty and pro Éamon de Valera. Macardle's bias prompted historian Joe Lee, in his seminal work *Ireland 1912–85: Politics and Society*, published in 1989, to refer to her as 'hagiographer royal to the Republic'.

Reducing Macardle to a one-dimensional writer or a narrow-minded keeper of the republican flame, however, is to do her a great disservice. While *The Irish Republic* generated considerable controversy, as de Valera's rationalisations and interpretation were followed faithfully without challenge and was a reminder of the way in which 'history' was being used for political purposes in the decades following the Civil War, Macardle was much more than a poodle of de Valera's. She had a strong liberal streak and an independent mind and was a prominent internationalist, humanitarian and committed feminist, who fell out with de Valera over the clauses in the Irish constitution of 1937 that discriminated against women. While she was a stout defender of the right of small nations to stake their claim to independence, she also had serious reservations about the morality of Irish neutrality during the Second World War, a defining foreign policy issue for de Valera.

Equally importantly, she had been personally immersed in the events of the revolutionary period and knew many of the combatants and politicians well. She had been arrested and interned during the Civil War, was deeply affected by the death and executions of republican friends and had been furious with the Catholic Church over its support for the provisional government established in 1922.

The prominence of people who had personal involvement with the revolutionary period is what has most obviously changed since 1960. Macardle's biographer, Nadia Clare Smith, has noted that her inclusion as a contributor to the Thomas Davis Lecture series that formed the basis of *The Shaping of Modern Ireland* was intriguing, 'as the broadcasts were mainly given by younger professional historians'.[1] When introducing the book, its editor Conor Cruise O'Brien also observed: 'some of the contributors are old enough to be "reminiscent" rather than interrogative'.[2] Macardle, inevitably, was influenced by her own experiences and memories; as she wrote in her essay, there was a danger of being influenced by 'emotional mists and wishful illusions',[3] but it is worth noting that Macardle's essay was also significant because of the simple fact that she was tackling this vexed period. The medieval historian at University College Dublin (UCD), F.X. Martin, who also turned his attention to the history of the 1916 Rising in the 1960s, had pointed to the tendency up to the early 1960s to 'fight shy' of the more controversial issues of that era, but that with Macardle's broadcast, 'the nettle was tentatively crunched'.

Macardle was conscious of being a defensive keeper of the flame of that revolutionary generation; in the words of Smith, by the 1950s when she delivered her Thomas Davis broadcast, 'as a member of an older revolutionary generation in Ireland, she felt increasingly unappreciated and believed that younger Irish people had forgotten the accomplishments of their predecessors'.[4] Macardle addressed this when referring to criticism of the 1916 leaders: 'It comes, sometimes, from young people who are free from the scepticism which is induced by much reading of history. These maintain that all we have achieved in four fifths of Ireland since 1916 would have come to us, without any Rising, without any violent effort, already, in the natural course of events.'[5]

Debate about that contention continues to this day. In the decades since Macardle's essay it has been complicated by new research, the Troubles in Northern Ireland and the peace process, but the core of the issue, the towering question, remains the same: was violence justified and necessary? Macardle was adamant:

> I think that few Irish people of my generation, who remember the desperate bitterness of subjection, and remember the obtuseness, at that time, of the British governing class concerning Ireland – the insolence of many of the most powerful, the facetiousness of a multitude, the ruthlessness of a few – will agree with that happy optimists' view; nor will those of us who have studied the long struggle of India and of other countries held down by great powers believe easily in that 'natural course'.[6]

Such a justification was coming under pressure even when Macardle made her spirited defence; the year of her broadcast, 1956, a new phase of Irish Republican Army (IRA) activity was inaugurated through the border campaign, and the legacy of the violence of the period 1916–23 was then further complicated by the outbreak of the Troubles at the end of the following decade. But an active IRA was not the only relevant factor influencing attitudes to the past. In the Republic, a revision of traditional interpretations of the revolutionary period coincided with the release of an abundance of new archival material from the mid-1960s. F.X.Martin published a provocative article in 1967 – '1916 – myth, fact, and mystery' in the journal, *Studia Hibernica*; it was a one-hundred page challenging and insightful overview of the background and consequences of the Rising. Martin criticised the neglect by historians of John Redmond, rehabilitated Eoin MacNeill, and in relation to whether the Rising was morally justified, asserted, 'the democrat and the theologian may question the means they [the rebels] used'.[7] In the following decade, with the backdrop of the Troubles in Northern Ireland, 1916 was more of a target for ire than the period 1919–23. For Conor Cruise O'Brien, for example, whose grandfather was David Sheehy, a nationalist MP who was embittered at the defeat of the constitutional nationalists in 1918 and very hostile to Sinn Féin, it was the origin of all later ills.

Undoubtedly some historians and political scientists, in response to the Troubles, began to paint their history in black and white instead of grey, absorbing messy reality into a neat narrative of constitutional progress. Many historians had a strong distaste for paramilitaries; some felt a moral obligation to draw lessons of contemporary relevance from revolutionary history, sometimes before non-academic audiences as an exercise in 'public history'. This was, according to David Fitzpatrick, 'widely regarded as a civic duty for near contemporary historians in a country, like Ireland, saturated with history and pseudo-histories'. [8] It was also about legitimately challenging those who were abusing history and falsifying the past for their own ends. Michael Laffan, for example

> felt that he was a member of a generation which had benefitted from the professionalization of history... he had been trained to be suspicious of the nationalist version of Irish history, just as he had been trained to be suspicious of the unionist version... In adopting new perspectives on such fundamental parts of modern Irish history as the Rising, historians were simply being true to their professional responsibilities, doing no more for Irish history than American and French scholars when they revised long-standing accounts of the revolutions which had transformed their own societies. Not to do this would be the real betrayal. [9]

Others, however, felt that in doing this, some historians were disingenuously engaged in efforts to explicitly support the state in its opposition to the IRA by deliberately downplaying the important role of violence during the years 1916–23.

Questions that came into the frame in the 1970s and 1980s included whether there was a need to challenge the 'assumption of inevitability' regarding the level of violence from 1916 onwards and the establishment of partition and whether the idea that the IRA had a mandate for violence during the War of Independence was flawed. But even at the height of the Troubles, a number of historians refused to shirk the question of the effectiveness of historic violence. Nicholas Mansergh, who taught Irish history at Cambridge University, and whose childhood in Tipperary coincided with the War of Independence, did not avoid these challenges in *The Irish Question: 1840–1921* (1975), suggesting that constitutionalism during this period 'was not enough', and that violence was inevitable. This was partly a reaction to the assertion of Leland Lyons in *John Dillon: A Biography* (1968), an account of the life of one of the leading nationalist parliamentarians of that era, that Dillon had learnt from harsh experience that 'patriotism was not enough'. Mansergh concluded that 'force, or the threat of it, delivered the goods, or most of them, where constitutionalism, after long trial, had not'. [10] In the same year, Charles Townshend, in *The British Campaign in Ireland* maintained convincingly: 'some form of military struggle was inevitable before Irish demands would be taken seriously'.[11] Nearly forty years after Townshend's conclusion, Ronan Fanning essentially echoed Macardle's view in his 2013 book *Fatal Path*: force 'was indeed necessary', and 'there is not a shred of evidence that Lloyd-George's Tory dominated government would have moved from the 1914-style niggardliness of the Government of Ireland Act to the larger, if imperfect generosity of the Treaty, if they had not been impelled to do so by Michael [Collins] and his assassins'.[12]

2 Connolly

What Macardle was not prepared to acknowledge, however, and this is where the icier winds of modern historical scholarship are so obvious, were the shortcomings and complex personalities of her subjects, Patrick Pearse and James Connolly. Pearse, she wrote, was 'brimming with talent, with radiant dreams and burning convictions ... attaining his boyhood's ideals and exercising all his faculties, Pearse was by definition a happy man ... Pearse filled those who heard him with hope.'[13] Connolly's teachings, Macardle maintained, 'had the strength of simplicity; no ambivalence, no disharmony, no inner conflict ever inhabited him ... an optimist, Connolly had high hopes for the outcome in Ireland'.[14] These are the sort of pious assertions that cannot withstand the force and depth of knowledge that has been accumulated through decades of research, revision and modern detachment. But a crucial point is that, at the time Macardle wrote her essay, there was no body of critical research into Pearse and his motivations, and Connolly's writings remained largely unpublished and his archive widely scattered.

Connolly has proved to be a remarkably enduring icon of Irish socialism, despite the fact that he had little success as an active trade union organiser or politician and failed to demonstrate how the labour movement would negotiate its relationship, if any, with parliament. His reputation and legacy were, instead, secured by his unique intellect and prolific writings, many of which are still in print; his sheer command over Irish and international history, and the insistence of the promoters of his legacy that his thoughts and words are directly relevant to the contemporary world. A year after publication of *The Shaping of Modern Ireland*, a biography of Connolly by Desmond Greaves, was published.

Greaves, a leading light in the Connolly Club when it was formed in 1941 (later the Connolly Association), which was committed to the ending of partition through peaceful means and the influencing of the British labour movement, was a committed Marxist; one of his advantages as a biographer was that he was able to interview contemporaries of Connolly. He was also able to establish that, contrary to popular belief and some members of Connolly's family, Connolly was born not in Ireland, but Edinburgh, and that he had been a member of the British army, at that time a sensational finding. More importantly, however, Greaves did justice to the different phases and aspects of Connolly's very full life. Another biography in 1973 by Samuel Levenson also focused on the 'many faces of Connolly', but Levenson was also keen to point out that even by that stage, little was known of Connolly's role as a pioneer in the international socialist movement and the issue of reconciling his socialism with participation in the 1916 Rising.

These biographies reflected a determination to generate more interest in Connolly, as did new publications of his work, and some of the support for the Labour Party in the late 1960s was as a result of this new focus on his writings. But this also raised an obvious question: were Connolly's teachings and targets being followed at that time, as one who had, in Macardle's words, 'hurled himself against the one enemy – capitalistic imperialism'? Macardle acknowledged that 'Connolly's kindly socialist state ... may never exist'; [15] she did not, however, dwell much on that, suggesting, exaggeratedly, that 'to men gifted with patience and wisdom', the failure to realise socialist aims 'might seem passing ills; phases'. But those reflecting on the failure to realise Connolly's vision were less sanguine. In 1964, as a young political scientist, David Thornley wrote a provocative article in the Jesuit published journal *Studies*, when the Labour Party was contemplating its continued relevance to Irish politics and its intellectual foundations:

Ask the Irish Labour Party supporter today what he believes in and he will most certainly not say, with Marx, the class war, the total smashing of the bourgeois state and the establishment of the dictatorship of the proletariat. He will almost equally certainly not say, with clause four of the British Labour Party – the ownership of the means of production, distribution and exchange. It is indeed unlikely that he will even say the Welfare State. What he is most likely to say is 'I follow the principles of James Connolly.'[16]

Of course, as Thornley recognised, few of the Labour Party followers did anything of the kind, and as far as Thornley was concerned, the party at that stage was terrified of the word 'socialism' and belonged to the 'broad stream of the revisionist Social Democrat parties of the continent'.

The following decade, *Saothar*, the journal of the Irish Labour History Society, was established. Its early editions provided a platform to broaden the parameters of labour history, and by 1983, Emmet O'Connor asserted that 'an age of agitation' could not be reduced to just looking at James Larkin and Connolly, who had been 'fetishised and then buffeted between iconography and iconoclasm'. [17] Labour history began to move beyond hagiography and demagoguery to restore the complexity of individuals who were prominent while Macardle was politically active. Given these trends, which have continued to the present, Macardle's assertion that 'no inner conflict' ever affected Connolly seems far-fetched. The more recent accounts of Connolly's life have documented his darker side, frequent displays of volatility and the confusing and ambiguous relationship he had with Ireland and his contemporaries.

In 2005 Donal Nevin, a well-known trade unionist and tireless chronicler of labour history, quoted extensively from 200 letters that revealed aspects of Connolly's relationship with his colleagues, and recorded Connolly's acute disappointment at the reception he received in his earlier years of activism: following the failure of the tiny Irish Socialist Republican Party and the *Worker's Republic* newspaper in 1903, he wrote: 'I regard Ireland, or at least the socialist part of Ireland which is all I care for, as having thrown me out and I do not wish to return like a dog to his vomit.'[18] Nevin underlined how Connolly was also frequently cut-off from family and friends and ironically, given his widespread travel, seemed to blame them more than himself. These inner conflicts are laid bare in recent historiography, in contrast to 'a simple serenity' suggested by Macardle, but so too is the enduring power of his exceptional intellect and prodigious output, or what Macardle referred to as 'his power to study somehow, anywhere, his clear brain and energy'.[19]

3 Pearse

In relation to Pearse, Macardle's laudatory assessment was made without the benefit of a body of critical published work and when the stained-glass approach to Pearse was still paramount. This reverence had begun in earnest while the War of Independence was only beginning, as is apparent in Pearse's devoted disciple Desmond Ryan's 1919 biography, *The Man called Pearse*, which established Pearse as the chief leader of 1916 and referred to him as 'a perfect man, whose faults were the mere defects of his straight and rigid virtues'. [20] Louis Le Roux's 1932 biography of Pearse was also predicated on the idea that canonisation was warranted: 'My design was to make Pearse appear, in the light of historic truth, among the models and the glorious builders of the history of Ireland'. [21]

But this adulation did not endure, and instead, a focus on Pearse's cultural legacy and downplaying his association with violence came to serve a political purpose from the 1960s. In 1966, in the run up to the fiftieth anniversary of the Easter Rising, Seán Lemass, as Taoiseach, was concerned in private about celebrating Pearse as revolutionary. The tone of the correspondence emanating from the Department of the Taoiseach suggested Lemass was not keen on vigorous debate on the Rising, particularly in the context of his determination to promote 'the building of Anglo-Irish good will'. When pondering the suitability of Pearse's poem 'Invocation' as an inscription on the memorial wall in the Garden of Remembrance, Lemass was 'disturbed by the fierce and vengeful tone of the poem, which was entirely appropriate to the circumstances of 1916, but will be less so to those years after 1966'. [22]

An article published in the Jesuit publication *Studies* in 1972 by Fr Francis Shaw SJ, who had studied at UCD under early Irish history scholar Eoin MacNeill, who as Chief of Staff of the Irish Volunteers had tried to prevent the Rising of 1916, was another manifestation of the discomfort with the Pearse legacy. Shaw's article had been intended for publication in 1966 but, because of its perceived attack on the legacy of 1916, it was delayed. Entitled 'The Canon of Irish history: A Challenge', it maintained that 'Pearse, one feels, would not have been satisfied to attain independence by peaceful means.' It criticised the way Pearse 'consistently and deliberately and without reservation' equated 'the patriot and the patriot people with Christ' which Shaw argued was in conflict with Christian tradition. Conor Cruise O'Brien, in 1976, went much further, describing Pearse as 'a manic, mystic nationalist with a cult of blood sacrifice and a strong personal motivation towards death. A nation which pretends to take a personality of that type as its mentor, without really meaning it, is already involved in a disaster, a disaster of intellectual dishonesty and moral obliquity.' [23]

A detailed critical reassessment of Pearse's life, however, did not appear until Ruth Dudley Edwards's *The Triumph of Failure* was published in 1977; for some, this was a necessary corrective to the existing hagiographies, for others, it was infused with 'corrosive cynicism' which, in the words of Dudley Edwards at the time of the seventy-fifth anniversary of the Rising in 1991, had supposedly 'placed our national heroes in the dock and conducted the case for the prosecution'.[24]

What Dudley Edwards uncovered was a 'tortured and complex man'; a sincere, selfless, brave, kind man, but also delusional about his fellow people, and a Pearse who 'wrote, acted and died for a people that did not exist'. She suggested his obsession with self-sacrifice and failure to achieve the great conversion of people to his evolving republicanism drove him to martyrdom and left him fixated on immortality: 'he left behind him a self-justicatory political testament that turned out to be a Pandora's Box. Terrorism would have appalled him, but the IRA were logically his heirs'.[25] Dudley Edwards, it appeared, had become both 'fond of and sorry for' Pearse. But such perspectives were also paralleled by another new focus, what journalist Mary Leland referred to in 1977 as 'the ecumenical, democratic and joyous aspects of the character' of Pearse, which were 'hidden from the general public'.[26] What he strove for, it was argued, was something profoundly modern and radical in the form of child-centred education; he was an inspired educationalist 'who got sidetracked by other things'.[27]

Macardle did not ignore the cultural contributions of Pearse, especially in relation to his championing of the Irish language – 'the proudly bilingual Ireland Pearse dreamed of', while acknowledging that such an Ireland 'may never exist'. But that was secondary, she maintained, to his 'larger purpose', which was 'to rouse a nation half moribund from long failure; revitalize its withering pride and confidence; create a generation of insurgents, selfless and stalwart'. But what constituted a revitalising of pride and what could be construed as selfless and stalwart was much contested in the decades after Macardle's assessment.

The centenary of Pearse's birth in 1979 also raised sensitivities. At the end of 1977, all Irish government departments were asked to submit proposals as to how the centenary could be marked. The view was expressed that 'in the prevailing Northern Ireland situation such commemoration could raise delicate issues affecting relations between the communities in the North and possibly extending to Anglo-Irish relations' but that a decision not to mark the occasion 'could be open to misinterpretation and might leave the field to subversive elements who might seek to capitalise on the situation for their own ends'. [28]

There was a feeling that commemoration should concentrate on 'Pearse's contribution in the literary, cultural and educational fields'. [29] But the Pearse centenary cabinet sub-committee, while being aware of the 'strong Provoish element who will be emphasising the physical force aspect of Pearse and 1916', also agreed 'to restore the memory of Pearse to a place of honour in Irish society and to counter the denigratory effects of certain commentators in recent years'.[30] This underlined uneasiness about a perceived simplistic denigration of Pearse and his legacy, to the extent that, in 1977, Joe Lee concluded that, due to the Troubles in Northern Ireland, Pearse 'was in danger of falling victim to mindless condemnation having long been the victim of mindless adulation'. Such resentment lingered; in 1991 Lee further argued 'we are still at an early stage in trying to understand the mind of Patrick Pearse', but that the work of Seamus Buachalla on Pearse's letters and his role as an educationalist, published in 1980, provided much material to rectify that and made apparent the dangers of a 'fatally easy' approach to Pearse – to place him 'into a particular mould and then to fit everything in him into that mould'. The reality, no more than with Connolly, was that 'there were many Pearses'.[31]

By the time of the ninetieth anniversary of the Rising in 2006, Roisín Higgins and others were able to contextualise the reaction to revisionist perspectives on Pearse; because Pearse had come to symbolise both moral and political integrity for a generation, some had responded to a revising of the Pearse legacy 'as if it was the national psyche that was being raided'. [32] But what continued to be a focus, seen for example in the book *The Life and After-Life of PH Pearse* (2009), was the idea that he was a multifaceted figure, reflecting many tensions and identities during the early twentieth century, and this is where Pearse has been subjected to a broader historical analysis that reflects a desire, often propelled by new sources, to complicate the narrative of the revolutionary period: in the words of Higgins: 'he was both Irish and English, Victorian and modernist, respectable and revolutionary'.[33]

4 Conclusion

Joe Lee's assessment of Pearse for the landmark *Dictionary of Irish Biography*, published in 2009, underlines the polarisation generated by his status as a republican icon. 'The task of rescuing Pearse from the clutches of his idolaters and demonisers continues' but, significantly, Lee also suggested 'in the longer run, his cultural legacy will prove at least as significant as his political'.[34] This, however, is doubtful, given his position as the president of the republic declared in 1916, the events and violence it led to and the long and still controversial legacy associated with this foundational event of modern Irish republicanism, politically and militarily.

In that sense, the words of Macardle about the roles of Pearse and Connolly in 1916 – 'men without elected authority taking action calculated to involve their country in war…was justified, to their own minds, by the fact that no elected national authority was permitted to exist, or could be brought into existence, without a fight; it is justified in the minds of others because of its results'[35] – are as relevant to debate now as they were in the 1960s. What will also doubtless continue is selective citation of Pearse's and Connolly's words and actions to justify or condemn a whole host of contemporary sentiments and political priorities.

Macardle finished her essay by asking these two questions: 'And are we not free? And is not a free-born generation preparing to take the future of the Republic into able and faithful hands?'[36] Attempting to answer those questions in Ireland in 2016 will provoke a variety of conflicting responses; defining and evaluating Irish freedom and Irish republicanism is still no easy task and hardly conducive to consensus, which is why the questions raised by Macardle are still relevant and challenging today.

Further Reading:

R. Dudley Edwards, *Patrick Pearse: The Triumph of Failure* (London, 1977)

D. Fitzpatrick, 'Dr Regan and Mr Snide', *History Ireland*, Vol. 20, no. 3, May 2012, pp.12–13

D. Greaves, *The Life and Times of James Connolly* (London, 1961)

F.X. Martin., '1916 – Myth, Fact and Mystery', *Studia Hibernica*, no. 7, 1967, pp.7–127

J. McGuire and J. Quinn (eds), *Dictionary of Irish Biography: From the Earliest Times to the Year 2002* (Cambridge, 2009)

E. O'Connor, 'An age of agitation', *Saothar*, Vol. 9, 1983, pp.64–7

F. Shaw, 'The Canon of Irish History: A Challenge', *Studies*, Vol. 61, Summer 1972, pp.117–51

N.C. Smith, *Dorothy Macardle: A Life* (Dublin, 2007)

D. Thornley, 'Ireland: The end of an era?' *Studies*, Vol. LIII, no. 209, Spring 1964, pp.24–31

Notes

1   N.C. Smith, *Dorothy Macardle: A Life* (Dublin, 2007), p.132.
2   C. Cruise O'Brien, 'Foreword', *SMI*, p.8.
3   D. Macardle, 'James Connolly and Patrick Pearse', *SMI*, p.185.
4   See Smith, *Dorothy Macardle*, p.128.
5   See Macardle, 'James Connolly and Patrick Pearse', *SMI*, p.186.
6   Ibid., p.187.
7   F.X. Martin., '1916 – Myth, Fact and Mystery', *Studia Hibernica*, no.7, 1967, pp.7–127.
8   D. Fitzpatrick, 'Dr Regan and Mr Snide', *History Ireland*, Vol.20, no.3, May 2012, pp.12–13.
9   D. Ferriter, *A Nation and not a Rabble: The Irish Revolution, 1913–1923* (London, 2015), p.70.
10 N. Mansergh, *The Irish Question, 1840–1921*, 3rd edition (London, 1975), p.5.
11 C. Townshend, *The British Campaign in Ireland: The Development of Political and Military Policies* (Oxford, 1975), p.26.
12 R. Fanning, *Fatal Path: British Government and Irish Revolution, 1910–1922* (London, 2013), pp.133–7.
13 See Macardle, 'James Connolly and Patrick Pearse', *SMI*, p.190.
14 Ibid., p.193.
15 Ibid, p.187.
16 D. Thornley, 'Ireland: The End of an Era?' *Studies*, Vol. LIII, no.209, Spring 1964, pp.24–31.
17 E. O'Connor, 'An age of Agitation', *Saothar*, Vol.9, 1983, pp.64–7.
18 D. Nevin, *James Connolly: A Full Life* (Dublin, 2005), p.218.
19 See Macardle, 'James Connolly and Patrick Pearse', SMI, p.189.
20 D. Ryan, *The Man Called Pearse* (Dublin, 1923, first published Dublin 1917), p.103.
21 L.N. Le Roux, *Patrick H Pearse* (translated by Desmond Ryan, Dublin, 1932), pp.200–01.
22 D. Ferriter, 'Commemorating the Rising, 1922–65' in Mary Daly and Margaret O'Callaghan (eds), *1916 in 1966: Commemorating the Rising* (Dublin, 2007), pp.198–218.
23 D. Ferriter, *Ambiguous Republic: Ireland in the 1970s* (London, 2012), p.241.
24 R. Dudley Edwards, 'Is it unpatriotic to be honest?', *Irish Times*, 1 April 1991.
25 Ibid.
26 M. Leland, 'Pearse the Educator', *Irish Times*, 2 May 1977.
27 Ibid.
28 See Ferriter, *Ambiguous Republic*, pp.238–42.
29 Ibid.
30 Ibid.
31 J.J. Lee, 'In Search of Patrick Pearse' in Máirín Ní Dhonnchadha and Theo Dorgan (eds), *Revising the Rising* (Derry, 1991), pp.122–39.
32 R. Higgins and R. Uí Chollatáin (eds), *The Life and After-Life of PH Pearse* (Dublin, 2009) pp.xvii
33 Ibid.
34 J.J. Lee, 'Pearse, Patrick, Henry', *DIB*.
35 See Macardle, 'James Connolly and Patrick Pearse', *SMI*, p.192.
36 Ibid., p.195.

CHAPTER 16

The Guinnesses and Beyond

J.J. LEE

1 Introduction

The history of business in Ireland was, for long, even more neglected than business itself. Happily this is increasingly being rectified as the study of business as a legitimate subject of historical enquiry has become more widely acknowledged; however, much still remains to be done. The splendid 1969 volume, *Conor Cruise O'Brien Introduces Ireland*, edited by the inspirational Owen Dudley Edwards, reflected the still incubational state of business history in Ireland in having no chapter explicitly focusing on business. It should be acknowledged that the chapter 'The Economic Scene' by Patrick Lynch, Associate Professor of Economics at University College Dublin (UCD), a bank director and director of Aer Lingus, admirably reflects the optimism of the 1960s. However, it focuses more on government policy and public attitudes than on the performance of individual companies per se.[1]

For our purposes, it is fortunate that two iconic firms, Guinness in Dublin and Harland and Wolff in Belfast, have been the subjects of indispensable company histories.[2] Indeed, by happy coincidence Patrick Lynch himself was co-author with John Vaizey of the first volume of the two volume history of Guinness.

Yet, it is striking how little attention can still be paid to the performance of individual companies, even the most successful ones, as if they can be subsumed under the general heading of business, and how little attempt is often made in general histories to identify the reasons for, as distinct from occasionally recording the results of, their exceptional success. It often seems that success – or for that matter failure – just happened. As useful a pioneering compilation as E.J. Riordan's *Modern Irish Trade and Industry* allows Guinness, already a world leader in its field, one paragraph and doesn't allow another outstandingly successful company, Jacob's the biscuit makers, a solitary reference. W.P. Coyne's *Ireland: Industrial and Agricultural* remains a useful compilation, but compilation it still is, venturing little analysis of the material it so assiduously accumulated. These things apparently just happened.

That impression is being gradually overcome, though still companies occupy a subordinate place in as outstanding an economic history of modern Ireland as that of Cormac Ó Gráda, in which Guinness receives only one index reference.[3]

Even the splendid county history series by Geography Publications, which has pushed back so many frontiers of our history, has relatively little on business history.

These lacunae in even highly impressive works are perfectly understandable in the historiographical circumstances, and yet to neglect the business history of a country is to neglect a crucial factor in the quality of not just economic, but overall, national performance.

2 Guinness

Even if I took issue a long time ago with some of the emphases in the first volume of the commissioned history of Guinness, by Lynch and Vaizey,[4] I can only applaud their wider achievement in helping elevate business history into the mainstream of historical studies in Ireland, protracted though the parturition process has proven to be, as well as applauding the initiative of the company in commissioning the history, thus pioneering major business historiography as they had earlier pioneered many of the techniques of business success in building one of the great global companies.

A great merit of the Lynch and Vaizey volumes is that they make it crystal clear that there was nothing preordained about the rise of the firm. The main variable appears to have been the sustainability of management ability over several generations, a rare experience in firms that remained under family control. The experience of the brewing industry may have been exceptional, but it was far from preordained. A striking comparison can be drawn between the relative fortunes of Guinness of Dublin and Beamish and Crawford of Cork. An early nineteenth-century forecaster might have discounted as wildly improbable the relative future fortunes of the two firms. Beamish and Crawford's output of 119,400 barrels in 1807 compared with Guinness's 29,520, provided no hint of the turn-around by 1845, with Guinness now producing 81,441 barrels, nearly double Beamish and Crawford's 45,892 – and though the Cork firm recovered to 112,826 barrels by 1875, this now lagged far behind Guinness's 725,791.[5]

Guinness took rapid advantage of two fortuitous opportunities to grow itself into a firm with an all-Ireland and not simply a local Dublin market. A Dublin location allowed it to exploit potential markets which opened up in the decade after 1845 because of the railway lines radiating from Dublin to Cork, Limerick, Galway and Belfast, enabling Guinness to penetrate markets around the country, while investing in railways, and taking positions on railway boards, with the result that, by 1864, over half the beer sold outside Dublin was Guinness.[6] Given Ireland's declining population after 1845 it is sometimes difficult to recall that growing monetisation actually increased the size of the market in post-Famine Ireland when one considers pockets rather than persons. And the spread of railways in England also helped open up parts of the English market so that Guinness was able to consider at least parts of England as a home market, Liverpool and Manchester being closer to them, in terms of transport costs, than to many English or Scottish manufacturers.

The other expanding sector, which Guinness also participated in, was banking. It was no accident that leading Irish businessmen sought to ensure their access to both markets and capital by acquiring directorships in the main railway companies and banks. Those who are authorities on the rise of Guinness to preeminence among Irish breweries, when Beamish and Crawford appeared better placed in the early nineteenth century, attribute the remarkable achievement to Guinness's good fortune that the family produced four generations of able managers who took the company from its solid but unexceptional first-generation achievement to its unique standing a century later, not only in Ireland but in the United Kingdom.

Indeed, few could have predicted, as long as eighty years after its foundation in 1759, that Guinness would become such a global brand during the following eighty years. Whereas it accounted for only about 7 per cent of total Irish beer output in 1837, this had risen to 29 per cent in 1871 before increasing dramatically to 75 per cent by 1900, including no less than 96 per cent of the Irish export trade in beer.[7]

Though several reasons can be adduced for this spectacular spurt that transformed Guinness into the most renowned brewery in the world, a few of those reasons can be identified as crucial. Bielenberg, the outstanding authority on the subject, notes a sharp contrast between Guinness and its Irish competitors. The latter, including Beamish and Crawford, relied on the tied-house system to capture the market, thus tying up a substantial amount of their capital in property. Being tied up meant, in effect, being tied down, with capital being diverted from reinvestment in production to investment in control of outlets. Guinness, on the contrary, opted to concentrate on the production of a high-quality product, counting on reliability and taste to enhance their reputation and expand their markets. This, incidentally, allowed them to think in terms of export markets where their product had to compete on capturing consumer taste rather than control of public houses. Their reliance on quality and taste even went so far as inducing them to refrain from transporting their own products outside Dublin, confident that their quality would speak for itself. Taste, in turn, depended on reliability, and it can be no coincidence that Guinness invested heavily, by the later nineteenth century, on recruiting Oxbridge science graduates to sustain or even enhance the quality of their renowned porter and stout.

Guinness was, of course, a family business. But what a family! When MacDonagh insists that its history is *sui generis*, one must agree with him – subject to the proviso that the same can potentially be said of every firm and of every family. The challenge for the historian is to extract the highest common denominator, as well as to identify the unique, or at least distinctive, features. MacDonagh's characteristically probing and pungent preface to the 1886–1939 volume, by reaching back to 1868, compensates for the fact that the decade 1876–86 appears to have somehow slipped partly out of sight between the two volumes. But in this brief preface he virtually relieves later historians of the burden of interpretive uncertainty about the nature of the firm, identifying with characteristic acuity the distinctive features of its success, asking how it had, since 1800, 'emerged from the ruck of moderately sized Dublin establishments to become the largest brewery' in the world? [8]

What made it distinctive was not only the product but the family. Ireland had no shortage of breweries. But Guinness was essentially managed for over a century by what MacDonagh calls 'a monarchical succession of four' Guinnesses – the first two Arthurs, Benjamin Lee and Edward Cecil, the first Earl of Iveagh. This is accurate, except that the notion of 'monarchical succession', at least in accordance with the English model, is the wrong description, for – and this was crucial – 'primogeniture was not allowed to interfere with the best management'.[9] In fact, no eldest son succeeded. 'Eventually', MacDonagh confidently asserts, 'the finest was always chosen, or forced himself forward from the pool of young Guinness males'.[10]

And what a pool it was, for it was nothing if not a prolific clan. How precisely this occurred over time – how they managed to engineer, generation after generation, such 'selection of the fittest' for the running of the business – remains, however, obscure, as the internal functioning of family relationships often must. Nevertheless, it was a crucial factor in the firm's success. When one talks of 'family firms', emphasis must be placed on family as well as on firm. Strictly speaking we can never know if it was the finest who were chosen – and by what process – for there may have been lurking even greater potential among the also rans – or the nonrunners, particularly as the chosen one had to become involved at an early age. However, it is hard to imagine that the most celebrated of them all, Edward Cecil, was not, in fact, an inspired choice.

Edward Cecil, sole proprietor of the brewery when it was sold to the public in 1886, had been apprenticed to the business as early as 1862 at the age of fifteen, and developed his own formidable managerial talent under the guidance of an extraordinarily accomplished general manager, J.T. Purser.[12] While Edward Cecil was the fourth Guinness to assume control, J. T. Purser was the third of the Purser family to serve sequentially in a position of decision-making responsibility within the company. The first, John Purser senior, had been appointed as chief clerk in 1799, bookkeeper in 1811, and a partner in 1820, followed by John Purser junior, who progressed from a position as an apprentice brewer in 1799 to become a partner like his father in 1820. These two men were followed by John Tertius Purser (1809–93) – son of John Purser junior – apprenticed as early as 1824, who would become general manager in 1862 and serve in effect as Edward Cecil's right-hand man, retiring only in 1886. Indeed at times the firm might have more properly been called Guinness and Pursers rather than Guinness alone. It may even have been fortunate for the firm that Claude Guinness, Sir Edward's distant cousin and brother-in-law, educated at Winchester and New College,

Oxford and recruited in 1881 with a view to his succeeding J.T. Purser as general manager[13] died in 1894 after some years of declining health, for his potential seems to have been limited.[14]

3 The Context of Business Success

MacDonagh's conclusion is hard to rebut. Guinness succeeded in isolating itself as effectively from its 'times' as from the remainder of its trade in general. In the last analysis, it was, on almost every count, 'one of a kind'.[15] It almost sounds as if Guinness was in Ireland but not of it. It would be a foolhardy historian who would venture to express a reservation about so acute an analyst as Oliver MacDonagh. And yet, some queries remain.

Was the Guinness record due to the sheer chance of a sequence of talent, with one man emerging from four successive family generations endowed with exceptional business talent? If so, can any lessons of wider inference be drawn from that? Was it due to the sheer chance of the genes in a single family that allowed decisions to be taken about the succession that led to its extraordinary preeminence in due course? And if so, how much of the genetic thrust may have come from the distaff side? Given the importance of the gene pool in Ireland's greatest business success, one of the few reservations one can express about the authorised history is how little attention is paid in it to the wives and mothers. Not a single mother features in the index under Guinness in the second volume. Can it really be that all of the Guinness females have been completely irrelevant to the performance of the children?

Lynch and Vaizey do indeed pay attention to two wives. In 1873, Edward Cecil, who would buy out his brother in 1886, married Adelaide Guinness, daughter of his second cousin, 'a strikingly handsome woman, highly intelligent, as energetic as her husband, and, like him, forceful and determined in character'. [16] It seems improbable that she was wholly uninvolved in the issues that consumed her husband; this was in contrast to the wife of Edward's brother, Sir Arthur – later Lord Ardilaun, who would give Stephen's Green, where his statue still stands, to Dublin – 'Lady Olivia Charlotte White, the daughter of the third Earl of Bantry'. Lynch and Vaizey discreetly refer to how she 'was known to lack sympathy with her husband's connexion with the brewing trade'.[17] Was it a happy business chance that 'they were childless and Edward's children were heirs to the brewery'?[18]

The convention by which business history and family history tend to be segregated in the more austere recesses of economic history may disguise, from those preoccupied with economic performance, the potential importance of internal family relationships in business circles. It is arguable that family history may in some, maybe many, cases be an integral part of business history, and that business history should, therefore, be embedded *a priori* much more firmly in social history.

At its most elementary the distribution of the genes may have made a significant difference to business history, and not least in the Irish case. Might it have made a difference to Irish economic development if so outstanding an Irish business figure, the great railway builder and contractor, William Dargan, had not died childless? W.R. Le Fanu, himself a civil engineer and commissioner of public works, who had worked under Dargan, would recall twenty-five years after Dargan's death, 'in my life I have never met a man more quick in intelligence, more clear sighted and more thoroughly honourable'.[19] There can, of course, be no guarantee that these qualities, or indeed any of them, would have distinguished his putative offspring – but who can know?

It is easy to overlook the role of chance – not least the chance of personal connections – in assessing business history. The most spectacular, if not the most ultimately enduring, of all success stories in business in Ireland was that of Harland and Wolff, the celebrated Belfast shipbuilders. Yet the number of chance relationships out of which it emerged also warns of how it might never have emerged, at least in that form. Moss attributes the yard's initial success to Wolff's connection with Schwabe and his range of contacts that enabled him to bring regular business to the yard.[20] But who was Schwabe? He was related by marriage to Edward Harland's uncle, Thomas, a medical practitioner in Salford. By 1840 Schwabe was a partner in the successful Liverpool agency house of Sykes, Schwabe and Company, and in the 1840s he became a partner in the shipping company of John Bibby & Sons. It was this range of contacts, originally arising from family relationships, that made him so crucial to the early success of the great Belfast company.

The lack of coal, the crucial raw material of the first age of the industrial revolution, seriously restricted the potential openings for Irish business. Nevertheless companies of distinction did emerge, if mainly in the consumer goods sector. If they hadn't we'd probably not give it a second thought, so long were we habituated to assuming that Ireland was destined to be mainly an agricultural country due to the scarcity of the raw materials of the industrial revolution. And yet a number of individual firms, even if none so spectacularly as Guinness, emerged out of the darkness, so to speak; these defy generalisations based on assumptions about the inevitability of industrial backwardness.

4 Jacob's

Jacob's Biscuits is a classic case in point. During the 1840s William Beale Jacob (1825–1902) took over the modest family business in Waterford, including a bread and biscuit bakery. He soon invested in steam-based machinery in opening a Dublin location in 1853, and expanded sufficiently rapidly to begin exporting to North Wales in 1862. Jacob's became a limited company in 1883, and he would leave an estate of 82,000 pounds on his death in 1902 – maybe 5,000,000 in today's money. His son, George Newson Jacob, 1854–1942, became managing director of the company in 1883, and introduced the highly successful cream cracker to the English market in 1885, based on a biscuit he saw on a tour of the USA. His biscuits soon enjoyed sufficient success in England for him to open a depot in Liverpool and appoint an agent in London.

Although a relatively benevolent employer, as one would expect from a businessman in the Quaker tradition, during the Lock-out of 1913 he took a very hard line against his workers, including the women, imposing demeaning conditions to permit their return after their defeat in the Spring of 1914.[21] He surfaces further in general history by virtue of having his factory occupied by rebels in 1916, but he did well out of the First World War, supplying the army with 1,200,000 packets of biscuits. In spite of this, he threatened to leave the country in 1922 if tariffs were introduced and he even considered splitting the company into English and Irish entities. Jacob's became a public company in 1928, becoming one of the state's three top exporters.[22] Jacob's is yet another example of a successful company that, if it didn't exist, we might be inclined to assume it never could have.

Much of Irish economic history is a record of defeat, or at least of defeatism. There are a number of companies, including the whiskey companies, Jameson's, Power's and Paddy, or the fertiliser company, Goulding's, – that have achieved success globally, though, as with Jacob's, if they had not, we may have assumed they could not. And yet what a different country it might have been, or at least what a different atmosphere might have prevailed, if there had been more like them. For much of the century after the Famine, including the period when the country was asserting its political independence, Ireland may have suffered as much from economic defeatism as from political domination or administrative conservatism. Those who succeeded economically deserve to have the sources of their success explored, and to have the question posed, 'Why weren't there more like them?'

Answers to this question ideally require a comparative perspective on business performance in the Irish diaspora no less than in Ireland. Given the role many in the diaspora have played in the domestic politics of Ireland, and given the variety of circumstances which emigrants experienced in different destinations, it may be argued that a full understanding of the business experience of Ireland itself can be acquired only by placing it in a rigorous comparative perspective to ascertain what factors operated across the diaspora, and what were distinctive to specific places and periods. Such a project, crossing continents and centuries, would, of course, be hugely ambitious, perhaps indeed chimerical, but it is only by placing the performance in Ireland itself in the totality of global Irish performance that we can reasonably confidently hazard generalisations about the impact of 'national' identity, and of transnational experience, on the relative roles of character, culture and circumstance in Irish economic performance. From a wider perspective, one of the most rewarding approaches for understanding ourselves at home may be to follow the routes to economic success – or indeed failure – not forgetting that one of the most distinctive features of Irish emigration is the remarkably balanced gender ratio of our emigrants, at least since the Great Famine.

A host of other questions suggest themselves for further exploration. Does the Max Weber thesis of the relationship between Protestantism and economic growth find support in the Irish experience? For that matter, how would one assess the actual historical experience in Ireland against reasonable expectations of what would, or rather might, have happened in other political circumstances, whether South or North?

The conceptual challenge now is how most effectively to advance our understanding of Irish economic performance through an ever deeper engagement with economic history in the broadest sense. This kind of analysis requires an understanding of how we have come to be where we are, to probe beneath the headlines and the surface manifestations, as best we can, to identify the crucial factors influencing economic performance. One important factor within the context of this kind of analysis is the recognition that so small and open an economy will often be at the mercy of factors beyond its control, and must value a capacity for adaptability, both to immediate circumstances and to longer-term trends, in so far as they can be identified. These are crucial but immeasurable variables in Irish economic performance, both in private and public sectors and in the conduct of our affairs both internally and externally and, in order to respond to them, we must have quick minds, and must devise structures and stratagem by pulling together across the board, in the public sectors, state institutions and private sector organisations. That, of course, is a counsel of human perfection which we need never delude ourselves will ever be fully achieved, but the closer a small, open economy comes to it, the more effective its performance.

The internationalising of Irish business, not least the arrival of American companies, the growth of exports to the European Union and wider world markets, has transformed the external environment in which Irish business – one should rather say business in Ireland – operates, while the establishment of business schools in universities has helped transform the image, and the ambitions, of a younger generation of business people. Family connections remain important, as they inevitably will in small, face-to-face, societies, but conditions have, nevertheless, altered almost beyond recognition as Ireland has changed with striking speed since the late fifties, and more emphatically still since our entry to the European Economic Community, and as our horizons have lifted beyond the confines of 'these islands'. But much though circumstances continue to change, there are still valuable lessons to be learned, if only we can get them right, from an understanding of our business history, and of how we have come from then to now.

5 Conclusion

The men and women of 1916 were not primarily interested in business performance, although they dreamed of the benign consequences of impressive national economic performance, but without much idea of how to go about achieving it. If Pearse indulged an idealised image of the fruits of economic growth, he remained singularly silent on how one would actually achieve it. The Proclamation of the Republic declares its resolve 'to pursue the happiness and prosperity of the whole nation, and of all its parts' – was that meant to be a sop to unionists? – but it remains studiously silent on how the prosperity is to be attained. Means are, of course, crucial to ends, and there is not much point pondering the fair distribution of the fruits of prosperity if there is little idea of how to achieve it in the first place. It seems singularly appropriate that we should ponder these matters, however schematically, as the centenary of the Rising draws upon us.

Further Reading:

A. Bielenberg, *Ireland and the Industrial Revolution: The Impact of the Industrial Revolution on Irish Industry, 1801–1922* (London, 2009)

A. Bielenberg, *Cork's Industrial Revolution, 1780–1880* (Cork, 1991)

A. Bielenberg, 'The Irish Brewing Industry and the Rise of Guinness, 1790–1914', in R.G. Wilson and T.R. Gourvish (eds), *The Dynamics of the International Brewing Industry* (London, 1998), pp.105–22

L. Kennedy, *An Economic History of Ulster, 1820–1940* (Manchester, 1985)

C. Ó Gráda, 'Did Ireland 'under'-industrialise?', *Irish Economic and Social History*, xxxviii (2010),pp.117–23

Notes

1   O. Dudley Edwards and C. Cruise O'Brien, *Conor Cruise O'Brien Introduces Ireland* (London, 1969).

2   M.L. Moss and J.R. Hume, *Shipbuilders to the World: 125 Years of Harland and Wolff, Belfast 1861–1986* (Blackstaff, 1986).

3   C.Ó Gráda, *Ireland: A New Economic History, 1780–1939* (Oxford, 1994), p.304.

4   J.J. Lee, *Economic History Review*, xix, 1, 1966, pp.183–90, and their reply, pp.190–94.

5   A. Bielenberg, *Cork's Industrial Revolution 1780–1880* (Cork, 1991), p.58.

6   P. Lynch and J. Vaizey, *Guinness's Brewery in the Irish Economy* (Cambridge, 1960), p.201.

7   Ibid. p. 235.

8   S.R. Denison and O. MacDonagh, *Guinness 1886–1939* (Cork, 1998), p.x.

9   Ibid.

10 Ibid.

11 Ibid., pp.x-xi.

12 Ibid., p.6.

13 Ibid., p.7.

14 Ibid., p. 33.

15 Ibid., p.xiii.

16 See Lynch and Vaizey, *Guinness's Brewery,* p.190.

17 Ibid.

18 Ibid.

19 W.R. Le Fanu, *Seventy Years of Irish Life* (London. 1893), p.208.

20 M.S. Moss, 'Wolff, Gustav Wilhelm (1834–1913)', *Oxford Dictionary of National Biography* (online edition).

21 P. McCaffrey, 'Jacob's women workers during the 1913 lockout', *Saothar,* 16, 1991, pp.118–29.

22 P.J. Dempsey, 'William Beale Jacob', *DIB.*

CHAPTER 17

HANNA AND FRANK SHEEHY-SKEFFINGTON

MARGARET WARD

1 Introduction

Hanna Sheehy-Skeffington described the Proclamation as 'the only instance … where men fighting for freedom voluntarily included women'.[1] That declaration of an Irish Republic was addressed to 'Irishmen and Irishwomen', promising 'equal rights and equal opportunities' and pledging a government 'elected by the suffrages of all her men and women'. What influenced the seven men who put their name to that document? More specifically, *who* influenced them? A large part of the answer is contained in the contribution of Frank and Hanna Sheehy-Skeffington to the causes of women's equality, peace, social and economic justice and Irish national independence. Their careers are an integral part of our 'Decade of Centenaries'.

Hanna Sheehy, eldest daughter of David Sheehy, a former Fenian who later became a venerable member of the Irish Parliamentary Party, could trace a continuity within her family between different generations who had struggled for freedom. She boasted that her great grandmother had known Lord Edward Fitzgerald, the United Irelander killed in 1798 – 'she was 106 when she died, so I actually touched the withered hand that had clasped his'. As a young child, a 'chit of four' she called herself, she visited her uncle, imprisoned for Land League activities.[2] Political imprisonment held an honoured place in family history.

Frank Skeffington, Ulster-born and home-schooled by a school inspector father who thought all schools unworthy of his son, was an only child brought up to hold strong opinions on all manner of issues, although Dr J.B. Skeffington never envisaged his son developing into a person holding so many deeply-held, radical views.

Hanna and Frank met at university, where Hanna acknowledged that Frank was the person to introduce her to feminism. On their marriage in 1903, the joining of Hanna Sheehy with Frank Skeffington into a new entity, the Sheehy-Skeffingtons, symbolised what would be a partnership of equals. They supported each other in all activities, complemented each other's strengths, and struggled equally to be good partners and parents to Owen, their son. Hanna became an effective public speaker and polemicist, whilst Frank was the indefatigable editor of the *Irish Citizen*, an invaluable tool of the Irish suffrage movement and indispensable source for historians today. Hanna wrote articles and reviews for the paper, often under pseudonyms, while Frank wrote combative editorials and delighted in engaging with his critics. Despite his own views, he was always generous in his coverage, with all suffrage organisations represented in the paper. She was often the main financial provider in the relationship, at least until she lost work as a teacher following her first imprisonment in 1912. After Frank resigned his position as registrar of University College Dublin (in protest at the unequal treatment of women in higher education), his income from journalism was sporadic and not always paid. They were part of pre-revolutionary bohemian Dublin; their friends were also those who valued intellectual pursuits over material ambition.

2 Militant Feminists

Frank's close friend James Joyce had ridiculed him for remaining Catholic while calling himself a rationalist, provoking Frank to think seriously about religion. For the first years of their marriage both Frank and Hanna continued to be practising Catholics but before their son was born they had, as Owen said of his parents, 'thought themselves out' of all religious belief, becoming 'convinced rationalists and humanists'.[3] Hanna was now no longer able to teach in convents. Rejecting long-held beliefs was not easy. On her first hunger-strike, she briefly considered confession, eliciting an impassioned response from Frank: 'I don't see how you could ever have contemplated confession. Let them associate suffragism with atheism if they like – they will be right! This is one of the things on which I am drastic and can't understand compromise.' She never again capitulated. While dying, she urged her son to remember that she had no religion and a priest was unnecessary, declaring, 'I am an unrepentant pagan.'

Hanna and Frank, together with their close friends James and Margaret Cousins, formed the Irish Women's Franchise League (IWFL) in 1908, as a new departure in Irish feminist politics, developing a programme 'suitable to the different political situation of Ireland as between a subject-country seeking freedom from England and England, a free country'.[4] Unlike other groups, they would use militant tactics if necessary. By 1912 the IWFL claimed around 1,000 members, with 160 male associates. For Hanna, the organisation 'helped women to self-expression through service … for the first time in history, not for a man's cause but their own.'[5] This was a controversial claim, given the existence of the nationalist women's group, Inghinidhe na hÉireann, set up in 1900 by Maud Gonne. She had engaged in argument with the Inghinidhe feminists over the years, calling on them to 'set about working out their own political salvation', arguing that the vote was 'the keystone of citizenship' even if it had to be wrested from an 'alien government'.[6]

After years of deputations, petitions and demonstrations, militancy began in June 1912 when it was evident that women would be excluded from the terms of the Home Rule Bill. While planning their attacks, Hanna insisted on Dublin Castle, centre of British rule in Ireland, 'avenging the treasured wrongs of fifty years'. Women, she wrote, had resorted to violence 'on their own behalf' and Irish people should understand, because 'the stone and the shillelagh need no apologia; they have an honoured place in the history of argument'. With sarcasm she condemned 'the average man', who only applauds 'the stone-thrower as long as the missile is flung for them and not at them'.[7] She was sentenced to two month's imprisonment. Frank 'came pretty well every day; he enjoyed the experience vicariously and urged us on even to the hunger-strike. He was never amenable to the Governor's suggestion to advise his wife to be "sensible"'. Owen, aged three, also came, continuing the family tradition of prison visits. Frank's letters to Hanna, smuggled into jail, are revealing in their portrayal of a political and personal partnership based on total commitment and support. They also show Frank's vulnerability, realising the toll political activities were taking on their marriage, 'I'm afraid I've been inclined to forget the human needs of ourselves in our work for humanity. Not that I'm not proud of all you've done dearest; but in future I think I'll keep you a bit more to myself!' That was not to happen.

In those suffrage years both shrugged off ridicule, eviction from meetings and the wrath of the Hibernians, when it was unsafe to hold open-air meetings for fear of mob violence. Such was Frank's determination, he even argued against James Connolly when the latter urged temporarily stopping meetings after the two men had been forced to retreat to the safety of Dublin zoo. Connolly had travelled down from Belfast especially to show solidarity with the women's cause. Frank continued to stress the importance of the 'moral effect' of such meetings. As James Stephens described him, he was 'absurdly courageous'.[8]

The Sheehy-Skeffingtons were clear-headed on the challenges that existed. Having been supporters of the Irish Parliamentary Party, they came to reject it for its hostility to women's emancipation, vested interest in the licensed trade and acceptance of clerical influence. Achieving Home Rule was only the beginning. After meeting Frank in March 1913, Rosamund Jacob wrote in her diary, 'He expects rough times if Home Rule materialises, fighting clerical and capitalist influences, says we shall probably all be executed or banished.' He added that after suffrage was won 'the first battle must be against the priests'.[9] His widow would continue that battle in the ensuing decades.

3 Pacifism and Militarism

After the start of war, Frank combined newspaper polemics with anti-war speeches. It was a desperate effort to combat what he denounced as an imperialist war that the Irish Parliamentary Party would drag Ireland into, thereby providing a rationale for Irish retaliation and more bloodshed. His initial response was the furious headline 'Votes for Women – Damn Your War!' and he began a frenzied round of public meetings against recruitment, on the grounds that 'war can breed nothing but a fresh crop of wars. If we want to stop war we must begin by stopping this war. The only way we can do that is to hamper as far as possible the conduct of it. The best way to do that is to stop recruiting.' For him, war was the antithesis of feminism: 'Men, and more men, is the cry of the war-lords. Women count only as producers of men...start by assuming the emancipation of women...Humanity – man and woman – can proceed to construct its Utopias, to organise a social system based on peace and co-operation...'[10] He, Constance Markievicz and James Connolly were participants in a short-lived Irish Neutrality League; Frank believed a decisive victory for either side would mean 'Imperialism will be rampant.'[11]

Hanna was an equally impassioned propagandist, recognising that war would mean women being persuaded to 'roll up the map of suffrage... and forget their own pressing economic and political grievances'. Controversially, she argued against engaging in war relief work: 'it is not for us to mitigate by one iota the horrors of war', urging women instead to 'lend a hand – not at mopping up the blood and purifying the stench of the abattoir, but at clearing away the whole rotten system'. Until then, it was their duty to increase their activities, 'to preach peace, sanity and suffrage'.[12] By now she had experienced a second prison sentence and had undertaken a further hunger strike. She would also be arrested, briefly, when she and her colleague Meg Connery attempted to make speeches while Prime Minister Asquith visited Dublin on a recruitment mission. The nationalist women's organisation, Cumann na mBan, formed in support of the work of the Irish Volunteers, she dismissed as 'animated collecting boxes' because of their auxiliary status and perceived timidity in standing up for women's equality, but it was towards the men she directed her anger: 'women the ministering angel of the ambulance class, who provides the pyjamas and the lint, but who sinks below the human the moment she asks for a vote!' Both Sheehy-Skeffingtons continually challenged the Volunteers to explain why they would not define the words 'rights' and 'liberties' to make it clear that they intended to extend them 'without distinction of sex, class or creed'.[13]

Hanna was one of the Irish delegates chosen to attend the Women's International Peace Congress planned for the Hague in May 1915 and was jubilant that Ireland could have separate representation from that of the British, 'It is the hour of small nationalities.' The Irish resolution for the Congress urged: 'Subject Nationalities ... be offered a path to freedom ... by plebiscite of their men and women effectively to declare whether they are contented with their lot or would prefer a change of government.' By this they hoped further war could be prevented. In the end, the British government refused travel permits to Irish and British delegates, also closing the North Sea to shipping, so none of the Irish women could attend. They organised a protest meeting, at which Thomas MacDonagh, a suffrage supporter, close friend of the Sheehy-Skeffingtons and now Director of Training for the Irish Volunteers spoke in support of the motion of protest. Patrick Pearse sent a message hoping that the incident would 'do good if it ranges more of the women definitely with the national forces', provoking a furious reaction from Meg Connery, chairing the meeting, who retorted this was a 'masculine inversion' and the national forces should be on the side of women. MacDonagh, while in support of the women, argued that 'they were all helpless under the ruling oligarchies'; it was why he had 'helped to arm tens of thousands of Irish men for defence' and why he was now instructing men 'how to bayonet their fellow-man and how to put their foot upon his body and pull out the bayonet afterwards. It was disgusting and nobody could hate it more than he did.' This was an extraordinary contribution to a meeting ostensibly about peace. It was also an indication that some advanced nationalists believed it important to engage with feminists, and some feminists were very prepared to challenge the nationalists.

Not all feminists were sympathetic. Louie Bennett, suffragist and pacifist, wrote angrily to Hanna after the meeting that she would take no part in future 'peace meetings which put Irish nationalism above international tolerance and which are embittered by anti-English feuds'. Hanna's response revealed her to be willing to contemplate physical force, if it was conducted by those suffering from aggression and if there was a chance of success:

> A terrible war for reasons of commercial jealousy admits of no defence…But there are other pacifists (and I am one of them) who hold that while war must be ended if civilization is to reign supreme, nevertheless there may still be times when armed aggression ought to be met with armed defence…If I saw a hope of Ireland being freed forever from British rule by a swift uprising, I would consider Irishmen justified in resorting to arms in order that we might be free. I should still be radically opposed to war and militarism…But I hold no such hopes.[14]

Frank's pacifism was complex, and it did not necessarily rule out the use of arms, if this was for defensive reasons. His friend Con Curran had said he was always 'mounting barricades', possessing 'boundless' physical and moral courage[15], while J.F. Byrne, another old college friend said if you described him as a pacifist 'that was to classify him and you couldn't classify Skeffington'.[16] For example he was, initially, a strong supporter of the Citizen Army, formed during the bitter months of the Dublin

Lock-out, believing that when they were properly organised they would no longer be at the mercy of the police, and when that time came he accepted the necessity of acquiring arms for the use of the men. What he objected to was the cult of militarism, which he believed was becoming prevalent and which had been starkly displayed at the Hague meeting. His response was to issue a challenge to his friend, with the publication of an 'Open Letter to Thomas MacDonagh'. Frank shared some of the ambivalences expressed by both Hanna and MacDonagh, being 'in full sympathy with the fundamental objects of the Irish Volunteers', but, as MacDonagh had said of himself, his 'position was somewhat anomalous at a peace meeting'. The preparations the movement was making to kill were 'repellent'. What Frank hoped for was that 'the age-long fight against injustice clothe itself in new forms, suited to a new age'. Once again he questioned the omission of women, 'when you have found and clearly expressed the reason why women cannot be asked to enroll in this movement, you will be close to the reactionary element in the movement itself'. The only way out of this 'tangle' of achieving the objective of freedom without falling into the 'abyss' of militarism was to conceive of 'a body of men and women banded together to secure and maintain the rights and liberties of the people of Ireland...armed and equipped with the weapons of intellect and will that are irresistible'. He believed it to be 'the only way in which we, the oppressed and exploited, can reconcile our hatred of oligarchies and our hatred of organized bloodshed'.[17] Some of his questions would be answered in the assurances on equality contained in the Proclamation of the Republic, but not the fundamental challenge regarding the means deployed to achieve that goal.

Frank eventually made forty speeches against war, before being arrested at the end of May and given a six-month prison sentence. From the dock he made it clear he was an Irish nationalist as well as a pacifist:

> For twenty or thirty weeks I have pledged audiences of from 500 to 1,000 that they would passively resist Conscription...This prosecution...would be intelligible above all in a country held by force by another country...If you condemn me, you condemn the system you represent as being some or all of these things. Any sentence you may pass on me is a sentence upon British rule in Ireland.[18]

Proud to follow the suffragette example of hunger strike, he was released after seven days under the terms of the Cat and Mouse Act which, in rendering him liable to re-arrest for the balance of his sentence was, he said, 'a convenient method of getting rid of an opponent'.[19] As a consequence he spent four months in America, ostensibly to earn a living and to raise funds for the *Irish Citizen*, but much of the time desperately attempting to enlist American support for Ireland's right to be included in any peace talks as a small nation on a par with those in whose interests the war was supposedly being fought.

In a number of writings for the *New York Times* Frank attempted to convey to his new audience the urgency of the situation in Ireland. In November 1915 he wrote directly to President Wilson to ask for support for Irish recognition at any peace conference: if Ireland continued to be regarded merely as 'a province of England', Irish nationalists would 'continue their already well-advanced preparations to fight at the first opportunity'.[20] His article *A Forgotten Small Nationality* 'caused consternation in Dublin Castle', with the under-secretary suggesting to colleagues they read it to understand what was currently happening.[21] In it he described Ireland as 'still bleeding at every pore from the wounds England inflicted' and outlined two scenarios for the future: 'Must Irish freedom be gained in blood, or will the comity of nations, led by the United States, shame a weakened England into putting into practice at home the principles which are so loudly trumpeted for the benefit of Germany?'[22]

That same month the IWFL organised a public debate on the question 'Do We Want Peace Now?' Constance Markievicz argued that, as Britain was losing the war, it should continue in order to weaken Britain still further, while Frank argued strongly for pacifism. He appeared to be winning over the audience until James Connolly intervened with a powerful speech. Louie Bennett portrayed Connolly as 'the centre of danger' while Hanna, in a report for the *Irish Citizen*, wrote very differently of Connolly's twinkling eyes as he said 'I was afraid you might get the better of it Skeffington. That would never do.'[23] In the days before his execution, not knowing what had happened to Frank, Connolly would ask his family to make him executor of his writings, an indication of the esteem in which he held his friend.

4 The Easter Rising

In this period Frank continued to write and to warn of impending disaster, his friendship with MacDonagh and Connolly alerting him to a realisation that some kind of insurrection was being planned. He was a constant visitor to Liberty Hall so could not have failed to notice the heightened atmosphere, but still hoped that civil resistance to British rule could happen, talking to his father about a possible tax-resistance movement. Connolly's relationship with Hanna was different. He had given her a hint not to go away for Easter but to stay in Dublin. He also informed her that women had been given equal rights and equal opportunities in the Republican Proclamation. The leadership selected her to act as a member of a civil provisional government, to come into effect if the rising was prolonged. If that had occurred, she would have been the first woman to serve in an Irish government.

Frank was near Dublin Castle on Easter Monday, the first day of fighting. He risked his life trying to help a wounded British soldier, then walked around the centre of Dublin, pleading with rioters to stop the looting of shops which he feared would damage the idealism of an insurrection whose aims, if not methods, he supported. He returned to that task the second day, attempting to organise a civic police, while Hanna went to the General Post Office to offer her services to the insurgents. She had collected food from IWFL members and brought this to the College of Surgeons, where Markievicz later remembered her appearance through bullet-swept streets, adding 'I have nothing but pleasant and happy memories of the Sheehy-Skeffingtons. They always instinctively took the right side and were always ready to help.'[24]

Frank's arrest by Captain Bowen-Colthurst as he was going home that Tuesday evening was not surprising. Hanna said later that his previous arrest for opposing recruitment had proved he was 'offensive to the British authorities', and that his description had been 'circulated to the military immediately after the Easter Monday rising'. And of course Frank, with his knee-breeches, Votes for Women badge, red hair and beard was immediately recognisable. What was shocking, brutal and utterly indefensible was his summary execution and secret burial in the yard of Portobello Barracks and the subsequent cover-up by the British authorities, including ransacking his home and terrorising its inhabitants. There was international outcry and an outpouring of support for Hanna in her efforts to expose the truth. She met Prime Minister Asquith and made the British government agree to a public inquiry. Despite her efforts, the cover-up continued. Bowen-Colthurst, after a brief sojourn in a mental institution, was able to settle down in Canada while Sir Francis Vane, the officer who did so much to help her, was dismissed from the army. It was not a case of one temporarily deranged British officer. When Vane spoke to officers in Dublin Castle Major Price replied, 'Some of us think it was a good thing Sheehy-Skeffington was put out of the way, anyhow.'[25] That strengthened Vane's determination to seek justice.

Dismissing an offer of £10,000 compensation, Hanna travelled to America, to publicise her husband's murder and to gain American support for Ireland's right to be recognised as an independent small nation. Refused a passport, she had to smuggle Owen and herself over. Speaking at more than 250 meetings she assured her audience she was not there 'just to harrow your hearts by a passing thrill, to feed you on horrors for sensation's sake'. While admitting 'Sometimes it is harder to live for a cause than to die for it', she knew it would be a 'poor tribute' to her husband 'if grief were to break my spirit'. She described herself as someone who 'knew the Irish Republican leaders and (was) proud to have known them and had their friendship…they were filled with a high idealism'.

5   A Republican Feminist

Eva Gore-Booth was one of many who recognised that the 'relentless and irresistible way' in which Hanna had made public the full facts must have created 'little cold doubts' in the minds of many patriotic English regarding the severity 'by which the desperate struggle of insurgent nationality had been so quickly crushed'.[26] Despite the fact that her stature had warranted an audience with President Wilson, it was evident the British government now regarded Mrs Sheehy-Skeffington as an enemy of the state. On her return to Liverpool, in July 1918, she was refused permission to return to Ireland. She smuggled herself home, only to be arrested and returned to England, imprisoned in Holloway Jail with Maud Gonne and Kathleen Clarke. As an experienced suffragette she immediately went on hunger strike and was soon back in Ireland, now a member of Sinn Féin and shortly to become its Director of Organisation.

For a time she had seen her role only as witness for her husband's memory (and friends remarked that, all her life, 'she would bring his name into conversation as if they had been together but a moment before'), but her sense of self re-emerged, as did her determination to continue to fight for a free and egalitarian Ireland. She and Louie Bennett worked somewhat uneasily together, editing the *Irish Citizen* until its end in 1920. With IWFL colleagues and women from Cumann na mBan, she campaigned to ensure that the imprisoned Markievicz was successful in the 1918 election. She had wanted to stand for election herself, but was offered only an unwinnable seat. She opposed the treaty, condemning it as being for 'the vested interests…the propertied classes', undemocratically imposed on the Irish people, as an out-of-date electoral register meant many young men and no women between the ages of 21–30 could vote on the issue. Lobbying in support of extension of the franchise for those young women was, she wrote to a friend, almost like old suffrage times. She was conscious that partition ('a crazy patchwork frontier') cut off the Skeffington family from the twenty-six counties.

Frank was never far from her thoughts, but while she described him as a 'fighting pacifist', in reviewing Sean O'Casey's account of the Irish Citizen Army, she was uncomfortable with his idealisation of Frank and condemnation of Connolly. She would not allow Frank to be used as a way of criticising the insurgents: 'What matter which is the Socialist or Nationalist hero: both died as they lived for their ideals…One to Peace and one to Freedom and neither looked for fame or laurels, in death or in life.'[27]

Her allies were radical republicans like Peadar O'Donnell and Frank Ryan. When they were imprisoned she edited their journals. Banned from entry to the North, she was arrested in 1933 for crossing into Newry to speak on behalf of imprisoned women republicans, declaring from the dock 'I would be ashamed of my murdered husband if I admitted that I was an alien in Armagh, Down, Derry or any of the 32 counties.' After serving a one-month prison sentence thousands greeted her as she made a triumphal motorcade tour home.

In her last years, feminist rather than nationalist considerations again dominated her political activities. She was a leading figure in the opposition to much anti-woman legislation, above all in the fight against the 1937 constitution of Éamon de Valera, which she described as 'fascist', calling, as did many feminists, for the restoration of the 1916 equal rights and equal opportunities for women. In her last campaign, three years before her death, she stood unsuccessfully for the Dáil, one of four women who hoped their example would lead to the formation of a women's party. She wanted Connolly's ideal of a Workers' Republic and her platform was an unambiguous call for equality for women, complete independence for Ireland and the abolition of partition, but by then the radicalism she espoused was out of favour, and would be for several more decades. Her last article, supporting the Irish Housewives League showed that her caustic humour and feminist views had not diminished with age: 'These clumsy man-made words remind us how little free we really are, so "housewife" is accepted more or less meekly by most women as we accept men's names in marriage and live in their inconveniently-constructed houses.'[28] Her critique of the influence of patriarchy remains utterly relevant today.

6 Conclusion

This article has highlighted key moments when the Sheehy-Skeffingtons, individually or collectively, urged those planning revolution to define the interests in whose name they would fight, and to justify the methods to be used to achieve those ends. As a couple, their feminism was rooted in a conviction that women's emancipation could only be fully realised with national independence and their commitment to nationalism was as deeply felt as those who took the path of armed insurrection. The historic commitment to women's equality contained in the Proclamation was not due solely to their efforts (one must acknowledge the contribution of feminists in Inghinidhe na hÉireann and the Irish Citizen Army), but the issue was placed centre stage on the political agenda once the feminists of the IWFL, through their militant activities, brought to public attention the fact that the debate over future Home Rule ignored women. The revolutionaries, in choosing Hanna for their provisional government, recognised her capabilities. It is significant that those in positions of leadership afterwards did not support her desire to stand as candidate in the 1918 election. She became disillusioned by what she saw as a failure in revolution, regarding the Irish Free State as 'rapidly becoming a Catholic statelet under Rome's grip',[29] but never stopped supporting progressive movements. For a further three decades Hanna fought valiantly in an attempt to move the new independent state beyond tokenistic equality, to embrace the social and economic justice she and Frank had fought for and which was promised in the Proclamation.

Further Reading:

C. Beaumont, 'Women, Citizenship and Catholicism in the Irish Free State 1922–1948', *Women's History Review*, 6:4, 1997, pp.563–585

R. Cullen Owens, *Louie Bennett* (Cork, 2001)

R. M. Fox, *Rebel Irishwomen* (Dublin, 1935)

D. Hearne, 'The Irish Citizen, 1914–1916: Nationalism, Feminism and Militarism', *Canadian Journal of Irish Studies*, xviii, 1, July 1992, pp.1–15

L. Levenson and J.Natterstad, *Hanna Sheehy Skeffington, Irish Feminist* (New York, 1986)

M. Luddy, *Hanna Sheehy Skeffington* (Dundalk, 1995)

C. Murphy, *The Women's Suffrage Movement and Irish Society in the Early Twentieth Century* (Hertfordshire, 1989)

L. Ryan, *Irish Feminism and the Vote: An Anthology of the Irish Citizen Newspaper 1912–1920* (Dublin, 1996)

A. Sheehy Skeffington, *Skeff: A Life of Owen Sheehy Skeffington 1909–1970* (Dublin, 1991)

H. Sheehy Skeffington, 'Reminiscences of an Irish Suffragette' in *Votes for Women: Irish Women's Struggle for the Vote*, edited by A. Sheehy Skeffington and R.Owens (Dublin, 1975), pp.12–26

M. Ward, *In Their Own Voice: Women and Irish Nationalism* (Cork, 1995)

Notes

1   M. Ward, *Hanna Sheehy Skeffington: A Life* (Cork, 1997).

2   See Ward, *Hanna Sheehy Skeffington*, pp.4–5.

3   O. Sheehy Skeffington, 'Francis Sheehy Skeffington', *The Easter Rising*, edited by O. Dudley Edwards and F. Pyle (London, 1968), p.139.

4   J. H. and M.E. Cousins, *We Two Together* (Madras, 1950), p.28.

5   H. Sheehy Skeffington, *Reminiscences*, p.14.

6   H. Sheehy Skeffington, 'Sinn Féin and Irishwomen', *Bean na hÉireann*, November 1909.

7   H. Sheehy Skeffington, 'The Women's Movement – Ireland', *Irish Review*, July 1912, pp.225–7.

8   J. Stephens, *The Insurrection in Dublin* (Dublin, 1916), p.1.

9   R.F. Foster, *Vivid Faces: The Revolutionary Generation in Ireland 1890–1923* (London, 2014), p.180.

10   F. Sheehy Skeffington, 'War and Feminism', *Irish Citizen*, 12 September 1914.

11   Frank to Charlotte Shaw, in L.Levenson, *With Wooden Sword: A Portrait of Francis Sheehy-Skeffington, Militant Pacifist* (Dublin, 1983), p.170.

12   H.Sheehy Skeffington, *Irish Citizen*, 15 August 1914.

13   Frank to Thomas MacDonagh, October 1914, in Levenson, *With Wooden Sword* , 169.

14   M. Ward 'Nationalism, Pacifism, Internationalism: Louie Bennett, Hanna Sheehy Skeffington and the Problems of Defining Feminism', (Amherst, 1997), p.70.

15   C.P. Curran, *Under the Receding Wave* (Dublin, 1970), p.117.

16   J.F. Byrne, *Silent Years: An Autobiography* (New York, 1953), p.122.

17   *Irish Citizen*, 22 May 1915.

18   See Levenson, *With Wooden Sword*, pp.245–9.

19   F. Sheehy Skeffington, *A Forgotten Small Nationality: Ireland and the War*, New York, February 1916.

20   See Levenson, *With Wooden Sword*, p.194.

21   Ibid. p.208.

22   See F. Sheehy Skeffington, *A Forgotten Small Nationality*.

23   See Ward, *Hanna Sheehy Skeffington*, p.148.

24   C. Markievicz, *Irish World*, 3 May 1924.

25   Sir F. Fletcher Vane, *Agin the Governments: Memories and Adventures* (London, 1929), p.266.

26   S. Tiernan, *The Political Writings of Eva Gore-Booth* (Manchester, 2015), p.48.

27   Review in *Irish Citizen*, September 1919.

28   H. Sheehy Skeffington, 'Random Reflections on Housewives: Their Ways and Works', *The Irish Housewife*, Vol.1 No 1, 1946.

29   H. Sheehy Skeffington to Esther Roper, n.d. Sheehy Skeffington Papers, NLI, Ms 24, p.134.

INDEX